Before the 1960s, archaeologists did not much concern themselves with "theory": archaeology was an uncontroversial procedure for reconstructing the past. The rise of processual archaeology introduced a concern for explicit theory and methodology, linking the subject to generalizing anthropology as a model of scientific rigor. More recently, as part of the wave of post-modernism, post-processual archaeologists have controverted the scientific pretensions of the subject by situating it in the context of present-day political action.

This volume takes stock of the present position, mindful of the importance of archaeology as an academic subject and the growing scale of archaeological activity throughout the world. It asserts the real achievements of the subject in increasing understanding of the past. Without rejecting the insights of either traditional or more recent approaches, it considers critically the issues raised in current claims and controversies about what is appropriate theory for archaeology.

The volume looks first at the process of theory building in archaeology and at the sources of the ideas employed. The following studies examine questions such as the interplay between expectation and evidence in ideas of human origins; social role and material practice in the formation of the archaeological record; and how the rise of states should be conceptualized; other papers deal with the issues of ethno-archaeology, visual symbols, and conflicting claims to ownership of the past. The message that emerges is that archaeologists should be equally wary of naive positivism in the guise of scientific procedure, and of speculation about the unrecorded intentions of prehistoric actors.

Archaeological theory: who sets the agenda?

NEW DIRECTIONS IN ARCHAEOLOGY

Archaeological theory: who sets the agenda?

Edited by

NORMAN YOFFEE
University of Arizona

and

ANDREW SHERRATT
Ashmolean Museum, University of Oxford

CAMBRIDGE
UNIVERSITY PRESS

WD

Published by the Press Syndicate of the University of Cambridge
The Pitt Building, Trumpington Street, Cambridge CB2 1RP
40 West 20th Street, New York, NY 10011–4211, USA
10 Stamford Road, Oakleigh, Melbourne 3166, Australia

First published 1993

Printed in Great Britain at the University Press, Cambridge

*A catalogue record for this book is available from the
British Library*

Library of Congress cataloguing in publication data

Archaeological theory: who sets the agenda? /
edited by Norman Yoffee and Andrew Sherratt.
    p.   cm. – (New directions in archaeology)
Includes index.
ISBN 0 521 44014 9
1. Archaeology – Philosophy. 2. Archaeology – Methodology.
I. Yoffee, Norman. II. Sherratt, Andrew. III. Series.
CC72.A65 1993
930.1'01 – dc20   92–25825   CIP

ISBN 0 521 44014 9 hardback
ISBN 0 521 44958 8 paperback

Contents

Figures

Contributors

RICHARD BRADLEY
Department of Archaeology
University of Reading

CHRISTOPHER CHIPPINDALE
Museum of Archaeology and Anthropology
Cambridge

CLIVE GAMBLE
Department of Archaeology
University of Southampton

KELLEY ANN HAYS
Museum of Northern Arizona

PHILIP L. KOHL
Department of Anthropology
Wellesley College

TIM MURRAY
Department of Archaeology
La Trobe University

STEPHEN SHENNAN
Department of Archaeology
University of Southampton

ANDREW SHERRATT
Ashmolean Museum
University of Oxford

MIRIAM STARK
Department of Anthropology
University of Arizona

ALISON WYLIE
Department of Philosophy
University of Western Ontario

NORMAN YOFFEE
Department of Anthropology
University of Arizona

Introduction: the sources of archaeological theory

NORMAN YOFFEE and
ANDREW SHERRATT

Abstract

Archaeological theory is not independent of the problems that need to be solved: it arises out of particular problems and articulates them with others. This volume explores how widely discussed bodies of theory relate to the major problem-domains studied by archaeologists.

There has never been a unified school of archaeology: just as today, the subject has always been characterized by competing theoretical stances that often arise from different bodies of data and attendant problems of interpretation.

If "archaeology" is more than a word that completely changes its meaning according to context, however, there should be some common ground among its practitioners in various branches of the discipline. One expects some community of ideas and approaches, especially an explicit understanding of how "appropriate theory" is matched to the various problems with which archaeologists have to deal.

Typically, however, "theoretical schools" have arisen and claimed to have a privileged status in determining what constitutes valid explanation in archaeological research, and the recent literature shows that this is still the case. In historical perspective, such schools are clearly seen not only as grounded in partial bodies of empirical material but also as reactions to preceding theoretical positions and are themselves likely to be superseded.

Despite the evident dangers of advancing universal prescriptions, however, a significant part of the explicitly theoretical literature in archaeology today consists of polemical claims to novel and exclusive sources of truth. Thus, "post-processual" archaeology stigmatizes all earlier modes of explanation as inadequate – not because they are limited by particular types of evidence, but because they are fundamentally misconceived. These earlier approaches are characterized as "behaviorist," "functionalist," "positivist," or "evolutionist" and are seen as fatally flawed because they fail to consider "cognition," "structuration," "the individual," and "the arbitrary nature of the sign." Moreover, adherents of this school assert that their agenda represents the only way forward to a theoretically sound modern archaeology.

Rather than launch a "post-post-processual archaeology," this volume examines the claims of various archaeological theories against a wider historical and geographical perspective of archaeological work. We intend, thus, to consider both a representative sample of traditional archaeological problem-domains as well as to examine a variety of newer issues that confront archaeologists.

This volume is particularly timely in view of the fundamental changes affecting the role of archaeology in society today. The status of archaeology in the universities is uncertain and, in many cases, under threat. The relation of archaeology to its sister disciplines (sociocultural anthropology, history, classics), to its "parent organizations" (e.g., the American Anthropological Association), and to funding agencies necessitates practical consideration of archaeology as an autonomous academic subject. Archaeologists also face the repatriation of collections as yet unanalyzed, are denied excavation permits, and must battle looters for control of archaeological sites (Kintigh and Goldstein 1990).

Then, all over the industrialized world, the "heritage phenomenon" has placed archaeology in a central role in providing local sources of identity. Ancient sites are visited by vast numbers of people and hence are increasingly protected, and interpreted to the public. Much of the presentation of archaeological material is geared to the instant appreciation and visual stimulation demanded by the video generation; like fast-food, there is a "fast-past." While books for the mass market may naturally choose to emphasize visual images rather than verbal arguments and concepts, archaeologists cannot cede rights of interpretation to the Rupert Murdochs of the communication world.

Under these circumstances, archaeologists must especially avoid a retreat into obfuscatory and introverted arguments that have decreasing reference to problems of interest about the past. Furthermore, while views of the past are inevitably "theory-laden" and relative to the concerns of the present, this does not mean that archaeologists should choose to manipulate the past for their own purposes. Archaeologists must and do strive to see what happened in the past as objectively as they can while attempting to recognize what motivates certain kinds of investigations but not others.

Archaeologists now deploy increasingly sophisticated

means towards the acquisition of hitherto unobtainable data needed to understand life in the past. We do not seek to reduce the past to the mechanical application of a naive positivism dressed up as scientific procedure (in which methodology is confused with theory); equally we do not believe that criteria of testability and falsification should be abandoned in favor of speculations about unrecorded intentions of knowledgeable actors in the past in which anyone's opinion is as good as anyone else's.

The goals of this volume, therefore, are not to set a new agenda for archaeological theory, if by that is meant a rejection of traditional and important problems and existing archaeological activities: archaeologists have reason to celebrate successful research into important segments of the human past and the development of many persuasive and interesting accounts of social organization and social change. We shall consider what sorts of theoretical contexts are appropriate for the explanation of archaeological problems – as well as which theoretical claims are specious. We propose to identify those areas (within the scope of this volume) in which archaeological theory remains to be built, and what are the means by which we can get on with the job.

Our contributors deal with a wide range of archaeological theories that are adumbrated further in this introduction. The first section considers the attractions of theory-building in the context of the archaeological community. The second section focuses upon the appropriateness of theories that have been used to explain respectively the biogeographic spread of human populations in the Paleolithic, the "cultural logic" of societies that neither are based on hunting–gathering nor are states, and the rise of ancient states and civilizations. The third section presents case studies on the use and abuse of empirical methods in ethnoarchaeology, in the interpretation of visual symbols, and that sort out the various claimants to ownership of the past. An epilogue on the relativity of archaeological theory and the nature of archaeological imagination concludes the volume.

The origin of this volume

Most of the papers in this volume were written for a symposium (bearing the same title as this volume's) held at the 10th annual meeting of the Theoretical Archaeology Group (TAG) on 14 December 1988 at Sheffield University, UK. Thanks to a British Academy grant secured by Andrew Flemming, we were able to fund the travel of overseas participants to the symposium. Prior to the TAG meeting, most of the symposiasts met at Wolfson College, Oxford, to discuss our papers and the agenda for the symposium and projected volume. We acknowledge here the grant from the British Academy and express our appreciation to Andrew

Flemming and to the President and staff of Wolfson College for supporting the symposium and so making this volume possible.

The idea for the symposium germinated in Oxford over lunches at which the editors (and itinerant friends) regularly discussed the state of archaeological theory and especially the latest post-processual writings. We were concerned not only with what was being said by post-processual archaeologists but also, and perhaps more interestingly, with why it was being said. In particular, as archaeology students of the 1960s in the USA and the UK, respectively, that is, the *floruit* of the "processual" archaeology, we were surprised that "processual" archaeology was of any immediate relevance to archaeologists in the late 1980s, much less had such a pejorative connotation. To us, "processual" archaeology was an episode in the history of archaeology that had had a demonstrable effect on archaeological theory and practice but whose wretched excesses were as clear as its accomplishments. We also found it significant that adherents of the post-processual school based much of their criticism of processual archaeology on new domains of social theory outside archaeology itself and in this there were obvious parallels to processual (or "new archaeology") practices.

We thus decided to convene a symposium around the question of where did archaeologists find theory. In this we saw ourselves not opposed to the post-processual camp, since we wanted to place the most recent generations of archaeological schools of theory in intellectual and socio-logical perspective. Post-processualism served as a point of entry, therefore, in a wider-ranging investigation of the sources of archaeological theory and the practice of theory-building in archaeology.

For our symposium we wanted to gather archaeologists who were engaged in different kinds of archaeology. This included not only archaeology of different levels of socio-cultural complexity (and in this volume there are papers by Gamble on the Paleolithic, Yoffee on chiefdoms and early states, and Shennan on societies betwixt and between those two categories) but also archaeology as practiced in various parts of the world and by archaeologists of different social backgrounds and educational experiences (in this volume Tim Murray presents an Australianist perspective; Kelley Hays and Miriam Stark are graduate students working in the American Southwest and the Philippines, respectively). We also wanted a philosopher's analysis of changing trends in archaeology and were pleased that Alison Wylie accepted our invitation. Wylie's paper, furthermore, is grounded in a feminist perspective on archaeological theory, which we regarded as an important component in modern archaeo-logical discourse.

Philip Kohl and Christopher Chippindale write about the sociological context of archaeological schools of theory. Kohl notes the similarities of processual and post-processual movements, while Chippindale considers the questions of social status and political correctness that attend claims of theoretical purity. Both writers note that such claims, which usually are directed against the defects of a foregoing school and especially its lack of critical perspective on why and how it is historically situated, are notoriously un-self-critical in their own pretensions.

Miriam Stark and Kelley Hays take up two of the most important topics in modern archaeological practice, the relationship between studies of modern material culture in ethnographic field situations and the ancient distribution of artifacts, and the interpretation of prehistoric visual arts. Both consider the problem of elucidating cross-cultural regularities while insisting on context-specific cultural particularities, and both offer practical avenues of analysis in ethnoarchaeological and symbolic studies. Tim Murray considers, by means of examples from Australian prehistory and modern political affairs in Australia, how diverse interest groups compete both for ownership of the physical past and for control of the means by which the past might be investigated. In the presented case studies Murray shows that by fostering communication and by re-examining how and for whom the past is investigated and disseminated, the possibility of avoiding a footrace for the high moral ground can be facilitated. Finally, Richard Bradley offers an epilogue in which the process of archaeological discovery is connected to theory-building in such a way that theory is not only not distant from the archaeological record, but is rather the vehicle for open-mindedness and the exercise of critical imagination.

The post-processual critique

Since many new publications have evaluated the sources, trends, and diversity of post-processual theory (Binford 1987, Earle and Preucel 1987, Gibbon 1989, Hodder, 1991, Patterson 1989, 1990, Preucel 1991, Redman 1991, Shanks and Tilley 1989, Stutt and Shennan 1990, Trigger 1989, 1991, P. J. Watson, 1991, Watson and Fotiadis 1990, R. Watson 1990), we present here a critique – not all of which is unfriendly – of post-processual claims simply as an introduction to our theme of agendas in archaeological theory.

On the surface, little unanimity of what should be the sources of archaeological theory characterized the 1980s, as can be seen from the following statements about the nature of archaeological theory that have been drawn from major essays from that time:

(1) What archaeologists need is an evolutionary theory, a "theory that can be borrowed in unadulterated form," namely modern biological theory, because "biology is . . . struggling with similar problems in a similar context" as archaeology (Dunnell 1982: 20, 19).

(2) "I don't believe there's any such thing as 'archaeological theory.' For me there's only anthropological theory. Archaeologists have their own methodology and ethnologists have theirs; but when it comes to theory, we all ought to sound like anthropologists" (The Old Timer, cited in Flannery 1982: 269–70; this position is refuted by Flannery in Flannery and Marcus 1983: 361–2).

(3) "If archaeologists can gain a healthy skepticism regarding received conceptualizations of nature and seek to place themselves in positions relative to nature and experience where the adequacy and/or ambiguity of the received comments may be evaluated, then they can hope to gain some objectivity relative to the utility of their concepts." Such objectivity will proceed, the authors continue from an unusual vantage point: "Once archaeologists learn to look at systems from the realistic perspective of an observer in a well, they will see many new things which can aid in the organizational diagnoses of past systems" (Binford and Sabloff 1982: 150, 151).

(4) Archaeology is a mediated relation between what happened and its representation . . . Material culture [is] a constructed network of significations . . . irreducibly polysemous . . . a contextualized matrix of associative and syntagmatic relations involving parallelism, opposition, linearity, equivalence, and inversion between its elements (Shanks and Tilley 1987b: 134, 114, 115, 103).

Although there may seem to be little in common among the biological, anthropological, objectivist–positivist, and generative linguistic goals for archaeological theory-building, there is one unifying thread running through the disparate views cited above (save perhaps the Binford–Sabloff damp allegiance to objectivism): archaeological theory is a mining-and-bridging exercise. The archaeologist's task is to find theory in some other discipline – since *real* theory exists in biology, geography, sociology, sociocultural anthropology, and/or linguistics – and then to "operationalize" that theory, that is, modify it for archaeological purposes.

In the most atavistically positivist accounts of Binford and Schiffer, the mines need only be shallow while the bridges are mighty. Binford's call for "good instruments for measuring specified properties of past cultural systems" (Binford 1982: 129) and Schiffer's focus on site-formation processes that emphasize taphonomy, ethnoarchaeology, and experimental archaeology (Schiffer 1987), are built on assumptions that once it is known how the archaeological record is formed, there will be a more-or-less clear path to the behavior of the people who ultimately produced it. Unfortunately, the "good instruments" are still being forged and the site-formation processes still seem to be in formative stages of development. Grand organizational theory is usually eschewed until our observational powers are sufficiently sharpened (see Schiffer 1988).

For most archaeologists, however, the mining part of the exercise is straightforward and depends on the background of the "theoretician." Thus, catastrophe theory, central place theory, structuralist theory, and others have been borrowed and adapted by "archaeological" theorists. The result of these mining-and-bridging operations has been to force otherwise practically engaged archaeologists to consider the ideas of Thom, Christaller, Lévi-Strauss, and others before determining that mathematical topology, the economics of retailing, and mythological analysis, however worthy on their own terms, are of limited or at best indirect relevance to the study of past societies. By this time, of course, the miners have moved on and new bridges have been erected.

Processual archaeology in the post-processual critique

It is in this context of theoretical engineering that the claims of post-processual archaeology may be briefly evaluated. Since this discussion is not intended to duplicate or comment upon the above-cited articles that review the contributions of post-processual archaeology, we shall pass over whatever schisms may be apparent among the hardly unified congregation of post-processual archaeologists. We apologize to offended Albigensians and Monophysites for unfairly lumping them into what we delineate as the central post-processual creed.

The post-processual critique of the processual school can be divided into three parts: the processual models of culture, material culture, and explanation. Processual archaeologists, according to the post-processualists, argue that *culture* is a means of adaptation to the natural environment. Human behavior, being the instrument of such adaptation, is determined by material circumstances, while ideas and values are epiphenomenal and predictable by the material conditions of existence. The systemic nature of human organization is due to the functional relationship between material culture and the environment such that an equilibrium is established and maintained until upset by an external stress. Individual behavior is determined by these systemic forces. Since the relationship between artifact characteristics and distributions is functional and universal, the remains of past behavior can be measured without reference to specific contexts.

Processualists (again, according to post-processualists) consider that *material culture* is the passive product of human adaptation to the external environment. Culture may therefore be inferred from material culture after formation processes are taken into account. Once functional relationships within the system, and between the system and the external environment, are established, change can be explained as perturbations that lead to greater adaptive efficiency. Although material culture may serve ideological or social purposes, beliefs, ideas, and values are not reconstructable by archaeologists and, in any case, are of secondary importance in the function of material culture.

Explanation for processual archaeologists (in the post-processual view) consists in constructing universal laws through the hypothetico-deductive method. Objective procedures of analysis allow formulation and testing of hypotheses that can be statistically confirmed or at least falsified. Detailed methodological work and cross-cultural comparisons will result in law-like correlations between artifact distributions and social organizations. The constructed typologies will stand in evolutionary sequence based on their levels of adaptive efficiency.

This picture of what the post-processual archaeologists claim to be "processual archaeology" is, of course, a jarring collage. While it may be intellectually amusing to fit Schiffer and Binford into the same frame, it is only unlettered arrogance that forces Flannery into the same family unit. What post-processual archaeologists have conjoined as "processual archaeology" are certain programmatic statements made about a quarter of a century ago (while ignoring the historical context of those positions). Not only have post-processualists denied the diversity of views of archaeologists studying non-complex societies, but they have overlooked the fact that most archaeologists investigating ancient states and civilizations (since most post-processualists are not themselves interested in complex societies) were never processual archaeologists. Furthermore, there is nothing new in the attack on functionalism and the quest for cultural laws. Boasians of more than a half-century ago considered themselves to have refuted evolutionists and structural–functionalists on precisely these terms.

The post-processual attack on scientism in processual archaeology has, at least, made explicit that which most archaeologists have been content to accept without much comment. Those few archaeologists who insist on discovering "laws" have thus far failed to produce more than the most trivial of observations (as Flannery noted in 1973). Despite the most earnest claim that the development of more scientific methods of coping with the archaeological record is only a first step, many studies of the physical properties of archaeological materials seem to be conducted in the absence of any archaeological problem requiring investigation.

In the failure to discover "laws of behavior," there is of course little agreement on what constitutes adequate archaeological explanation – as the diversity of views on archaeological theory cited above illustrates. However, in their attack on scientism in archaeology, post-processualists have unfairly de-emphasized the necessary role for scientific analysis of archaeological materials in the investigation of the past; they have merely constructed a processual school in order to differentiate it from their own view of culture, material culture, and explanation.

Culture, material culture, and explanation in post-processual archaeology

According to post-processualists, human behavior is "culturally constituted"; that is, behavior is informed by meaning and through the agency of individuals. The ever-changing structure of meaning is context-dependent and negotiated through the actions of individuals to produce culture. *Culture*, therefore, can only be understood as an ideational code and must include function and meaning, process and structure, norms and variability, and subject and object.

Material culture cannot be reduced as a direct reflection of behavior because it is a transformation of behavior. In fact, material culture has transformative power; it is "recursive," and "acts back" on behavior as part of the strategies of social negotiation. Material culture thereby symbolizes the relationship between people and things: as Hodder puts it in an oft-cited passage, material culture and culture "are not caused by anything outside themselves . . . they just are" (1986: 4). Material culture, since it is used for purposes of communication and to effect changes in the social environment, constitutes a universal meta-language and hence must be read as a text. By contextualizing artifacts in the totality of the entire environment of cultural meanings and strategies, the symbolic messages of material culture can be deciphered.

Explanation in post-processual archaeology is the process of deciphering the meaning-laden constitution of material culture. As ethnoarchaeological researches have shown, adequate explanation of the parts of a cultural system depends on the richness of contextualization within specific, long-term historical trajectories. In order to reach the meaning of past social action, it is necessary, following Collingwood, to live the past experience through the mind. As Hodder puts it, in another of his elegant locutions, "it is only when we make assumptions about the subjective meanings in the minds of people long dead that we can begin to do archaeology" (1986: 7). Furthermore, since the real world is not independent of the observer, archaeologists must understand how particular reconstructions of the past are used in the context of modern society and the observer's place in it. The achievement of self-knowledge is important because "the need for cultural order is universal and the methods of producing and reading the cultural order are the same in the present and the past" (Hodder 1986: 8).

From post-processual critique to archaeological theory

Much of the post-processualist view of culture is obviously borrowed from post-modernist trends in literature and the resonance of such trends in sociocultural anthropology. For example, since, according to Clifford, "culture [is] composed of seriously contested codes and representations" (1986: 2), ethnographies are hardly empirical accounts but rather a species of fiction. In similar spirit, Hodder's "writing archaeology" (1989a, 1989b) and Tilley's call for site-reports to be like stage plays (1989) are like "thick description," self-reflexivity, "dialogic" rhetoric and the "writer's voice" in post-modernist anthropology. Although post-processualists are kindly dedicated to bringing various post-modernist writers into the purview of their less up-to-date archaeological brethren and sistren (see most recently Tilley, ed. 1990, and Bapty and Yates, eds. 1990, who are carrying on this mission), post-processual archaeologists are much like other archaeologists who borrow concepts of culture, material culture, and explanation from a variety of non-archaeological sources and with little recourse to the understanding of archaeological problems. In this activity they have functioned as theory-miners on a grander scale than other archaeologists. Perhaps it is the very scale of their mining exercise that has prevented even the most rudimentary of bridge-building operations. While Tilley's assertion that "digging is a pathology of archaeology" (1989: 275) has awakened the suspicion that some post-processualists aren't interested in the practice of archaeology at all (as a practical science that studies the past; see Bradley, this volume), Hodder has clearly sought to distance himself from this position (1991).

As many commentators have observed (see Kohl, this volume), most of the theoretical pronouncements of post-processual archaeologists began as structural oppositions to their constructed category of "processualists." But, as we argue here, although functionalist, adaptationist, positivist, and reductionist ideas of culture and material culture can be dredged up from some fossilized "new archaeologists," these views have never been held seriously by many (including leading) archaeologists. (Is or was Gordon Willey or Robert McC. Adams a "new archaeologist"?)

Yet the dichotomy of views between, for example,

Binford and Hodder, the academic patrons of new and post-processual archaeology, respectively, is of continuing interest to historians and philosophers of archaeology. First, Binford seems not to have grasped that if a model of culture is preferred to his own adaptationist one, then a different interpretation of material culture and explanation is warranted (Binford 1987, Binford and Stone 1988). Post-processual archaeologists, on the other hand, have resisted claims that there is anything important that is adaptive or functional in culture and material culture or that there are sound and successful empirical methods for dealing with residues of the past.

Preucel has recently sought to reconcile these opposing views (1991). He proposes that archaeologists must include scientific, empirical methods in explaining human behavior while also seeking to understand (*sensu* Dilthey's *verstehen*) the past so that "an empathetic linkage between the past and the present is established" and we may identify "the meaning of cultural systems for those participants within it" (Preucel 1991: Ch. 1). The practice of analysis must finally consider a self-understanding of why archaeologists ask certain questions and what is the "intellectual investment in a particular answer" (Preucel 1991: Ch. 1). Although Preucel accepts the terms of the debate as set by those working at its extremes, he still regards the various approaches in processual and post-processual archaeology as complementary and mutually reinforcing.

While Preucel's attempt at resolving these theoretical oppositions is admirable, one may question his synthesis on two grounds. First, not all working archaeologists are card-carrying members of one of the two schools that are delineated; also, the two diametrically opposed views of culture, material culture, and explanation cannot easily be compartmentalized into different aspects of, or as subsequent steps in, archaeological practice. Second, it seems disingenuous to claim that archaeological theory can be abstracted from the kinds of problems that archaeologists seek to investigate and that archaeological theory is a kind of abstract logic. These two points deserve some elaboration.

It is a relief to many archaeologists that they can do without either a nomothetic view of culture or one that holds that material culture is a text and site reports are a kind of story. Indeed, for most archaeologists it is obvious that the degree to which culture/material culture can be considered as a response to the environment is greater in the Paleolithic than in classical Athens. Similarly, in ancient states one must study a variety of social and economic orientations, especially the nature of political systems and resistance to them; in non-stratified societies one studies, among other things, wealth-levelling mechanisms, the moral economy of

kinship relations, and how these institutions are socially learned and reproduced. Since the nature of culture is very different along the spectrum of human societies, it follows that archaeological theory must vary commensurately with the societies and problems being investigated.

We must also point out in this otherwise high-minded discussion of the nature of archaeological theory that chronological resolution in archaeology is often coarse, that site-formation processes are critically important in assessing artifactual patterning, that population size is often a guessing game and, even if we could identify individuals in prehistory, one would then need to relate individual behavior to that of the group (or groups) in which the individual was embedded (see Shennan, this volume). Furthermore, as Kohl and Wylie discuss in this volume, if archaeologists are to think themselves into the past and regard the process of inference as a species of story-telling, we shall not only lose academic credibility as scientists, but also we shall bore the public who can always find more entertaining versions of the past than archaeologists are likely to produce. Although archaeologists can have no objective way of reconstructing a final and uniquely true human past, they do have the capability of eliminating some alternative versions, and reasonably prefer others (as Wylie shows in her paper in this volume).

While the methodological objections alone may be sufficient to put most archaeologists off post-processualism, it is still important to evaluate post-processual claims of what culture is, and hence how material culture is to be studied and explanation structured. Having rejected the adaptationist and functionalist views of the "new archaeologists," is the post-processual position the only viable alternative?

David Clarke wrote (in the R. Chapman translation) of his own concern about the relationship of culture to material culture in a way that still commands our attention:

> The anthropologists [may] look at aspects of the social system of cultures [whilst] the archaeologists . . . look at the material system of the same cultures – the systems are not the same yet neither are they unconnected. Serious dangers await those who transfer observations about the one class of system to the other and yet it is important that the coupling between the different systems and their attributes should be . . . made explicit . . . The archaeological entities reflect realities [that are] as important as those recognized by . . . other disciplines . . . [and] are equally real . . . and simply different (1978: 61, 369).

We may infer from Clarke that even if the post-processual view of culture as a network of individuals negotiating their status is not fallacious, it is a partial view of the range, origins, and changing nature of culture and need not determine the archaeological investigation of material culture. Archaeologists deal with certain kinds of problems, some of which are not studied or cannot be studied by sociocultural anthropologists. Archaeological theory, it follows, cannot simply be a subset of anthropological theory (see Flannery 1983, and Wobst 1978).

Understanding the transition to sedentary, food-producing societies or explaining how certain groups control access to scarce resources, including the field of symbolic resources (see Hays, this volume) in the evolution of ancient states and civilizations, or how and why movements of peoples resulted in culture change, cannot be reduced to theories about the negotiation of meaning.

In sum, no matter how salient in post-modern ethnographic theory the role of the individual might be, there is little theory on the individual's ability to affect more than the short-term ethnographic moment. Thus the issue at stake in theory-building in archaeology concerns what is the proper subject of archaeological research and what is the relationship between culture history and cultural generalization (see Stark, this volume).

Archaeological self-criticism and the future of archaeological theory

The most powerful rhetoric of post-processual archaeologists has focused on the relationship of the archaeological investigator to the number of important political issues that do and must obtain in every stage in the reconstruction of the past. The post-processualist position has been (especially in the writings of Shanks and Tilley, e.g., 1987a, 1987b, Tilley 1989) that processual (and all other non-post-processual) archaeologists, under the guise of being neutral and scientific reporters of the past, have been in fact willing conspirators in exercising a control over the past in the interests of the conservative, ruling apparatus of modern Western societies.

Post-processualists have argued, by way of example, that principles of systemic order and economic rationality are simply Western concepts that apply to capitalist societies and have been writ (wrongly) by processualists as universal principles of analysis. Similarly, the goal of constructing universal "laws" of behavior has tended to rob indigenous, subject peoples of their own pasts: their histories and their views of their histories are insignificant compared to the scientific enterprises carried out by objective archaeologists. While great museums have nobly argued that they safeguard the remnants of past human achievement, post-processualists charge that the museums are really claiming that they are the spiritual heirs of the past; the objections to foreign ownership by institutions in lands whence the artifacts originated are petty and wearisome. Furthermore, the presence of these foreign artifacts happily reminds the Western museums' clients of the former or current power of their own lands and of the generosity of benevolent philanthropists who were able to secure the prized residues of the past.

While these powerful and often cogent arguments are not and have not been the sole property of post-processualist archaeologists, the force of post-processual arguments has focused the attention of the archaeological community and is especially not lost on modern students of archaeology. Archaeologists of all theoretical persuasions, however, are working to reorganize governmental policies concerning reburial, repatriation, sacred sites, and excavation procedures. Jim Allen (1987) has shown that archaeology cannot be and never was an ivory-tower discipline; Tim Murray, in this volume, has presented an example of how archaeological theory is implicated in the practice of archaeology in Australia.

As Murray's, Wylie's, and Kohl's essays in this volume emphasize, moreover, the branch of post-processualism that argues that there are multiple versions of the past and that all or many of them might be equally valid (especially as is espoused by Shanks and Tilley) contradicts the important call to political action by archaeologists. Just as they have refuted claims of the Third Reich and some South African and Israeli governments, for example, archaeologists today cannot afford multiple versions of the past to proliferate. Rather, it is critical that archaeologists assert that there is at least a partially knowable antiquity and that archaeologists are the guardians of its integrity.

Conclusion

In this introduction we have argued that post-processual archaeologists, like their equally theory-borrowing adversaries, have looked to other fields' theories to understand the archaeological record. However, while most theory-borrowers have ingeniously attempted to show that their theory explains observed patterns of data, post-processual archaeologists have advanced a theory that is unlinked and apparently unlinkable to archaeological practice (O'Shea's 1992 review of Hodder 1990; compare Hodder [1991], who insists that outdoors is where he wants to be). Post-processual theory in archaeology has been taken substantially from post-modernist trends in social theory which, however weakly transmuted into archaeological terms, are less concerned with specific cases and concrete problems than with a self-denigrating polyvocality. Practical and substantive arguments are not held to carry conviction – this despite a century of progress in archaeological knowledge that ought to have made archaeology an ornament of modern academic life as it is a subject of endless public fascination.

Of all the social sciences (in which category we include the historical sciences), archaeology stands alone in its failure to insist on and build a contextually appropriate range of social theory. Such theories must afford linkage between matters of data collection and primary analysis of data, and the process of inference in which patterns of data are held to reflect social phenomena. Thus far the process of inference has relied on assumptions and analogies – theories or parts of theories – that have been drawn from other disciplines. These theories have been used to model extant archaeological data by specifying the logically entailed, but non-existent, data required by the overarching assumptions and analogies. Having borrowed these "prior probabilities" (Salmon 1982) from other fields, archaeologists have condemned the past to resemble some aspect of the present.

It is only when archaeologists are able to build social theory on an intra-archaeological data base and using an intra-archaeological comparative method – one that demands the possibility of discovering and explaining contrasts as well as similarities – that archaeological theory can be said to flourish. Using this foundation of archaeological theory, then, we will be able to select critically and to evaluate theories that might be taken over from other fields and that are claimed to fit past organizational structures and trajectories of change. This volume is dedicated to the ideal of constructing a range of archaeological theory that is appropriate to the problems archaeologists face.

Post-processual archaeologists have effectively emphasized that archaeology is an interpretive science, that symbols, ideologies and structures of meaning are not merely reflections of how humans cope with the vagaries of external environments. Furthermore, as post-processualists have stressed, archaeologists have special responsibilities, not only in recovering the past, but also in ensuring that the past is not maliciously used in the present. Post-processual archaeologists, however, have no monopoly on these matters. Indeed, the post-processual school is no school at all (nor have its proponents ever declared that it was) in that it does not attempt to formulate a constructive archaeological agenda, launches no coherent body of theory and method for interpreting the past, and sets out deliberately to obfuscate the genuine gains made in over a century of systematic archaeological research.

The ideological danger posed by the grimmest processual scientism pales in comparison to the threat of those who seek to undermine the framework of traditional archaeological *practice* and who, at their most systematically critical, are indeed nihilists. In this time when the existence of archae-ology in the academy is being debated and the integrity of archaeologists is being questioned in public forums, archaeologists cannot be excused the responsibility for setting our own theoretical and contextually appropriate agenda.

Acknowledgments

Parts of this introduction were initially written by Norman Yoffee during a seminar on "Post-processual archaeology" which he supervised at the University of Arizona during the Fall semester, 1988. The paper Yoffee presented at the TAG meeting (entitled "Archaeological theory: something borrowed, something blue") had as co-authors the members of that seminar: John Carpenter, Astrid Golomb, Timothy Jones, Kelley Hays, Maria O'Donovan, Louise Senior, Miriam Stark, Mary Van Buren, Ruth Van Dyke, and Maria Nieves Zedeño. We both thank these co-authors for allowing us to incorporate sections from our joint paper in this introduction. We are also grateful to Alison Wylie, Hugh Gusterson, and Joyce Marcus for their good advice on this introduction.

References

Allen, Jim 1987 *The Politics of Archaeology*. Inaugural Address of the Professor, Dept. of Archaeology, La Trobe University, Bundoora, Victoria, Australia.

Bapty, Ian and Tim Yates, eds. 1990 *Archaeology after Structuralism: Post-Structuralism and the Practice of Archaeology*. Andover: Routledge.

Binford, Lewis 1982 Objectivity-Explanation-Archaeology 1981. In *Theory and Explanation in Archaeology*, edited by C. Renfrew, M. Rowlands, and B. A. Segraves, pp. 125–38. Academic Press: New York.

1987 Data, Relativism and Archaeological Science. *Man* 22: 391–404.

Binford, Lewis and Jeremy Sabloff 1982 Paradigms, Systematics, and Archaeology. *Journal of Anthropological Research* 38: 137–53.

Binford, Lewis and Nancy Stone 1988 Archaeology and Theory. *Man* 23: 374–6.

Clarke, David 1978 *Analytical Archaeology*, 2nd revised edn. by Robert Chapman. Cambridge: Cambridge University Press.

Clifford, James 1986 Introduction: Partial Truths. In *Writing Cultures*, edited by James Clifford and George Marcus, pp. 1–26. A School of American Research Advanced Seminar book. Berkeley: University of CaliforniaPress.

Dunnell, Robert 1982 Science, Social Science, and Common Sense: The Agonizing Dilemma of Modern Archae-ology. *Journal of Anthropological Research* 38: 1–25.

Earle, Timothy and Robert Preucel 1987 Processual Archaeology and the Radical Critique. *Current Anthropology* 28: 501–38.

Flannery, Kent 1973 Archaeology with a Capital S. In *Research and Theory in Current Archaeology*, edited by Charles Redman, pp. 47–52. New York: John Wiley and Sons.

  1982 The Golden Marshalltown: A Parable for the Archaeology of the 1980s. *American Anthropologist* 84: 265–78.

  1983 Archaeology and Ethnology in the Context of Divergent Evolution. In *The Cloud People*, edited by Kent Flannery and Joyce Marcus, pp. 361–2. New York: Academic Press.

Gibbon, Guy 1989 *Explanation in Archaeology*. Oxford: Basil Blackwell.

Hodder, Ian 1986 *Reading the Past*. Cambridge: Cambridge University Press.

  1989a Writing Archaeology: Site Reports in Context. *Antiquity* 63: 268–74.

  1989b This is Not an Article about Material Culture as Text. *Journal of Anthropological Archaeology* 8: 250–69.

  1990 *The Domestication of Europe*. Oxford: Basil Blackwell.

  1991 Interpretive Archaeology and its Role. *American Antiquity* 56: 7–18.

Kintigh, Keith and Lynne Goldstein 1990 Ethics and the Reburial Controversy. *American Antiquity* 55: 585–91.

O'Shea, John Review of Ian Hodder, *The Domestication of Europe*. In *American Anthropologist* (forthcoming).

Patterson, Tom 1989 History and the Post-Processual Archaeologies. *Man* 24: 555–66.

  1990 Some Theoretical Tensions within and between the Processual and Postprocessual Archaeologies. *Journal of Anthropological Archaeology* 9: 189–200.

Preucel, Robert 1991 Introduction. In *Processual and Postprocessual Archaeologies: Multiple Ways of Knowing the Past*, edited by Robert Preucel, pp. 1–14. Carbondale: Southern Illinois University Press.

Redman, Charles 1991 In Defense of the Seventies – The Adolescence of New Archaeology. *American Anthropologist* 93: 295–307.

Salmon, Merilee 1982 *Philosophy and Archaeology*. New York: Academic Press.

Schiffer, Michael 1987 *Formation Processes of the Archaeological Record*. Albuquerque: University of New Mexico Press.

  1988 The Structure of Archaeological Theory. *American Antiquity* 53: 461–85.

Shanks, Michael and Christopher Tilley 1987a *Re-Constructing Archaeology*. Cambridge: Cambridge University Press.

  1987b *Social Theory and Archaeology*. Oxford: Basil Blackwell.

  1989 Archaeology into the 90s. *Norwegian Archaeological Review* 21: 1–54 (with comments by Hodder, Olsen, Herschend, Nordbladh, Trigger, Wenke, Renfrew, and authors' response).

Stutt, Arthur and Stephen Shennan 1990 The Nature of Archaeological Argument. *Antiquity* 64 245): 766–77.

Tilley, Christopher 1989 Excavation as Theatre. *Antiquity* 63: 275–80.

  1990 *Reading Material Culture*, edited by Christopher Tilley. Oxford: Basil Blackwell.

Trigger, Bruce 1989 *A History of Archaeological Thought*. Cambridge: Cambridge University Press.

  1991 Constraint and Freedom: A New Synthesis for Archaeological Interpretation. *American Anthropologist* 93: 551–69.

Watson, Patty Jo 1991 A Parochial Primer: The New Dissonance as Seen from the Midcontinental U.S.A. In *Processual and Postprocessual Archaeologies: Multiple Ways of Knowing the Past*, edited by Robert Preucel, pp. 265–74. Carbondale: Southern Illinois University Press.

Watson, Patty Jo and Michaelis Fotiadis 1990 The Razor's Edge: Symbolic-Structural Archaeology and the Expansion of Archaeological Inference. *American Anthropologist* 92: 613–29.

Watson, Richard 1990 Ozymandias, King of Kings: Postprocessual Radical Archaeology as Critique. *American Antiquity* 55: 673–89.

Wobst, Martin 1978 The Archaeo-Ethnology of Hunter–Gatherers or the Tyranny of the Ethnographic Record in Archaeology. *American Antiquity* 43: 303–9.

PART I

The social context of archaeological theory

1

Limits to a post-processual archaeology (or, The dangers of a new scholasticism)[1]

PHILIP L. KOHL

handwritten note: Who's we phil?

In search of the truly critical

Post-processual archaeology is an amorphous phenomenon; it assumes many different shapes and forms, deriving inspiration from fields as diverse as contemporary literary criticism, women's studies, and human geography. As Earle and Preucel (1987) have recently suggested, post-processual archaeology may, in fact, constitute more a radical critique of the long dominant, "new" Anglo-American archaeology of the sixties and seventies than a unified research pro- gramme or disciplinary paradigm in its own right simply due to this diversity. It is such a mixed bag that it is difficult to define a common core, a new orthodoxy that has already replaced or, at least, is trying to dislodge the positivist, systemic ecological functionalism (or what I prefer to dub "animalism" – as opposed to the overused "vulgar" or the misnamed "cultural materialism"), championed most stridently by L. Binford and his disciples.

Yet if the adjective *new* had the most positive conno- tations in American culture and American archaeology in the late sixties, defining a rebellion against all that was old, traditional, and therefore suspect, the adjective *critical* today seems to be accorded the highest status, possibly uniting the diverse strands of post-processual archaeology into a single *critically* self-conscious, reflexive enterprise. Whether we have read our Adorno, Horkheimer, Marcuse, and Habermas or have not mulled over the profundities of the Frankfurt School in our search for a meaningful – dare I use the sixties word? – relevant archaeology, we post-processualists by definition are involved in a *critical* process of self- examination, engaged introspection, reflective inquiry on the multiple meanings of the past for the present, the present for the past, and all possible permutations thereof. If the

hypothetical deductive scientists of the "new" archaeo- logical paradigm saw themselves as the ultimate social planners, discovering laws of cultural evolution that would lead us knowingly into the 21st century, we post- processualists have more modest aims. We can predict neither the past, nor the future; in fact, we claim not really to know the past at all. Rather, we tell stories about it and discover stories told by previous generations of scholars, including, of course, those constructed by the Binfordian mad-scientists and their ilk. But – and this is the important point – we proceed *critically*, seeing how these stories are used and manipulated for present purposes, sometimes condemning the tale, sometimes approving it – always, of course, from a *critical* perspective.

We are also constantly *critically* examining the social setting in which knowledge is produced, the disciplinary academic context or class background of particular scholars or schools to which they belong. Knowledge is never absolute, nor certain, but must be contextualized, related to a particular time and place. Thus, Shanks and Tilley have exhorted us in their breathlessly inspired, albeit "provisional, frail, and flawed" personal encounter with the past and its present that "any adequate conceptual and theoretical frame- work developed in studying the past must incorporate reflection upon archaeology as a professional discipline in the present" (Shanks and Tilley 1987: 2–3). In a *critically* self-conscious spirit, this chapter will attempt to follow these words of wise advice and reflect upon the current state of Anglo-American archaeology, for – it must be emphasized – in post-processual archaeology we are dealing with a phenomenon largely limited to the British Isles and North America; it is a curious fact (which also must be *critically* examined) that archaeology as practiced in most areas of the world has yet to experience its processual phase, much less benefit from its post-processualist critique.

Post-processual archaeology: the good, the bad, and the dangerous

Our cynicism must be tempered. Although this chapter is written from a perspective that is critical of post-processual archaeology (or at least some of its practitioners) and, in that sense, concentrates on certain defects or limitations, we must first acknowledge some real accomplishments. First, a "radical critique" of processual archaeology was long overdue and welcome. The debunking of the naive, "golly gee, Mr. Science" positivism characteristic of the worst of the new archaeology (e.g. Watson, Redman, and LeBlanc 1971), as well as of the perhaps more insidious and ubiquitous ecological materialism, characteristic of pro- cessual archaeology, had to occur, and, in retrospect, it is not surprising that critiques appeared more or less simultaneously on several theoretical fronts from Marxism to the structural and symbolic/contextual approaches advanced particularly by I. Hodder (1986).

There is no need to retread familiar ground; suffice it to say that nearly a generation of young scholars grew up and sometimes were uncritically indoctrinated in the canons of the new archaeology. Rare are the scholars like Mark Leone, who were first schooled in the heady days of the establishment of the "new archaeology" or archaeological paradigm, who later perceived the error of their ways. Retreats to the safety of middle-range theorizing or the none-too-subtle Red-baiting that characterizes Binford's defense (Binford 1986: 402–3) of the movement he pioneered illustrate how obstinate most positivists are in the belief in objectivity and in a knowable, external world. More of this defense later, but here from a truly critical perspective it is worth noting how ingrained American belief in the omnipotence of science actually is; how easy it is in an American context for technique and rigorous methodology to masquerade as theory, a tendency that formed one of the dominant features of processual archaeology; finally and from an equally critical, contextually sensitive perspective, it is striking that the most vigorous assault on positivism and a rejection of the dichotomy between idiographic and nomothetic or between historical and comparative evolutionary approaches has emerged in England, a country whose experiences this century, like those of all European countries, have been considerably more complicated, nuanced, and fraught with reversals and declines than those of the United States. European positivism and belief in unlimited progress died on the battlefields of World War I only to be resurrected phoenix-like on the relatively unscarred terrain of the United States. Or, as B. Trigger (1989: 19) correctly reminds us, the relatively low prestige accorded history in the United States is related to American history (our collective escape from Europe) and the "present-mindedness" of American culture.

In Great Britain the distinctive internal disciplinary development of prehistory came as an extension of history while in the United States archaeology came to be considered part of anthropology, which itself developed within institutions of natural history, like the Smithsonian and the American Museum of Natural History. From such a perspective one can better understand why British archaeologists today are sensibly turning to historians and philosophers of history and are suggesting, like Hodder, that archaeology is a form of long-term history, a discipline with its own distinctive methods and techniques of analysis, but one whose task is essentially the same as history's: the reconstruction of the human past. Binford's continuing insistence that "history as the model for archaeological investigations is . . . totally inappropriate" (Binford 1986: 401) simply does not understand the nature of historical sources, particularly their inherent limitations and ambiguities, nor the art of historical interpretation, and nothing that I have read which he has written suggests that his understanding of contemporary historiography has advanced beyond the grossest, dated caricature of history as a particularizing, idiographic discipline. Post-processualists, thankfully, have rejected this one-sided and now completely outmoded perspective on the discipline with which archaeology forms a natural alliance, indeed extension: history.

The diversity of post-processual archaeology and its advocacy of multiple perspectives for perceiving the past is, generally speaking, a strength; it certainly is a welcome development compared to the orthodoxy or dogmatic features of the new (or) processual archaeology. A French archaeologist with whom I worked used to delight in parodying the structure of a typical article gracing the pages of *American Antiquity* during the late sixties and the seventies: refutation of all previous explanations for problem X; development of an alternative, more satisfactory and inclusive hypothesis for explaining problem X; test and confirmation of the proposed hypothesis often without newly excavated evidence to support the theory but never without rigorous statistical confirmation, always demanding, as the seventies proceeded, access to a computer. The references cited in these articles, as my French colleague fondly noted, were always exclusively written in English. Hopefully, we have moved beyond such mechanical allegiance to a formula, beyond such parochialism. Hopefully.

How refreshing today to see a thousand alternative approaches to the past blooming! Since subjectivity and the bias of the observer can never be eliminated, let us not insist upon mathematical rigor for its own sake, but form impressionistic, qualitative judgments; the intuitive, gut feelings of traditional archaeologists often resulted in great discoveries, and we should emulate them as much as the unimaginative scientific drones who succeeded them.

A feminist archaeology? Why not? There is no question that models of cultural evolution largely have had a male bias; attention to gender distinctions in the prehistoric record cannot help but yield a more representative and complete understanding of past societies. Many contemporary social historians (e.g. Davis 1975–76), archaeology's natural disciplinary bedfellows, have successfully rewritten or reexamined past societies by focusing their research on the contribution and role of women in the societies and historical periods of concern; clearly a similar emphasis in prehistory is overdue. There is no debate that gender should be recognized as "a central category of human social life," that the past should be "engendered."[2] Nor is there any argument with the extremely salutary goal of correcting the androcentric, often largely speculative reconstructions that constitute most attempts at piecing together the past. As sympathetic investigators have noted, the inherent limitations of the archaeological record have not inhibited archaeologists from attempting to reconstruct intangible features of social organization or ideology. The avoidance of engendering the past on epistemological grounds, thus, appears unfair and biased.

Or does it? Part of the critical reading of post-processual archaeology advanced here relates ultimately to the nature of the archaeological record. Whether one writes of conceptual oppositions supposedly driving significant processes of cultural evolution (e.g., the imagined domus/agrios distinction for the domestication of Europe [Hodder 1990]) or engenders a very deficient record that is essentially silent on male/female tasks and roles within a particular society or archaeological culture (like the Upper Paleolithic Magdalenian culture of southwestern Europe), the problem of evidence cannot be ignored or swept aside simply by conjuring up one plausible, "peopled" reading of this record. Or, to use an older metaphor, sometimes the "Indians" are not particularly visible behind the artifacts, and, when that is the case, one should restrain or modify one's poetic, fictional impulse to concoct a just-so story. As archaeologists, we should not aspire to be Jean M. Auel. It is just an unfortunate fact that a purely prehistoric record is all too frequently silent on this important problem of determining gender differences and contributions. The point is not to condemn beforehand imaginative efforts at teasing out gender distinctions in the archaeological record; the data we collect and analyze and the interpretations we impart to it clearly are conditioned by our theories and perspectives, by the questions we ask. It is just that one should not gloss over the difficulties involved in interrogating that often intractable material culture record. To insist that "gender attribution" is unimportant or inessential to the task of constructing a feminist archaeology is to mislead. If one cannot determine whether some socially important group labor was performed by women or men or, more mundanely, whether this pot or this tool was made by a male or a female, one should simply admit it and ask other questions of these materials. Alternatively or even more, if a given record lacks the information needed to engender the past, the archaeologist interested in these questions should not just spin a plausible engendered tale but should feel compelled to gather to the best of her/his ability the data that would allow for such reconstructions. Binford probably was correct in his revisionist reading of Bordes' interpretation of the Middle Paleolithic, but, unfortunately, he never bothered to "test" his theory by collecting better information

through his own excavations. This is not a model one should emulate.

The same epistemological difficulty must be addressed for all the alternative readings of the past that we can envision. Since there were nearly as many important social divisions in the past as there are in the present, we must be open to and explore all sorts of possibilities. An homosexuals' archaeology? A workers' archaeology? An archaeology for and about the elderly? Why not? Name a cause which any fair, liberal, open-minded folk would support, and we should be able to devise a material culture reading of the past addressing its concerns. This is not an unhealthy development. An archaeology that focuses on questions of social inequality is appropriate and exciting, as is the nascent and flourishing archaeological examination of plantation complexes and slavery in the American South and elsewhere.[3] One nevertheless must keep analytically distinct the admirable social cause from the archaeology and the evidence that the archaeological record may or may not contain. Unfortunately, not all of these new approaches to the past will be equally amenable to archaeological analysis, to the direct interpretation of the material culture record. If the post-processualists triumph in their struggle against the old fogeys and reactionaries, entirely new departments of archaeology can be envisioned. No more job announcements for areal, period, or even theory specialists; rather, departments will hire archaeologists trained to represent "different interest groups" (see Hodder 1986: 149). Such a development could bring healthy change in the hallowed halls of academe – if it leads to the rigorous and appropriate archaeological examination of these issues. If, on the other hand, it results only in unconstrained multiple readings of the past, the discipline of prehistoric anthropological archaeology will come to resemble a poor stepfellow's department of fictional literature.

Diversity is a strength, but we cannot abandon tests of adequacy or those approaches to the past which are more satisfying, which may also mean more explanatory, than others. For accounts of specific problems, this may mean recourse to environmental-, demographic-, or technological-based explanations. Not for every issue, not inevitably; but when the archaeological evidence is most satisfactorily accounted for through such an interpretation, we should not be afraid to make it simply because it smacks of the vulgar materialism long dominant in processual archaeology. The problem with the metaphor of story telling is not just that links to an external real world are severed or, in some sense, trivialized, but also that the relativity of the exercise may be implied: one yarn is as good as another. Here, diversity becomes liability as any review of racist or chauvinist, nationalist readings of the past would demonstrate. The point is obvious and should not require belaboring, but, apparently, many post-processualists in England and the United States operate under the illusion that such dangerous, undesirable tendencies are behind us and represent nothing more than an unfortunate episode in the history of the discipline. In the real world (e.g., Southeast Asia, China, the former Soviet Union, the Middle East, continental Europe) such "readings" are still ubiquitous and still dangerous: the material culture record all too frequently is used to justify nationalist aspirations and land claims. In this light, post-processual archaeology seems absurdly academic.

Diversity is a strength, but it may also result in an archaeology that refuses to confront significant problems, to address unresolved difficulties in our understanding of the past. When I am lectured to on the significance of decorated calabashes among the Ilchamus of Baringo, Kenya or subjected to an excruciatingly detailed analysis of contemporary Swedish and British beer cans – besides yawning and falling asleep or turning to a really good story, i.e., a novel to be read for pleasure, I note, as others have done before me, that the advocated contextual critical approach seems to offer its most telling insights on the contemporary or ethnographically and historically documented world. The translation of these examples to the prehistoric past, however, and their relevance to what should be the major activity of most archaeologists, is either unclear or largely an article of faith.

Being critical, I also contemplate how trivial our sense of problem has become. The greatness of Childe consisted not only in his consistent application of the most powerful and generally appropriate and amenable social theory for archaeological purposes, Marxism, but also in his concern and focus in his major works on important prehistoric questions ranging from the introduction and utilization of wheeled vehicles to the spread of food-producing economies up the Danube or the interrelations among the early riverine civilizations of Mesopotamia and the Nile and Indus valleys. What will consign some of the output of today's most visible post-processualists to early obscurity is their choice of fundamentally irrelevant, at times even ludicrous, subjects for analysis. Phrasing this even more critically, it seems to me that the intellectual game-playing quotient (or sophistry) of post-processual archaeology, at this stage at any rate, is even higher than that which characterized the early writings of the first generation of new archaeologists. Whether questioning the food-sharing proclivities of our Plio-Pleistocene ancestors or sniffing around F. Bordes, drinking his wine, and jousting with him over the interpretation of the Mousterian, Binford, at least initially, addressed major problems in prehistory.

Binford is also correct in insisting that there is an external world out there, a reality, which the archaeological record – however palely and imperfectly – reflects. His current emphasis on the problems of interpreting that record, the distinction between contemporary artifacts and the past activities that produced them, middle-range theorizing, and the like – all these mark a significantly more sober appraisal of archaeology's ability to reconstruct the past than the unrestrained optimistic evaluation of his and other new archaeologists' writings of the late sixties and early seventies. These trends have not – quite explicitly and forcefully not – succumbed to the ultimate relativist or subjectivist temptation: that reality is a chimera or, at least, unknowable, and that one interpretation of the present or past is as valid as any other. Some of the more unguarded, hyperbolic statements of his post-processual nemesis, Hodder, unfortunately have implied that this Pandora's box should be opened, resulting inevitably, of course, in the realization that Mr. von Däniken's readings of prehistory are as true and meaningful as those of Mr. Hodder.

Overstated, malicious? Perhaps, but my criticism is intended to polemicize and ruffle certain feathers. One other significant limitation of Hodder's prescriptions for reading the past should be noted: his vaunted idealism. Methodological and theoretical difficulties beset the realization of this goal. I have written about the latter before (Kohl 1985), and, from my perspective, Hodder's more recent writings only confirm my suspicions that, if we follow his advice, we enter a world of cultural mystification, or what R. Fox labels "culturology," a world in which peoples differ simply because they differ, their cultures irreducible Platonic essences, givens that somehow exist outside the stream of historical experience. Let me cite Hodder himself:

> But to claim that culture is meaningfully constituted is ultimately to claim that aspects of culture are *irreducible* . . . The cultural relationships are not caused by anything else outside themselves. They just are.

Moreover,

> If we say that meanings are context dependent, then all we can do is come to an understanding of each cultural context in its own right, as a unique set of cultural dispositions and practices. We cannot generalize from one culture to another. (Hodder 1986: 4, 6)

Additional comment might not be necessary. Here I have not parodied Hodder but quoted him directly. This view not only will not take us very far in understanding the past, but, I would argue, is simply wrong and mystifying, treating culture as something not produced and constantly made, remade, and sometimes even consciously invented, by human groups in specific historical situations for specific, partially ascertainable reasons. Archaeologists should consider meaningfully constituted cultural explanations for certain phenomena, including long-term regularities often traceable in the archaeological record; but our task only begins, not ends, with the identification of specific cultural patterns (see Wolf 1984).

Methodological objections also are apparent to this call for getting "inside" the real meaning of archaeological data. Philosophically, R. G. Collingwood may make a more attractive guru for understanding the human past than C. Hempel, but the strictures Collingwood advocates are often too difficult for historians to apply, much less archaeologists who always must interpret mute, meaningfully ambiguous artifacts. This difficulty has been well stated by A. Gilman:

> The problem is that past ideas are represented as such through symbols, which are by definition arbitrary with respect to their referents . . . For prehistory, where no such bilinguals (as in ethno- or historical archaeology) exist, how are the symbols in the archaeological text to be read? (Gilman 1987: 516)

The point is not that cultural meanings, ideas, and values are unimportant or can be treated satisfactorily as epiphenomena to more basic material conditions. I also suppose it is useful for us to be reminded of M. Weber's famous (if contested) hypothesis on the significance of the Protestant ethic for the emergence of capitalism and to be told how unsatisfactorily archaeologists, including (perhaps even especially) Marxists, treat things ideological. All this is fair enough, but it does not solve the problem of interpreting meaningfully ambiguous material culture remains – except, of course, through various sleights of hand, subtle introductions of historical or ethnographic examples posing as prehistoric. We are once more confronting a world of relativism where my interpretation of meaning is as valid as yours.

Astoundingly enough, the optimism of some post-processual archaeologists even exceeds that of the early new archaeologists. It is better just to lower our expectations, adjust to reality, and accept, to some provisional extent, the assessments of more sober evaluations of the archaeological record, such as those long ago advanced by C. Hawkes and E. Leach. Knowledge of the past still can advance, and our reconstructions of it will only ring true if we are attuned, *as sensitively as the evidence permits*, to considerations of intentions, meanings, cultural values, and the like. In other words, a basic uniformitarian principle must be invoked: our understanding of the past must resemble our understanding of the present, and a world in which meanings, cultural differences, and beliefs play only an inconsequential, secondary role is an incomprehensible world, not the one in which I live. For me, this is the ultimate objection to the "animalism" of the new processual archaeology: the contemporary world is not exclusively shaped by demographic and environmental factors, an external reality that makes me strongly suspicious that the past was either. If we should consider prehistory as an extension of history, the ultimate *longue durée*, and if we need intellectual gurus for guidance, I suggest we read practicing historians who have reflected soberly on their craft and the limitations of their data. M. Bloch and E. H. Carr strike me as far better guides for archaeologists than Collingwood.

Processual and post-processual archaeology compared: continuities as progress or regress?

Such suggestions are perhaps too sensible, commonplace; our *critical* edge is no longer sharp. Clearly, we have not sufficiently followed Shanks and Tilley's dictum to reflect *critically* "upon archaeology as a discipline in the present." We will conclude not by contrasting, but by comparing post-processual to processual archaeology. Certain features must be shared, for, as noted above, when considering processual and post-processual archaeology we are dealing with phenomena largely of the Anglo-American world of scholarship and research.

How should we analyze this social reality *critically*? We cannot here cast our analysis so broadly as to review all the distinctive, relevant shared features of British and American culture evident in the new and post-new archaeology. We can only briefly examine some common characteristics internal to the discipline itself. Perhaps we can profitably proceed as structuralists, following one fruitful means for reading the past that Hodder advocates? Let us try:

> Processual archaeology:post-processual archaeology :: Binford:Hodder :: materialism:idealism :: etic:emic :: Hempel:Collingwood :: testing hypotheses:reading the past :: Academic Press:Cambridge University Press (and now perhaps Blackwell's) . . . *ad nauseam.*

This approach may have limited possibilities for a truly *critical* social analysis, but it has uncovered a certain symmetry: post-processualists define themselves in opposed relation to their processual forbears. Fashions in Anglo-American archaeology resemble one another – however inverted the forms they assume.

Perhaps, a literary critical analysis, a deconstruction of the canonical texts of processual and post-processual archaeology, will take us further? Certain shared stylistic traits can easily be traced: the polemical, combative styles of Binford and Hodder; the rushed, relevant, urgent prose of Watson, Redman, and LeBlanc, on the one hand, and Shanks and Tilley on the other; a certain style of preaching, akin to religious proselytization, carried out with the certainty that one has been blessed with special inspiration and insight for predicting or reading the past; the use of little archaeological vignettes or examples, as opposed to extended analyses of significant prehistoric problems, to illustrate one's insight; a rush to publication and an admitted ability to get published all types of articles from graduate student seminar reports to the personal recollections of remarkably young scholars.

Behind such shared traits, the *critical* analyst perceives broader social forces at work. These range from the structure of the publishing industry in the Anglo-American world (dominated, of course, by profit-making capitalist considerations) through the ways in which knowledge is produced and sold in British and American universities to the most significant criterion of all: how academic careers are established and lifetime sinecures obtained within these universities. Far less than in countries with centralized research archaeological institutes, like France or the former Soviet Union, is there any real structural imperative actually to dig. If one simply writes enough and in a polemical and, above all, sufficiently innovative style so as to convince a publisher that this material will sell, and be assigned for graduate and undergraduate instruction, one has fulfilled one's duty to the profession and to oneself. Here it is relevant to relate an anecdote illustrating the immense structural difference separating the praxis of continental European/ Soviet archaeology from American archaeology.

Soviet archaeologists who visited Washington, D.C. in the spring of 1986 to attend the third USA–USSR archaeological symposium were informed on the last day of the conference that their work was tradition-bound, tied to cultural-historical reconstruction of the sort Americans engaged in roughly half a century ago. Further, in the words of this concluding critique, relative to their Soviet colleagues, American archaeologists peered through more theoretical "windows of observation" on the past. Rather than being humiliated at this assessment, one Soviet archaeologist was overheard to ask – not rhetorically, but sincerely – a colleague who had visited the States before, "Do American archaeologists *ever* excavate?"

In an otherwise intelligent article, frequently cited for noting Anglo-American archaeology's tendency for joining tardily different theoretical bandwagons, Mark Leone wrote what I have always considered the silliest and, in a sense, most telling assertion of the then actually *new* processual archaeology.

. . . the reconstruction of events in the past is nearly complete; it offers little in the way of challenge today. And once the outline is in hand, there will remain nothing more than the prehistoric analogues to those studies produced in history under the rubric, "History of the three-tined fork." (Leone 1972: 26)

There is no reason to refute the idiocy of this statement. Anyone who has sincerely attempted to reconstruct the prehistoric past appreciates that what we do not know or understand always is far more impressive than what actually has been discovered and plausibly reconstructed. Nor is it sufficient to say, such were the follies of youth, that, of course, there was much naiveté evident, even predictable, in those exciting days when a new archaeological paradigm was forged. The same follies are being enacted today in a different guise. One important thread of continuity linking processual to post-processual Anglo-American archaeology is the sort of casual dismissal, bordering on disrespect or disregard, for what should be the primary archaeological task: adequately accounting for – that is, reconstructing and, as best we can, explaining – an ever-expanding, never complete material culture record. Post-processual archaeology's frequent lack of concern with significant prehistoric problems illustrates this tendency and is thoroughly consistent with Leone's mistaken belief in a completely known prehistoric past.

This is not a call to return to the trenches, to dig for its own sake. Despite certain irritating self-indulgent, narcissistic features, the self-conscious theorizing and epistemological soul-searching characteristic of both processual and post-processual Anglo-American archaeology has an undeniably positive, stimulating side. As it results in a more satisfactory and complete account of the past, we applaud it. The problem is that writing little books or editing collected volumes for Cambridge University Press's *New Directions in Archaeology* series should not substitute for, but rather complement, more traditional archaeological activities – including, one hopes, uncovering new data through excavations, materials that could significantly alter our understanding of the past. The truly *critical* suspicion, of course, is that what should constitute a subsidiary, ancillary, part-time activity has become primary. Writing papers for symposia is what we do to qualify as professionally active archaeologists in the Anglo-American academic setting.

To conclude, in reflecting *critically* upon processual and post-processual Anglo-American archaeology, we are reminded of the immortal Yogi Berra's immortal words: "It's *déjà vu* all over again." That is, it is the central thesis of this chapter that there is far greater continuity between processual and post-processual archaeology than the various proponents, opponents, or commentators on these approaches have yet admitted. We have only been able to suggest in the sketchiest terms that a satisfactory explanation for the various trends in Anglo-American archaeology must incorporate a sociological analysis of the way the discipline is structured here and in England, the way knowledge is produced, and the purposes to which it is put.

Unfortunately, academic disciplines do not always, nor necessarily, advance. Sometimes, they get sidetracked or structured around false problems, as is the case for theology, for example, or all the mismeasurements of man that Stephen J. Gould has so brilliantly and wittily recorded. The history of reversals, false starts, even wrong directions, often takes decades, if not centuries, to correct. When I was asked to write this paper in 1988 on theory in post-processual archaeology, I thought of medieval scholastic philosophy – the fellows who sometimes debated the number of angels who could fit on the head of a pin – as a potential source of fruitful analogy with contemporary Anglo-American archaeology. It would be fun to pursue this metaphor further; almost certain to irritate and estrange, I would love to sharpen my pen and proceed. In all honesty, however, the comparison would be strained, far too harsh or, in the words of this paper, *critical*. Processual archaeology has unquestioned merits, as do its post-processual successors. Our purpose was to focus on the negative for self-praise is all too evidently another shared trait of the new and the post-new archaeology.

Notes

1 An earlier version of this paper was presented at the "Theory in post-processual archaeology" symposium, organized by Dr. James Chiarelli, at the Society for American Archaeology meetings in Phoenix, AZ, April 1988.

2 The phraseology is that of M. Conkey and J. Gero, whose paper "Building a feminist archaeology" was presented at the symposium in Phoenix. See now Conkey and Gero (1991).

3 This important observation I owe to Elizabeth Brumfiel, who offered many trenchant criticisms of an earlier draft of this paper. I have tried to tone down some of my parody of the new developments in post-processual archaeology in light of her observations, though

probably not enough for her liking, nor enough to escape her characterization of my being an "old fogey." *Mea culpa.*

References cited

Binford, L. 1986 Data, Relativism and Archaeological Science. *Man* 22: 391–404.

Conkey, M. W. and Gero, J. M. 1991 *Engendering Archaeology: Women and Prehistory.* Oxford: Basil Blackwell.

Davis, N. 1975–76 Women's History in Transition: The European Case. *Feminist Studies* 3/3–4: 83–103.

Earle, T. K. and R. W. Preucel 1987 Processual Archaeology and the Radical Critique. *Current Anthropology* 28(4): 501–38.

Gilman, A. 1987 Comment to T. K. Earle and R. W. Preucel's Processual Archaeology and the Radical Critique, *Current Anthropology* 28(4): 516.

Hodder, I. 1986 *Reading the Past: Current Approaches to Interpretation in Archaeology.* Cambridge: Cambridge University Press.

1990 *The Domestication of Europe.* Cambridge, MA: Blackwell's

Kohl, P. L. 1985 Symbolic Cognitive Archaeology: A New Loss of Innocence. *Dialectical Anthropology* 9: 105–17.

1989 World Prehistory: Comments on the Development, Peculiarities and Requirements of a Forgotten Genre. *Culture and History* 5: 133–44.

Leone, M. 1972 Issues in Anthropological Archaeology. In *Contemporary Archaeology*, edited by M. Leone, pp. 14–27. Carbondale: Southern Illinois University Press.

Shanks, M. and C. Tilley 1987 *Re-constructing Archaeology: Theory and Practice.* Cambridge: Cambridge University Press.

Trigger, B. 1989 History and Contemporary American Archaeology: A Critical Analysis. *Archaeological Thought in America*, edited by C. C. Lamberg-Karlovsky, pp. 19–34. Cambridge: Cambridge University Press.

Watson, P. J., C. Redman, and S. LeBlanc 1971 *Explanation in Archaeology.* New York: Columbia University Press.

Wolf, E. 1984 Culture: Panacea or Problem. *American Antiquity* 49: 393–400.

2
A proliferation of new archaeologies: "Beyond objectivism and relativism"

ALISON WYLIE

Skepticism about the archaeological past

Archaeologists have debated a remarkably consistent core of issues since the turn of the century. In 1913, for example, Roland B. Dixon inveighed against research that showed "too little indication of a reasoned formulation of definite problems" and an inexcusable "neglect of saner and more truly scientific methods" (1913: 563); "the time is past," he insisted, "when our major interest was in the specimen . . . We are today concerned with the relations of things, with the whens and the whys and the hows" (1913: 565). The problems he recommended for archaeologists' consideration had to do with "the development of culture in general," with what he described as cultural processes, and the scientific methods he recommended were explicitly those of hypothesis testing: archaeologists should proceed by formulating "a working hypothesis, or several hypotheses" and then seeking material that might fill available gaps and "prove or disprove" them (1913: 564). Four years later, Wissler advocated a very similar (problem-oriented, hypothesis-testing) program, and explicitly aligned it with anthropology; he described it as "the real, or new archaeology" (the article was entitled "The New Archaeology"). There was not to be another such round of methodological soul-searching until the 1930s and 1940s when Kluckhohn, Steward and Setzler, and Bennett, among others, again called for a decisive break with "antiquarianism" – this time they confronted it in the form of a zeal for systematizing, rather than a passion for specimens – and advocated an immediate reorientation of research around anthropological aims and the adoption of scientific modes of practice. It was yet another thirty years before the most recent "New Archaeology" became "everybody"'s archaeology," promoting (again) a scientific hypothesis-testing methodology, and immediate attention to anthropological problems about culture process.

Apart from the prescience of these antecedent "new archaeologies," what impresses me most is that at every juncture where such self-consciousness has emerged about the (anthropological) aims and (scientific) status of the discipline, there has been a commensurably strong opposition both to the proposals made for upgrading practice and to the introduction into archaeology of a reflective, philosophical, mode of discourse; often this opposition has strongly skeptical undertones. Dixon's 1913 article was published with a lengthy critical response by Laufer, who evidently believed that existing specimen-oriented modes of practice were perfectly adequate; he attributed any apparent failure to realize "ethnological" understanding to the limitations of the archaeological record and the immaturity of archaeological investigations of this record. If only archaeologists would give up their vain speculations about aims and methods and get on with the work of collecting the necessary data, they would be assured of eventual success; an understanding of the past would surely be forthcoming. He is best known for a spirited condemnation of "theoretical discussion" of all kinds:[1]

> We should all be more enthusiastic about new facts than about methods; for the constant brooding over the applicability of methods and the questioning of their correctness may lead one to a Hamletic state of mind not wholesome in pushing on active research work. In this sense allow me to conclude with the words of Carlyle: "Produce! Produce! Were it but the pitifullest infinitesimal fraction of a produce, produce it in God's name! 'Tis the utmost thou hast in thee: out with it then!" (1913: 577)

In the 1930s and 1940s, the demand for greater theoretical sophistication and for an immediate shift of attention to explanatory problems ("problems of cultural process," Steward and Setzler, 1938: 7; problems of "functional interpretation," Bennett, 1943: 215) also met with strong resistance. W. D. Strong, for example, insisted that this shift of focus was premature; "archaeology is a youthful science whose primary concern is still [and should still be] the accumulation of essential data" (1936: 365). He added that interpretive and "generalizing" problems could safely be deferred to "a future time of greater leisure and fullness of data" (1935: 3). The subsequent thirty-year reversion to a preoccupation with space–time systematics suggests that many shared Strong's views. The New Archaeology of the 1960s has faced similar objections, but the dynamics of reaction here are more complicated in ways I will consider shortly.

What this makes clear is that archaeologists have debated questions concerning the status and security of archaeological claims about the cultural past since at least the turn of the century; this is not a concern that emerged *de novo* in the 1960s. In each case the underlying – indeed, the motivating – concern has been that archaeology seemed not to have the resources, specifically the necessary data, to take up the more ambitious anthropological and historical problems that have been identified as its ultimate concern. Periodically this gives rise to more general skeptical worries: is it the case that the archaeological data cannot or will not ever support such aims? These questions can be suppressed only as long as it can be claimed that the problem is simply one of gap-filling: the present data base is just contingently inadequate because it is incomplete; as further data accumulate, "the picture" will emerge complete, hence explanatory problems can be deferred to later stages of research. Those I have identified as taking a "traditionalist" line routinely pin their hopes on the promise of this "sequent stage" approach. Over the years, however, it has become progressively harder to sustain the (millenarian) belief that we are approaching a time of "greater fullness of data" in which explanatory questions will be resolved; the volume of accumulated data has increased exponentially and the main result has been a comparably vast increase in complexity and puzzlement. At those junctures when the expanding difficulty of the enterprise overwhelms faith in the prospects for succession to a stage of explanatory clarity, skeptical worries take hold in earnest and the dialectic of debate generates the search for a "new" archaeology – a new research regime – capable of dispelling these worries by transforming practice. The emergence of the "New Archaeology" of the 1960s and 1970s, and of the new reaction against it, is, then, a variant on persistent themes of opposition, generated by a stable core of epistemic problems.

Two considerations typically combine to produce skeptical conclusions in this context: theoretical (ontological) considerations on one hand, and epistemological considerations on the other. The first, the theoretical, arise when the cultural subject is conceived, first and foremost, as a system of intentional, conventional action informed by shared cultural "norms" or ideals. Where the "normative" dimension is emphasized the worry arises that past cultural forms may be entirely idiosyncratic and may diverge radically from any we know or could recognize. If this is the case, no uniformity can be assumed as the basis for interpretive reconstruction, hence, reconstruction of the specifically *cultural* past seems impossible. This is, of course, a central focus of current debates over the viability of the New Archaeology of the 1960s and 1970s in its eco-determinist incarnation. I take it, however, that it is an empirical question whether, or to what extent and in what areas, human behavior is systematic, constrained, or uniform enough to support reconstructive inference from accessible to inaccessible contexts (whether analogical or otherwise); it is not a question that can be settled a priori, by conceptual argument.[2] So I leave aside this dimension of the argument.

What I will consider here is the second, epistemological, set of considerations that generate skepticism: that archaeologists would not know (could not determine) whether, or in what respects, past contexts diverge from hypothetical reconstructions of them given the nature of their evidence. Because they address this problem directly rather than suppressing it, advocates of the various "new archaeologies" provide the clearest account of why it arises. Since 1913, their diagnoses have converged on the assessment that the reason why the mechanical accumulation of data cannot be expected to yield answers to explanatory questions is because these data are meaningless as evidence of the cultural past taken on their own; the data "do not speak for themselves," they have evidential significance only relative to specific problems, under interpretation. This point is made obliquely by Dixon and Wissler early in the century, but with vigorous clarity by critics of the 1930s who insist that "no fact has meaning except in the context of a conceptual scheme" (Kluckhohn 1940: 47) or, again, that "facts are totally without significance and may even be said not to exist without reference to theory" (Steward 1944: 99). The most recent new archaeology produced exactly parallel arguments after a hiatus of 25 years, with little evident awareness of these archaeological antecedents but with new philosophical reference points (i.e., the general contextualist, Kuhnian, arguments about the theory-ladenness of observation that had been formulated in the interim). In the latter two cases, optimistic conclusions were drawn to the effect that if only the "sequent stage" model were abandoned in favor of an "integrative" approach, one in which research is oriented around the problems of ultimate concern, and incorporates an explicitly theoretical component, then what we understand of the archaeological record need not be limited to what we can observe of it; a sufficiently rich interpretive/ theoretical framework will allow even very fragmentary data to be constituted as evidence of manifestly unobservable past events and conditions of life.[3]

As recent critics have argued to good effect, however, these contextualist arguments for a "new" archaeology prove too much. If the data stand as evidence only under interpretation, could they not be interpreted in any number of different ways, and thus support a myriad of alternative reconstructive and explanatory hypotheses? Even more worrisome, does this contextualism not entail that inferences concerning the past are unavoidably circular, that archaeologists will necessarily find in the record just, or only, what their conceptual framework prepares them to recognize as evidence? Implicitly, traditionalists since the 1910s have recognized this problem inasmuch as they reject any position which privileges theory, or calls for attention to explanatory questions before all the data are in, on grounds that this is simply a license for speculation. Their answer is to restrict attention to the data themselves and defer the problem of interpretation. After the 1930s, more specifically after Kluckhohn's arguments to the effect that theory-free or theory-neutral data collection is not an option, traditionalist responses were not so sanguine. Some did still insist that culturally significant structure could be "objectively discovered" in the data (e.g., Spaulding in debate with Ford; 1953, 1954), but throughout this period there were a number of self-avowed subjectivists who concluded that *descriptive* systematizations of archaeological data are "merely tools of analysis," arbitrary constructs that reflect more about our interests than about any inherent, "real" structure to be discovered in the record (Brew 1946: 76). In their view this is an unavoidable feature of practice and counsels tolerance of a broad plurality of approaches and perspectives. Those who were unwilling to endorse what approached an "anything goes" epistemic policy gravitated to conventionalism. Thompson's (pragmatist) subjectivism is perhaps the best-known example (Thompson 1956); it was he who was vilified by Binford for reducing the evaluation of interpretive hypotheses to a process of polling archaeologists. In fact, his analysis is considerably more sophisticated than this, but he does conclude that, given the theory-laden nature of archaeological data-as-evidence, testing procedures incorporate an irreducibly subjective element, hence our only recourse is to assess the credibility (intellectual honesty, skill) of the researcher who has formulated the hypothesis in question.

While these conventionalist arguments functioned as a catalyst for the most recent new archaeology, the most thorough-going skepticism formulated to date has emerged in reaction against it. A number of critics and successors to this New Archaeology now argue that, if its contextualist insights are really taken seriously, it must be accepted that the archaeologist "creates 'facts'" (Hodder, 1983: 6); archaeology must be "re-constructed" to take account of the fact that the "metaphysics of presence" and foundationalisms of all kinds have now been thoroughly discredited. Although the strongest proponents of this latter, postprocessual move insist that they "do not mean to suggest that all pasts are equal" (Shanks and Tilley, 1987: 245), they do seem to embrace the conclusion that claims about the past are all equally speculative; "truth is a [mobile] army of metaphors" (Shanks and Tilley 1987: 22), and so, it would

seem, are any of the criteria of adequacy or grounds that might be used to judge competing knowledge claims. So long as alternative accounts are internally consistent, this leaves no non-conventional, non-subjective grounds for choosing among them, taken in their own terms (for further analysis of these arguments, see Wylie 1992c).

The final irony is that now, at the very time when these most profoundly skeptical and relativist critiques are emerging, a counter-trend in archaeology has been to return to strict data-oriented research and the conviction that culture-historical reconstruction will be unproblematic if only archaeologists can establish sufficiently complete knowledge of the record. With this the circle is closed. Skeptical worries are thus alternately embraced and denied, but in neither case routed.

Philosophical and feminist responses

Although this polarization of positions may seem highly specific to archaeology and its particular methodological difficulties, I am struck by a number of potentially instructive parallels between the pattern of argument unfolding here and that emerging in other contexts where similar "crises of representation" have taken hold. I have discussed elsewhere parallels with debates about the import of feminist critiques of science, specifically, whether they entail a radical and politically disabling relativism (Wylie 1992a), and with the challenges posed by "interpretive" social scientists, particularly those practicing in socio-cultural anthropology (Wylie 1922b). Let me comment on the feminist debates briefly but then focus on another, perhaps less obvious, set of parallels that arise when you consider current philosophical discussions of the opposition between broadly objectivist and relativist positions, specifically that due to Bernstein in *Beyond Objectivism and Relativism* (1983).

Although feminist critics of the social and biological sciences began by identifying instances of androcentric or sexist bias which seemed largely the result of "bad science," their analyses have come to pose a profound challenge to "good" science, science as a whole, calling into question the gender-neutrality of virtually all aspects of the research enterprise (see Harding 1986). The result has been intense debate over the relativist conclusions that seem to follow; however compelling they may seem, feminist theorists have been persistently wary of them (see, for example, Strathern 1987, and the "ambivalence" in Harding 1986, Wylie 1987, and also the articles included in Tuana 1987, 1988, and di Leonardo 1991). One recurrent theme in this literature, which has direct relevance for archaeology, is the suspicion that the constructivism and relativism of postmodern positions embodies what is patently an ideology of the powerful: it reflects a presumption of control over the "realities" of our lives, both as participants and as observers, that belies the oppressive network of constraints which any who are subdominant or dispossessed must continuously negotiate. While it is a central part of the experience of feminists that these realities are by no means an immutable given – as political activists, feminists are committed to challenging the ideologies of legitimation that make them seem "natural," and to taking action that will reshape oppressive conditions of life – it is also an equally central experience that the conditions of life we confront are not infinitely plastic ephemera; it is possible to be (disastrously) mistaken in what one believes about them and often a great deal depends on determining where the gaps and distortions, the self-delusions, lie in the understanding that guides our action. Given this it is a profound irony, often noted in this literature, that a crisis of representation should threaten to destabilize all understanding *just* as minority voices begin to be heard and to challenge the (coercive, oppressive) partiality of dominant world views (see the introduction to di Leonardo 1991).

Although recent philosophical analyses generally lack any such clear motivating insights as these, they do, increasingly, explore the question of how we proceed *in practice* to evaluate contending theories and identify errors when it is no longer plausible to assume that there are any given, cross-contextually stable standards of adequacy – no "foundation" – against which they can be judged. Bernstein's analysis is a particularly interesting, if substantially incomplete, exploration of options implicit in our practice which may lie "beyond objectivism and relativism" (1983), options which have been obscured by the pitched battle between objectivists and relativists.[4]

Bernstein's model

Bernstein's characterization of these alternatives "beyond" turns on a central metaphor: an amended version of Peirce's suggestion that scientific arguments are more like cables than chains. He observed that the arguments used to evaluate incommensurable theories typically proceed not by "a linear [link-by-link] movement from premises to conclusions or from individual 'facts' to generalizations," but rather by exploiting "multiple strands and diverse types of evidence, data, hunches, and arguments to [assess and, ultimately, to] support a scientific hypothesis or theory" (1983: 69). Although this process is often exceedingly complex – assessments of relative strength on different criteria may not pull in the same direction, and the criteria themselves may be open to revision as the process unfolds – Bernstein maintains that "the cumulative weight of [disparate, multi-dimensional considerations of] evidence, data, reasons, and arguments

can be rationally decisive" (1983: 74). Extreme relativism in which there are no grounds for choice between alternatives does not automatically follow from the fact that no one set of considerations is fundamental across the board, no one strand of argument conclusive.

Bernstein gives very little account of how or why this stabilization (tentative though it may be) is realized through "cables" of argument, but I think there is a clue to this in a second metaphor he invokes in passing, an adaptation of Geertz's suggestion that anthropologists must proceed by "tacking back and forth" between their own cultural context and that of the people they seek to understand. Geertz's view is that although anthropologists must grasp the system of "experience-near" concepts in terms of which members of a culture ordinarily understand and represent their own actions, beliefs, and feelings, these "must be balanced by the appropriate experience-distant concepts, concepts that are not necessarily familiar to the people being studied but that . . . make intelligible the symbolic forms [of their culture]" (1983: 95), e.g., concepts like that of a "person" which Geertz himself has used in comparative study. The aim of inquiry is, then, to construct an account of how these abstract concepts are instantiated in the experience-near concepts and practices of particular "subject" cultures.

On my analysis, this process of tacking has several more dimensions than Geertz or Bernstein acknowledges.[5] What they envision is, in effect, a diagonal tack between their own ("our") "experience-distant" – their/our explanatory concepts – and the practice of the subjects of inquiry, including their practice-embedded "experience-near" concepts. But for this tack to get under way, some form of "dialectical tacking" must occur on a vertical axis within the context of the researcher: "we" must formulate a set of general, explanatory (experience-distant) concepts appropriate to research, no doubt through some process of reflection on "our own" experience-near concepts and practices. Where anthropological subjects can be expected to have their own conceptual schemes that explain and, in fact, order their cultural practice – their own repertoire of experience-distant concepts – the process of tacking between contexts is further complicated by the fact that its aim cannot be solely to establish how *our* experience-distant concepts are instantiated in *their* practice. For many purposes, researchers must also seek an understanding of the indigenous ("experience-distant") concepts that structure life in the subject context. Moreover, with regard to both near and distant concepts, inquiry must proceed inferentially, usually by way of a suppressed analogy; explanatory and reconstructive hypotheses inevitably depend on a wide range of background knowledge about the sorts of conditions, beliefs, and structuring principles that are capable of producing the action we observe. If we are to avoid arbitrary imposition, a process of tacking between our models and their practices must unfold in which we ask directly (if we can) if our hypotheses are accurate, and otherwise (or, in addition) seek evidence that the conditions we postulate do, indeed, hold and are responsible for the action we seek to understand. Frequently this process will be interactive; the process of hammering out cross-framework understanding will often involve an enlargement and realignment of our own explanatory concepts and of the criteria of adequacy that govern the evaluation of rival accounts. When the tacking metaphor is unpacked, then, it reveals a process which is at least four-dimensional and it is bi-directional on all dimensions.

Archaeological tacking

I suggest that archaeologists routinely exploit a tacking process of roughly the structure I have described, but because they typically lack access to the articulate beliefs of their cultural subjects, they adopt strategies of inquiry that throw into sharp relief crucial inferential steps that are suppressed when we can directly negotiate an understanding of unfamiliar forms of life with those who participate in them. In the process, the factors that stabilize such inferential processes are also thrown into relief.

Whatever its specific aims, archaeological interpretation depends on background knowledge of contemporary contexts; it is explicitly and heavily dependent on vertical tack arguments within the source context (broadly construed) which produce both experience-distant concepts – generally theories about cultural development, differentiation, interaction, and adaptation – and detailed, experience-near models of specific past practices. These constitute a locus of constraint which has been very effectively exploited in the increasing number of instances where "source-side" (experimental or ethnoarchaeological) research is used to determine how a given archaeological record "could possibly" or "could likely" be produced. While current work in this area has produced numerous cautionary tales, it has also demonstrated that the plausibility and relevance of interpretive options can be systematically evaluated on substantive, evidential (i.e., not wholly arbitrary or subjective) grounds. The degree to which this yields a determinate conclusion depends on the nature of the subject phenomena; as I argued above, not all are equally plastic or equally uniformitarian. The most striking examples come from analyses of the material (physical) conditions necessary for the production of specific archaeological materials or traces (e.g., use-wear analyses which allow a sharp delimitation of the range of plausible interpretive alternatives).

In addition to this vertical tacking on the source-side of the interpretive equation, archaeologists engage a series of horizontal and diagonal tacks between source and subject which are frequently conducted as a deliberate test of interpretive hypotheses; evidence is sought (following something akin to Collingwood's logic of "question and answer," 1978) that is specifically relevant to the question of whether it is likely that a particular past context instantiated the reconstructive models archaeologists bring to it. Although this is a tenuous and highly complex process, it can be strikingly decisive in settling what can reasonably be claimed about a past cultural context. One classic example of this is due to Strong and to Wedel, two of the key proponents of the "sequent stage" model in the 1930s; they conclusively disproved the entrenched assumption that prehistoric plains Indians could not but have been nomadic hunters, like those groups encountered in the plains at the time of contact, given the harshness of the environment and the primitive nature of their material culture (1935 and 1938, respectively). They found direct evidence of cultigens in prehistoric contexts and indirect evidence of cultural continuity between the prehistoric cultures and displaced agricultural groups which established that agriculture was indigenous to the plains; the direct-historical analogy drawn between prehistoric groups and contact-period hunters, and the eco-determinist presupposition which underpinned it, proved to be unsustainable.

Although the negative examples are often most compelling, such subject-side testing can also provide at least limited confirmation of reconstructive hypotheses and can canalize interpretive theorizing. I take this to be the case in recent analyses which reveal that, contra the assumptions of latter-day eco-determinists, the variability evident in many assemblages of material culture cannot be accounted for in functional-ecological terms, and which are directed, by the highly redundant complexity of this material, to structuralist modes of analysis (e.g., in the contributions to Hodder 1982a). In some cases testing is decisive because crucial test data can be recovered whose evidential significance is unambiguous, given well-established interpretive principles. More often, questions about the applicability of a given interpretive hypothesis are settled when a number of independently constituted lines of evidence converge in either supporting or refuting the proposal that the particular conditions it postulates were instantiated in the past context in question.

In all cases, however, interpretive conclusions depend on various lines of argument developed on vertical and horizontal tacks in both source and subject contexts. And, in this, their strength derives both from the diversity of their evidential support and, more specifically, from the fact that their constituent strands concern different dimensions of the archaeological record and draw on different ranges of background knowledge to interpret its evidential significance; *they are compelling taken together because it is highly implausible that they could all incorporate compensatory errors.* This is just to say that archaeological tacking can, and frequently does, exploit a "network of resistances" (to use Shanks and Tilley's terminology, 1987: 104) that is set up both by the (subject-side) archaeological data and, indirectly, by the data that have shaped the theories (on the source-side) that inform the interpretation of these data as evidence (see Wylie 1992a for a further account of how these constraints operate).

Conclusion

These features of archaeological practice suggest a general strategy of response to archaeological skeptics which, in turn, yields some further insights about the nature of the "options beyond objectivism and relativism" defended by Bernstein and by many feminist theorists. Two points are relevant here. The first is that theoretical commitments do not *monolithically* control both the interpretation of archaeological data as evidence and the generation of reconstructive hypotheses which these data might be expected to test. In any given reconstructive–evaluative argument, it will be necessary to exploit a range of different, *independent* sources to accomplish these diverse tasks. It is the independence of sources, and therefore of the constituent arguments about evidential significance, which ensures that the strands of the resulting cables are not just mutually reinforcing but are also, and crucially, mutually constraining.

The second related point is that, as much as the vagaries of research practice make us aware that we very largely see or understand what our background knowledge and theoretical commitments prepare us to see, it is also a central and daily part of this experience that we can be surprised, we can quite literally discover things we did not or could not expect given this framework. In short, our presuppositions, theoretical or otherwise, are not *all-pervasive*. We frequently find out that we were wrong, that the data resist any interpretation that will make them consistent with our expectations, and that we are dealing with a subject (cultural or otherwise) which is very different from anything with which we are familiar. We are then forced *by the evidence* to consider interpretive possibilities completely different from those which we had entertained in the past, and even to rethink deep-seated orienting presuppositions about the nature of cultural phenomena. Although there are certainly no such things as wholly neutral factual "givens," it is also not the case that data are entirely plastic, that they are so theory-permeated

that facts can be constituted at will in whatever form a contextually appealing theory requires. I assume it is an appreciation of this which leads archaeological theorists like Shanks and Tilley to declare themselves realists (1987: 111) and to invoke the "network of resistances" imposed by data (1987: 104), even though this would seem to entail abandonment of the strong anti-foundationalist arguments with which they open their critique of processual archaeology.

The various new archaeologies proposed to date have certainly been flawed in significant ways. Nonetheless, they share a common and compelling core, *viz.*, the advocacy of research strategies which exploit resistances on the various dimensions captured by the tacking and cable metaphors. I suggest that what we need now is not a "postmodern" or "post-processual" archaeology, but renewed resolve to come to grips with the problems that modern, processual archaeology and its antecedents have addressed.

Notes

1 This was quoted with a kind of bemused admiration by Johnson in a review article, "A quarter century of growth in American archaeology," which was presented at the 25th anniversary of the SAA in 1960 (1961).

2 In fact I note that, despite their strong programmatic commitment to a contextualism that would seem to undermine any empirical treatment of such questions, the recent advocates of humanistic, "normative" particularism make extensive use of (empirical) ethnographic evidence to demonstrate the plasticity of social, cultural processes. They do not rest their case on appeals to the political implications of endorsing determinist models of human action (e.g., Hodder 1982b) which their epistemological/methodological arguments suggest should be their only recourse. I have discussed this irony in some detail elsewhere (Wylie 1989a).

3 This proposition is present in embryonic form in the arguments of Dixon and Wissler, and acquires programmatic force in the 1930s, but it is with the New Archaeology of the 1960s and 1970s that it receives full articulation.

4 Objectivists assume that there *must* be "objective foundations for philosophy, knowledge, or language"; if "certainty" and "absolute constraints" cannot be secured, we face the threat of "madness and chaos where nothing is fixed" (1983: 18), and since this is clearly untenable, it is taken as a reductio of relativist objections. Relativist critics are equally unmoved in their conviction that the "quest for some fixed point, some stable rock upon which we can secure our lives" (1983: 18) is manifestly

bankrupt. The result is an impasse in which the counter-posed positions harden into rigid opposition.

5 This analysis was originally developed in Wylie 1989b.

References

Bennett, J. W. 1943 Recent Developments in the Functional Interpretation of Archaeological Data. *American Antiquity* 9: 208–19.

Bernstein, Richard J. 1983 *Beyond Objectivism and Relativism: Science, Hermeneutics, and Praxis.* Philadelphia: University of Pennsylvania Press.

Brew, John O. 1946 The Use and Abuse of Taxonomy. In *The Archaeology of Alkali Ridge, Southeastern Utah*, Papers of the Peabody Museum, 21: 44–66.

Collingwood, R. G. 1978 *An Autobiography.* Oxford: Oxford University Press.

Dixon, Roland B. 1913 Some Aspects of North American Archaeology. *American Anthropologist* 15: 549–66 (with comments: 566–77).

Geertz, Clifford 1979 From the Native's Point of View: On the Nature of Anthropological Understanding. In *Interpretive Social Science: A Reader*, edited by Paul Rabinow and William M. Sullivan, pp. 225–42. Berkeley: University of California Press.

Harding, Sandra 1986 *The Science Question in Feminism.* Ithaca: Cornell University Press.

Hodder, Ian (ed.) 1982a *Symbolic and Structural Archaeology.* Cambridge: Cambridge University Press.

1982b *The Present Past.* London: Batsford.

1983 Archaeology, Ideology and Contemporary Society. *Royal Anthropological Institute News* 56: 6–7

Johnson, Frederick 1961 A Quarter Century of Growth in American Archaeology. *American Antiquity* 27: 1–6.

Kluckhohn, Clyde 1939 The Place of Theory in Anthropological Studies. *Philosophy of Science* 6: 328–44.

1940 The Conceptual Structure in Middle American Studies. In *The Maya and their Neighbors*, edited by C. L. Hay, *et al.*, pp. 40–51. New York: Dover.

Laufer, Berthold 1913 Comments on: "Some Aspects of North American Archaeology." *American Anthropologist* 15: 573–77.

di Leonardo, Michaela (ed.) 1991 *Gender at the Crossroads of Knowledge: Feminist Anthropology in the Postmodern Era.* Berkeley: University of California Press.

Shanks, Michael and Christopher Tilley 1987 *Re-Constructing Archaeology.* Cambridge: Cambridge University Press.

Spaulding, Albert C. 1953 Review of *Measurements of Some Prehistoric Design Developments in the Southeastern States. American Anthropologist* 55: 588–91.

1954 Reply to Ford. *American Antiquity* 19: 392–3.

Steward, Julian H. and Frank M. Setzler 1938 Function and Configuration in Archaeology. *American Antiquity* 1: 4–10.

Strathern, Marilyn 1987 An Awkward Relationship: The Case of Feminism and Anthropology. *Signs* 12: 276–92.

Strong, William Duncan 1935 *Introduction to Nebraska Archaeology.* Smithsonian Miscellaneous Collections, volume 93, No. 10. Washington: Smithsonian Institution.

1936 Anthropological Theory and Archaeological Fact. In *Essays in Anthropology* edited by Robert H. Lowie, pp. 359–70. Berkeley: University of California Press.

Thompson, Raymond H. 1956 The Subjective Element in Archaeological Inference. *Southwestern Journal of Anthropology* 12: 327–32.

Tuana, Nancy (ed.) 1987, 1988 *Feminism and Science I & II.* Special issues of *Hypatia*, vols. 2.3 and 3.1.

Wedel, Waldo R. 1938 The Direct-historic Approach in Pawnee Archaeology. *Smithsonian Miscellaneous Collections* 97: 1–21.

Wissler, Clark 1917 The New Archaeology. *American Museum Journal* 17: 100–1.

Wylie, Alison 1987 The Philosophy of Ambivalence: Sandra Harding on *The Science Question in Feminism, Canadian Journal of Philosophy.* Supplementary Vol. 13: 59–73.

1989a Matters of Fact and Matters of Interest. In *Archaeological Approaches to Cultural Identity*, edited by Stephen Shennan, pp. 94–109. London: Unwin Hyman.

1989b Archaeological Cables and Tacking: The Implications of Practice for Bernstein's "Options Beyond Objectivism and Relativism." *Philosophy of the Social Sciences* 19: 1–18.

1992a The Interplay of Evidential Constraints and Political Interests: Recent Archaeological Work on Gender. *American Antiquity* 57: 15–34.

1992b Feminist Theories of Social Power: Some Implications for a Processual Archaeology. *Norwegian Archaeological Review* 25: 51–68.

1992c On "Heavily Decomposing Red Herrings": Scientific Method in Archaeology and the Ladening of Evidence with Theory. To appear in *Metaarchaeology* edited by Lester Embree, Boston Studies in the Philosophy of Science, Kluwer, Boston (in press).

3
Ambition, deference, discrepancy, consumption: the intellectual background to a post-processual archaeology

CHRISTOPHER CHIPPINDALE

A post-processual archaeology is, by the definition of its name, something that arises out of a processual archaeology. Post-processual archaeology itself is a reflection, in our own little discipline, of the larger post-modern movement that has so influenced academics and intellectuals in the 1980s; the "modern movement" in archaeology itself seems to have been provided, in large measure, by the American school of the New Archaeology, and by contemporary work in Britain. As post-processual has arisen both out of and against processual, so it has come largely to be shaped by processual habits – either to develop those manners further, or to turn against them. A great deal has been written about the character of post-processual archaeology, by the "pp"s themselves and now by their several critics; some of that debate is now conveniently brought together in Preucel's excellent edited collection (Preucel 1991), to which this book adds more. This paper therefore looks not at post-processual by itself, but at four elements in the intellectual climate within archaeology of which post-processual is a part.

I chance to have been in the University of Cambridge, the place where the "p" versus "pp" argument has been most openly fought, at some busy periods: first as an undergraduate during 1970–73 when David Clarke held an intellectual initiative; and again from 1982 onwards, as a graduate student and in junior staff positions, in the era when "pp" has arisen there.

Like all participant observers, I have an interest in the matter – two interests, in fact. As editor of a journal, *Antiquity*, that wishes to keep in close touch with new, valuable, and influential work, I want to understand where the subject is going, so that my journal reflects what good people are interested in. As a researcher myself in fields

where post-processual is already an influence, I want to see how the intellectual topography of that landscape may be changing.

Adequately defining post-processual would take most of a paper: there is a recent argument about just what "pp" actually is in Bintliff (1991b), Thomas and Tilley (1992), and Bintliff (1992). I take post-processual as primarily referring to the ideas of the Cambridge radicals, as these were first displayed in Hodder's survey *Reading the Past* (1986), subtitled *Current approaches to interpretation in archaeology*, developing ideas from his earlier writing (e.g. 1982a; 1982b; 1982c) with two edited books (1987a; 1987b); and in Shanks and Tilley's black book *Re-constructing Archaeology* (1987a), subtitled *Theory and practice*, and red book, *Social Theory and Archaeology* (Shanks and Tilley 1987b). Important in the early critical literature were Gardin (1987), Barrett (1987), Earle and Preucel (1987), and Patrik (1985). For the American group, who may appear to be first cousins to the Cambridge radicals, there was to start with Leone, Potter and Shackel (1987), and Leone and Potter (1988). The literature has grown at an astonishing rate in the years up to the writing of this published paper in April 1992, but the essential character of the "pp" school has not – in my view – changed in that period.

I have divided my remarks under the four headings of my title: ambition, deference, discrepancy, consumption. To indicate the way in which these character traits are those of the larger discipline, rather than the exclusive concern of the "pp"s, I illustrate them with examples from scholars of "p," of "pp," and of uncommitted persuasions. Points which are near to self-evident are made briefly; others demand justification at some length.

Ambition

I begin with ambition. Embree (1987) provides an elegant proof that archaeology is the most fundamental, intractable, and important of all empirical disciplines. Its special place at the most difficult end of a range of studies arises from the complexity of the subject-matter that it addresses in relation to the paucity of reliable empirical evidence with which it is able to work. Embree remarks (1987: 76):

> Clearly, Archaeology is ambitious. In view of the data it begins with and what little it has thus far attained in the way of results, it would also be easy to call Archaeology preposterous.

The discrepancy between ambitious and preposterous, between ends and means, between ideals and reality, has shown itself in a thousand patronizing cartoons, and in two tendencies in the archaeological literature that have run side by side for decades.

The ambitious tendency sees archaeology as the great human story, the large historical study across so many millennia in which those recorded activities of literate peoples which historians are able narrowly to observe are only the last curiosities. That is why Gordon Childe called his studies of European prehistory not just *The Dawn of European Civilization* (Childe 1925) but *What Happened in History* (Childe 1942); it was these rather distant events, to be grasped from archaeological materials, which could explain how *Man Makes Himself* (Childe 1936). Notice the years when these last two books were published, times when there were pressing reasons for a European to believe that more contemporary historical events were what mattered in the world.

The preposterous tendency, with its eye more on the means, sees archaeological materials as limited and therefore limiting. So much has been lost! The task of the archaeologist must be to chronicle the ruins, hazarding only a cautious and occasional guess as to what they are the ruins of.

Some regions and periods are famously sparse in their evidence, others overwhelmingly rich. Yet there is no simple correlation between large ambitions and large materials. Those brave enough to face the Lower Paleolithic seem concerned to build large views of large issues; those with the overwhelming quantity of artifacts and encircling historical sources from Roman Europe seem less concerned with the biggest questions. If anything, it looks rather the reverse: perhaps those with poor sources are obliged to look to the large issues; perhaps those with good sources never need to look to the large issues. Each tendency can regard the other as absurd – inflating castles in empty air, or mindlessly stamp-collecting. The art-historical traditions, growing out of connoisseurship, offer especially for Classical archaeology a third tendency – the study of the qualities immanent in the objects themselves, to which the archaeological questions of context and interpretation are often secondary.

Sir Mortimer Wheeler (1954) famously said, forty years ago, "the archaeologist is digging up, not *things*, but *people*." Now Wheeler, like the rest of us, dug up things and nothing but things – however much he may have *wanted* to dig up people. The closest he got was human bones, bones like those from the "war-cemetery" at Maiden Castle that could be linked directly into the drama of invasion, battle, death, and subjugation as the Roman military swept over Britain. Wheeler dug up things, and then inferred from the things to the people: *here* the battle was fought, *here* the soldiers fell, *here* they were buried, *here* we now find their bones. The

recent re-examination of Maiden Castle is cautious in identifying these burials as amounting to a war-cemetery at all (Sharples 1991).

Ambition has been a conspicuous commonplace of the archaeological scene certainly since the time around 1968, the *annus mirabilis* of the New Archaeology, as the year when its American and English founding texts were published (Binford and Binford 1968; Clarke 1968). An immediate cause is a real and well-founded sense of achievement: we do have so much more information, more varied and more reliable, than colleagues of previous generations. The career and funding framework, increasingly competitive, rewards large ambitions.

In Cambridge at least, it was at this same period of the late 1960s and into the 1970s that the ambitious tendency took decisive command. The engine of Cambridge archaeology then was competition between two ambitious tendencies. From the "bone room", Higgs and Jarman led bands of "Higlets" into one school of truth: in their "economic" view, an ecological/evolutionary determinism, as summarized in Wynne-Edwards (1962), was combined with the simple and robust field-methods of site catchment analysis and a concern with the plant seeds and animal bones, the stuff of past human survival, rather than the made world of artifacts (Higgs and Jarman 1969; Higgs 1975). At Peterhouse, David Clarke made the new synthesis of an "analytical archaeology," with its formal mathematics, numerical taxonomies, and systems theory explanations. Each tendency respected the other and would work in the other's world: Higgs co-wrote a conventional account of Pleistocene artifacts (Coles and Higgs 1968), while Clarke made the most compelling of the ecological/economic case studies (Clarke 1972). The common thread was the optimism of their ambition, an optimism that was shared in the parallel movement of the American New Archaeology. Notice – and it is more than a coincidence – that 1968 was the year that unreasonable ambition took wider command in American society: you could levitate the Pentagon, if only enough people with enough faith surrounded the place and tried to levitate it. Notice – and this is important for post-processual attitudes – that if the Pentagon declined to be levitated, that was not because the ambition seemed defective to those who held it, but simply because too few people had too little faith to move that particular mountain.

Archaeological ambition, as it has now settled down to a routine of the trade, has two variants. Each begins with a large aim, which the best method of study does not seem able to deliver. In the ambitious tendency, the end is declared to have fulfilled the ambition, although it has patently failed to do so. In the preposterous tendency, the venture is declared to be impossible.

The ambitions tendency: expectations not reached but declared

A characteristic example of ambition patently unfulfilled is the proposal that prehistoric British society experienced, towards the end of the third millennium BC, a distinctive social upheaval. The Neolithic society is seen as egalitarian, structured by kinship and worshipping its ancestors. The Early Bronze Age society is seen as stratified, with petty chiefs ruling their fiefs by their individual power. The model for this transformation is the classic band–tribe–chiefdom–state sequence of social evolution, and some distant ethnographic analogy is, or used to be, sought in Hawaii (see Yoffee, this volume). This belief is so general now that it has by degrees been transformed from a reasonable *a priori* expectation into a "factoid," that is, something which is treated as if it is an uncontroversial fact when it falls far short of certainty. Even Tim Darvill toes the line in his standard book on *Prehistoric Britain* (Darvill 1987).

Certainly, it is reasonable to think of social complexity increasing in prehistoric Britain from scattered bands of hunter–gatherers in the immediate post-glacial to the ordered and well-populated petty states that are historically recorded by the Latin sources for Britain. If you choose to believe that social evolution *must* follow the band–tribe–chiefdom–state sequence in orthodox order, then it is a fair first guess that British tribes might turn chiefly somewhere in the middle of this time-span: bands in the Mesolithic? tribes in the Neolithic? chiefdoms in the Bronze Age? states in the Iron Age? But is there actually sufficient evidence for their turning this *particular* way at that *particular* time?

I doubt if there is.

In Darvill, and before that in the Edinburgh exhibition catalogue, *Symbols of Power at the Time of Stonehenge* (Clarke, Cowie, and Foxon 1985), which told the same social story, a contrast is made between a tribal Neolithic and a chiefly Bronze Age. A variety of lines of evidence are used, for example:

The egalitarian treatment of the Neolithic dead in megalithic tombs and long barrows is contrasted with the differential treatment of Bronze Age dead, only a few of whom are given the splendor of round barrows and grave goods;

but

Atkinson (1968; also 1972) showed that the Neolithic population of Britain arrived at by assuming that all dead were buried in monumental structures was quite impossibly low – and that even before radiocarbon calibration stretched the prehistoric chronology rather more; it follows that only a small proportion of the Neolithic population had this special treatment in death, just as in the Bronze Age only a small proportion had a special treatment.

The building of henges in the "chiefdom" phase is taken "to symbolize power and prestige" (Darvill 1987: 92) of those chiefly individuals who showed their wealth through personal ornaments and fine objects; the building of causewayed camps in the earlier "egalitarian" period is a communal matter, not taken to symbolize anyone's power or prestige;

but

causewayed camps are of broadly similar form – circular within encircling ditches – require similar labor investment and seem as equally domestic and undomestic in their artifactual evidence as henges; no distinction is identified to show why the first type goes with an egalitarian society, and the second with a stratified society.

The considerable changes in monuments and artifacts between 3000 and 2000 BC are seen as diagnostic of a fundamental break; the equally considerable changes between 1500 and 600 BC – during which the pattern of society "completely altered" (Darvill 1987: 108) – are said to demonstrate no "discontinuities in the development of society";

but

no coherent theory is offered to link the artifactual transformations to social transformations, and therefore no reason is offered as to why the first artifactual changes amount to demonstration of a social discontinuity but the second do not.

And so on.

Signs of strain are evident in Darvill's schema, as British society reaches beyond tribalism and achieves its first chiefdoms by 2500 BC; yet – after 1900 more years of upward mobility – it contrives by 600 BC still to be at a stage of "tribes and chiefdoms." Prehistoric Britons, having risen so far in their social evolution, are obliged to mark time for two millennia until the next stage arrives, that of being swallowed up by a larger empire.

There may well have been Wessex chiefdoms. Reliable evidence may well exist, overlooked or unrecognized. But they have in no way been demonstrated. Meanwhile they exist only as "factoids."

The Edinburgh exhibition of 1985, *Symbols of Power at the Time of Stonehenge*, and its catalogue (Clarke, Cowie, and Foxon 1985) took this line of reasoning a step further. The proposal was made that the change in the 3rd millennium BC from the building of chambered monuments to henges represented a shift in ideology and social control – "the re-writing of history, a re-interpretation and manipulation of the old order to justify the new" (Clarke, Cowie, and Foxon 1985: 41). Empirical evidence was offered in support of this proposition. The "re-writing" of the old monuments was said to take three distinctive forms – re-modelling or re-use, demolition, and abandonment. Each one of these was interpreted in the Edinburgh exhibition as a proof of that kind of social transformation, and of that political use of older monuments. Re-modelling or re-use of a monument was the new ideology showing its force: it appropriated the old. Demolition was the new ideology showing its force: it destroyed the old. Abandonment of a monument was the new ideology showing its force: it spurned the old. But pause and think. These three kinds of attitude and act are practically the *only* things that can be done with an obsolete structure; it is what has been done before, during, and ever since the third millennium BC to every built thing which is no longer useful. You can see just these three attitudes in what is now inflicted on old textile mills across Europe and North America. Any or all three responses indicate only that the structure is going out of use, for some reason. The reason *may* be a radical social transformation; it may be one of many other things.

The Edinburgh exhibition took ambition one stage further in its labels, by seeming to know what prehistoric people said to each other. The display panel explaining that shift from chambered monuments to circles and henges read in part:

> Gradually communities began to form regional groupings and a clearer hierarchy of leadership appeared. The resources of these regional groupings made it possible to build huge communal monuments. The ancestors and their ability to mediate with the gods were no longer so important since the new leaders, through the communal monuments and the rituals associated with them, claimed they were able to communicate directly with the gods and, what's more, could be seen to be doing so.

No evidence at all was offered for the last part of this statement, with reason.

The habit of dealing with these dubious entities can be spreading. Andrew Sherratt, an editor of this volume, was talking about the morphology of European megalithic structures a few years ago (Sherratt 1988). He had played around with site plans, found Kinnes had already invented the best game in a fine earlier paper, invented some evolutionary schemes to set shapes in order, and gave one scheme a fancy and elegant name. His scheme happened to have simple box-shaped plans at the beginning and, a couple of millennia later, simple box-shaped plans right at the end. Then he set out what he thought was going on: people were *consciously* reviving and re-making the same form as at the start of it all. Pause again, reader, and think again. How does one distinguish with the evidence available in prehistory the conscious revival of a structural type from the *chance*

repeating of a simple shape that would easily arise in any case? Perhaps the distinction could be made, but I do not begin to know how; and I doubt if Sherratt knows either. A method to distinguish chance repetition from conscious revival would indeed be a joy in making sense of the patterns of European prehistory.

There are good reasons why a book for a wide audience and an exhibition drawing a wide public should offer a full kind of archaeological knowledge. These display-windows of what archaeology has to offer are not places to under-sell ourselves, but nor is it useful to declare that we know much more than we do.

The factoids of the ambitious tendency, with its egalitarian Neolithic tribes and socially stratified Bronze-Age chiefdoms, provide a real obstacle for the future. What research interest and funding will address that social question, and make possible a real discovery, when it seems clear already? And if by some remarkable new work, that discovery is made, it will not excite those who had already "known" this for a decade.

The preposterous tendency: ambition patently unfulfilled and admitted

The converse attitude to ambition is more visibly a post-processual habit, early and still best displayed in Ian Hodder's *Reading the Past* (1986). The book's starting propositions are (Hodder 1986: 1):

(1) that material culture is meaningfully constituted,
(2) that the individual needs to be a part of theories of material culture,
(3) that despite the independent existence of archaeology, its closest ties are with history (rather than anthropology or natural sciences).

The bulk of the book explores a range of approaches and judges whether they can answer these requirements, which seem reasonable to me. Hodder's book, which apologizes for the limited range of approaches it covers (1986: x), nevertheless encompasses materialist, systems, formal-analytical, generative-grammar, structuralist, Marxist, indigenous, feminist, processual, ethnoarchaeological (plus "other alternative Western archaeologies") approaches, together with his own "contextual" approach. Each is set out, and then – his own included – shown to be inadequate. Gardin (1987: 322) summarizes the procedure:

> Hodder's account of the various approaches listed above is therefore double-edged: first come definitions and examples, with an emphasis on the kind of insight gained along each line; then critical comments follow, showing that the outcome regularly falls short of the requirements

stated in chapter 1, with respect to meaning, individuals, history.

All of the approaches failing to live up to the expectation placed on them, Hodder duly notes that "archaeology now appears hopelessly difficult" (1986: 178).

In another view none of the approaches has "failed." No single approach can tell all; each may offer some insights, some progress towards the stated ambitions. One can equally say that each approach lives up to expectation, so archaeology appears splendidly easy. Again, it is a matter of attitudes in the archaeological community. If the archaeologists say that what they do is preposterous, then others will believe them.

Deference

Even before ambition was so visible, there was deference in archaeology, deference to those many disciplines which have reached a higher degree of understanding than has timid archaeology. Deference, for whatever reason, is embedded into the disciplinary foundations since the beginning. Classical archaeology defers to art history and to the written sources. American archaeology is the perpetual junior in an unequal partnership with a generalizing anthropology. Prehistory, since its beginnings a century ago, has thought of itself as wanting to become a science, an attitude affirmed again by the spirit of the New Archaeology. Insofar as "science" is systematic knowledge, almost all academic disciplines are science. Unfortunately, the word is ambiguous in English; as well as *Wissenschaft*, it means more narrowly that knowledge expressed in universal general laws on the model of physical sciences and especially of classical mechanics. But archaeology is not any old science; it is a *historical* study, and has the special features of a historical science, like paleontology and historical linguistics, that addresses more-or-less remote historical events by means of the fragments that survive. It is unfortunate that so many views of archaeology as science have overlooked this, so that deference to non-historical physical and biological sciences remains strong among archaeologists of processual or no declared persuasion. To an extent this must be so, since archaeology has always been and must always be uniformitarian in its methods; in making sense of regularities in the past, it depends on knowledge of regularities in the present. The pressures of prestige and of funding encourage it. "Archaeological science" sounds better than "archaeology," and the academic world knows – and expects – things called "science" to cost more. An unhappy side-effect are the studies in archaeological science that seem more to generate numbers than understanding;

they may create many tables of the trace elements in ancient bronze objects, but the tables, it is found, cannot be reliably translated into a better knowledge in wider terms of what prehistoric metal-working amounts to.

There seems to be no good cause for archaeology to enjoy a low status. By its materials and its methods, archaeology has a partial and particular view of the world. So has each academic discipline. Archaeology addresses artifacts for the most part, and therefore has an artifactual view of the world. The geneticists have a wry joke: "Human beings are the means by which DNA reproduces itself." It is a statement equal to the usual one, that DNA is the means by which humans reproduce themselves. The archaeologist can offer a matching statement about the social world: "Human societies are the means by which artifacts reproduce themselves." This is not a whole truth, but expresses much about how the archaeologist sees human societies as they are reflected in the artifacts. Notice then how much archaeology may hope to offer for understanding of the contemporary world, as modern western society has more things, more material objects than other societies ever had. Here, then, is one of several ways forward from a cultural cringe, to apply material knowledge to the modern material world, which archaeological knowledge can offer once it shakes off its deference.

Distinctive in the post-processual programme is a reaction against the deference to physical science seen in a processual archaeology. Instead there are offered new deferences, among them to contemporary social theory, and in particular to Giddens' body of theories about "structuration" (Giddens 1977; 1979). Archaeology, once it has been much improved in this way from its present sad intellectual state, will rise to take its proper place, where it "can contribute to debate within modern social theory" (Hodder 1986: 178, from the closing sentence of *Reading the Past*). Much contemporary social theory, abstract in its concepts and ideas, does not address the place of the material in the western world. In endorsing Hodder's hopes, I would think that the particular contribution of archaeology is to work with the material – not to re-mould itself after another, abstract ideal. However universalizing its own ambitions, social theory of the 1980s, like earlier social theory, carries much of its force from its capacity to make sense of the *particular* aspects of society in its own time. In the same way Freud's insights, intended to be universalizing, can now be seen as arising in large part from the particulars of bourgeois life in turn-of-the-century central Europe.

Giddens' theories are being imported into post-processual archaeology as a general prospect of society, therefore applicable to all societies that archaeology addresses. In the reality of Giddens in his home ground of sociology, you find a more probable proposition – a body of work addressing the *particular* character and structures of recent "post-industrial" societies, in terms of that rather full body of information about them that is available for study. Reading and hearing Giddens, I am struck by the elegance and fluency with which his ideas articulate with the exceptional aspects of the society we inhabit as members of a prosperous western university, and by a distinction he chose to make in response to questions. If required to divide all the range of human societies into just two categories, he would place in one category the western societies of the last century or two – so remarkable and peculiar are they – and in the other, all the other human societies there have ever been. This places almost all societies that archaeology studies into the category other than the one Giddens addresses.

One can notice a further characteristic of Giddens' work. His "structuration" was developed in the 1970s as a reaction to the idea of the "industrial society," which depended on the cosy belief that capital and labor could live in harmony for mutual prosperity and advantage – a tolerable idea in the somnolent 1950s but clearly a hopeless proposition at a time when workers and students had been fighting the forces of capital on the streets, and the very foundations of capitalist nation-states could be made to tremble. Essential to structuration and allied theories had been a central role for conflict as the driving force of social change. The 1990s provide a different stage, not just in Britain, as they begin quietly with capital and (un)organized labor at peace or truce, the trade-union forces or organized labor in retreat, the radical left everywhere on the decline as a mass political force, and Stalinist communism collapsed into ruin. The rhetoric of the intellectual left is no longer heard, that our societies have reached the final stage of "late capitalism" which will surely bring their collapse through their overwhelming contradictions. Now instead is to be the time of market forces and the old ideals of liberal democracy. The "industrial society" model, of a coalition of interests between capital and labor, begins to ring true again.

In this way, archaeology is asked – once more – to subordinate itself to an imagined ideal which is not a general theory of archaeology at all, but a particular theory developed with diligence and skill at a particular time to address alien questions that have vanishingly little to do with those that archaeology addresses. Our odd society is full of parochial curiosities, most of which have an artifactual aspect. One can examine the place of bow-ties in pet-food factories (Hodder 1987c) – a curiosity of curiosities from our strange times – but should not expect this oddity to show common relations between things and people in all times and places, or in remote societies of a different nature.

Another post-processual deference is to Jacques Derrida,

the master of deconstruction, whose distinctive contribution has been to take to the limit the observation from language that signs are arbitrary: the word for chimpanzee is related to the creature only by convention. If all signs, symbols and meanings are arbitrary, then all is arbitrary. There is no system. If that is the case, then archaeology is impossible: all the links that make up the uniformitarian method are severed. Here a special case – that of the text – is made into a universalizing principle, and then applied to the subject-matter of archaeology, which is not text.

Discrepancy

Both the ambitious and the preposterous tendencies, as they have been sketched, share the quality of discrepancy – between what is sought, what is achieved, and what is declared. As well as new ambitions and new deferences, the post-processualists are importing new methods, many ultimately from literary criticism. They declare that artifacts are texts to be read, but they do not explain why artifacts and texts – which share so little in the way of observable characteristics – can or should be treated as if they are just the same thing. Perhaps this is another part of deference: among the distinctive aspects that set western post-industrial societies apart from any others is the dominance of texts, and understanding of others expressed as texts, over all other kinds of knowledge. Texts and the study of texts has a corresponding dominance in thinking life.

Rather than proving the relevance of literary criticism, the post-processualists take the relevance for granted and simply set out to treat artifacts as if they were texts. Hodder (1986) calls his book *Reading the Past*. Shanks and Tilley (1987a) offer, as their major case study of the relationship between "material culture and social practices" (1987a: 172–240), what they call an examination of "the design of contemporary beer cans" from contemporary Britain and Scandinavia. They do seem to believe that that is what they are exploring. It turns out that they are not studying the artifact or its design in any way whatsoever; the many pages say nothing at all about the drawn-aluminium cylindrical can with its composite metal top and ring-pull opening. This container, the artifact, the piece of material culture, is not mentioned at all. The study is of, and exclusively of, the texts and the pictures that are printed as labels *on* the can. This is a study of the relationship, not between society and a set of artifacts, but between society and a set of texts/pictures. Notice, also, that Shanks and Tilley's case study addresses not just a text and its accompanying iconography, but a quintessentially modern class of text. Advertising, in any form, does not go back much beyond 1600 (Turner 1959). Labels for packets of food and commodities begin about

1700 (Lewis 1969). Packaging as a class of artifact begins in the early 1800s (Opie 1980). The artificial manipulation of "images" to contrast brands of almost identical consumer products is particularly characteristic of this century, and its post-war years. No wonder the texts on cans may be amenable to a modern social theorist's and text-critic's analysis! No wonder the understanding it may bring seems much removed from an obvious relevance to a knowledge of ancient artifacts!

The attitudes, drawn from literary criticism and deconstruction, have another aspect with which I am not comfortable. As an editor, I have become very conscious of the reciprocity within the research community of archaeologists: good people write things for *Antiquity* which I reject; I, in my turn, write as best I can and good journals like *Man* and *Past and Present* reject my efforts. Each of us works and offers our work for criticism by others, whose work we criticize in its turn. Creative work and critical work go together, with their positive and negative moods. Literary criticism is not like that, because the critic criticizes without a matching obligation to create. Deconstructionists deconstruct, and do not feel obliged to construct. This critic's spirit is sadly evident in the post-processual literature of archaeology, in the thoroughness of the gloomy grumbling and the slightness of creative alternative that is offered. Shanks and Tilley (1987a: 107–8), for example, see natural scientists as involved in a single hermeneutic, for the "inanimate objects" they study (whatever happened to biology?) have no human meaning; sociologists are involved in a double hermeneutic in that they live and work within a world of pre-interpreted meanings; and archaeologists are enmeshed in a quadruple hermeneutic. Hodder (1986) – whose writing has a cheeriness in the face of so much obstacle – has by his page 3 already reached the point of saying, "the problem then becomes, not 'how do we study symbolism in the past?', but 'how do we do archaeology at all?'" On his last page, "rather than taking the line that archaeology now appears hopelessly difficult," Hodder gives positive advice; after his book-length exploration of so many orthodox and alternative approaches, and the noting of their many and thorough inadequacies, archaeologists are inexplicably advised to return to their basic principles, and "well-developed" methods of excavation and interpretation.

Consumption

Stonehenge, object of scholarly interests over eight centuries, offers a unique opportunity to see how research attitudes have developed over the very long term. Exploring that long history of Stonehenge studies (Chippindale 1990), I was surprised to find how constant have been the research questions. The fundamental materials of archaeology do not change, nor the fundamental frames of reference. If one looks at the history of archaeology, and of systematic history and social sciences generally, one can see that there is a rather small stock of fundamental ideas with which they work. Very little contemporary work is entirely new; most revises and advances are by means of refinements and revisions of old concepts. From its beginning archaeology has been concerned with classification, with time, with how assemblages come about, with relating the still lives of artifacts to the living lives of the people who made the artifacts, with the discrepancy between fragmentary evidence and complicated wholes. These and a small number of other questions are fundamental to the business. And there has arisen a correspondingly limited range of concepts and frames of thinking to address these issues, a few home-grown, some borrowed, the majority copied or adapted from other disciplines. They make a set which is not very large and which does not change or grow very rapidly.

One interest of mine is in formal mathematical methods, particularly in the geometry of shapes and the potential of generative geometrical grammars as a research tool. This is a fairly new field in non-archaeological studies of artifacts, and certainly a new field in archaeology. It has reached the stage of a small handful of papers, a conference session whose organizers were pleased to get an audience that at one point went over the number of 50; we have been hoping to get a book out. It looks like a modest idea, mostly for enthusiasts, quite technical, taking quite a lot of work; if we are lucky, it will be splendid for a very few archaeological questions, of some use for a fair number, and quite irrelevant to most. I would rather it was neither over-sold, nor discarded as worthless. But we are already too late. There in *Reading the Past* is a little section entitled "formal analysis and generative grammars" (Hodder 1986: 36–40). In these few pages it takes the work of Dorothy Washburn, a pioneer in the field, identifies some weaknesses in it which are specific to her approach, takes these to be characteristics of formal methods in general, dismisses them for that reason, and moves on to the deficiencies of the next approach, structuralism. So, even before formal methods have been tried, they have been declared wanting.

Looking at the pattern of archaeological work over the last twenty years, one can see a rapid turnover of ideas that come into fashion, are briefly modish, and are then ditched for their failings. The speed at which they come and go is disconcerting; when I spent a few years out of the business in the 1970s I missed one mode, optimal foraging theory, completely – it came, "failed", and was sent on while I chanced briefly to be looking the other way. The trouble has not been in the ideas at all, but in the unreasonable expectations we have placed upon them, in our refusal to learn and sympathize with what they are about, and in our lack of patience to give them the time and attention they need to produce results.

Consider simulation. I see it as a valuable technique, with the inescapable strengths and weaknesses that any technique must possess. It received a brief flurry of interest and a book was edited by Ian Hodder in the Cambridge New Directions series where these passing fancies are published (Hodder 1978b). In Hodder's view at the time, the approach, when subjected to an "optimistic yet critical" appraisal (Hodder 1978a), was said to "offer the chance of taking the interpretation of archaeological remains onto a level where clear thinking and precise procedures are encouraged, yet where the archaeologist's 'imagination' also plays an important role." The papers in the book offer some useful case studies. Then what happened? Simulation, quickly out of fashion, does not even figure in the large range of approaches that are tested and found wanting in *Reading the Past.*

An archaeological fundamental is time, and the archaeological view of time is distinctive. Archaeology is both required to develop ways of dealing with time that suit its special considerations and enabled to offer its special knowledge of time to other disciplines. Yet there is little in the archaeological literature on this essential subject, and the habit of deference again sends us to look outside our own experience for better understanding. Not much is on offer from the harder sciences that seems relevant, nor from documentary history, but an exemplar has been spied in the ideas of the Annales school (if "school" it be) of French historians. Accordingly there are now three books relating the Annales to archaeology, one edited again by Hodder (1987a), one by Bintliff (1991a), and a third by Knapp (1992).

Annales is a large movement extending over several decades, and over a range of scholars working in diverse ways and with changing intent within some common ideas. Like many intellectual groups, it cannot fairly be reduced to a handful of phrases or rote methods. And Annales needs to be well understood, if its attitudes are to be grasped properly and applied archaeologically. Of course, a cartoon version of Annales can be sketched for the speedy: take one author from the Annales (Braudel), take one book (Braudel's *La Méditerranée et le monde Méditerranéen à l'époque de Phillippe II*), take one edition of that book (the later one that is conveniently available in an English translation), and let that stand for Annales. (Conveniently, the structure of its two large volumes is visible from an inspection of the table of contents. You may not actually have to read the thing.)

Hodder's book is entitled *Archaeology as Long-Term History*, a phrase which echoes the *longue durée*, one of the phrases that commonly stand for Braudel. There is much reference in its introductory essay (Hodder 1987d) to the *Mediterranean*, and one to a 1958 Braudel essay on the *longue durée*.

For the rest of Annales, nothing. Bintliff's book is more specific in its title, *The Annales School and Archaeology*, and notices a little more, but not so much. Delano Smith (1992), reviewing it, remarks:

> To judge from *The Annales School and Archaeology*, Braudel was the "*Annales* school", and in particular Braudel as represented by his admittedly monumental thesis *La Méditerranée et le monde Méditerranéen à l'époque de Phillippe II* (1949) . . . It is odd, though, that in an avowedly methodological book it is virtually the only one of Braudel's major writings to be considered . . . It is also perhaps inevitable that Braudel's catchy concepts – *géohistoire*, time-scales of *courte* and *longue durée*, *conjonctures*, *structures* – like those other *Annales* flag-words (*mentalité*, *l'histoire globale* or, for Braudel, "total history") should come to pepper archaeological as well as much of modern historical writing. Less understandable is the absence of any systematic discussion of their meaning and relevance to archaeology. Like the debris of once-magnificent constructs now littering outer space, uncontextualized thoughts are a hazard to the unwary.

At least one could hope that the essentials of Annales would be made available to archaeologists in a book on the Annales and archaeology. Delano Smith (1992) again:

> Nowhere, least of all in the editor's discussion of "The contribution of an *Annaliste*/structural history approach to archaeology", are the key concepts identified as operational constraints and matched with specific steps in the archaeological gaining and understanding of knowledge about the past. Instead, we are offered an over-simplified, often sloppy, account of an alleged *Annales* "school".

What has happened to *Annales* in these two archaeological books, one post-processual and one processual in allegiance? It looks as if the *Annales* have suffered a consumption – picked up, played with, dropped. Clearly, nothing has been destroyed; like simulation or formal methods, an *Annales* approach to archaeology remains available to anyone who wishes to develop it. Work that builds on earlier study of the nature of time in archaeology (e.g. Bailey 1983) is likely also to use some of the Annales concepts. Yet it has lost a freshness in what has already been done; whoever works with Annales ideas in archaeology in the future may expect the response from a sated audience, "We tried that already – several times! – and it doesn't work."

Consumption has another meaning, as a wasting and debilitating disease. I do not think consumption, the burning-up of ideas in this way, whether by the post-processualists or by the rest of us, is likely to be healthy.

Discussion

The tone of this paper is gloomy. It identifies unhappy or unhealthy tendencies that seem now to be established in the archaeological research community. The tendencies, not new in archaeology, are congruent with that post-modern fashion of deconstruction that has run through western intellectual life spreading despair along its path.

Despite them, I remain cheerful, but this is due less to what intellectuals have talked about in western Europe than to what intellectuals have done in eastern Europe. In a vivid metaphor, Timothy Garton Ash (1990) talks of an intellectual hypermarket in the west, its many shelves crammed with brightly packed ideas to be taken away by the trolley-full, played with, and discarded. Central Europe saw smaller, barer shelves, as it suffered harder times. Yet precious ideas, and respect for those ideas which are good, provided a moral strength that in the end brought down the Communist occupation of the central European countries and installed an intellectual, the absurdist playwright Vaclav Havel, briefly as one of its presidents. That is a lesson for intellectuals in the west, archaeologists among them. The post-modern movement, and the fashions of deconstruction that it embodies, is to an extent a game played by intellectuals for their own incomprehensible concepts of amusement, just as English persons of a certain type indulge in the incomprehensible performances and cruelties of croquet. The experience of central Europe shows these things to be more serious than games. If the archaeological concepts really are enduring and if archaeology is important, then the ideas we work with deserve better treatment than being tossed around in pursuit of ambition, deference, discrepancy, and consumption.

Acknowledgments

A version of this essay was first written for, and presented at, the TAG conference session from which this set of papers has arisen. It was revised considerably in April 1992, but within its original structure as that seemed to me the right framework within which still to work. I am grateful to colleagues at the original TAG session and to Jeff Reid and referees for *American Antiquity* for comments.

References

Atkinson, R. J. C. 1968 Old Mortality: Some Aspects of Burial and Population in Neolithic England. In *Studies of Ancient Europe*, edited by J. M. Coles and D. D. A. Simpson, pp. 83–93. Leicester: Leicester University Press.

1972 Burial and Population in the British Bronze Age. In *Prehistoric Man in Wales and the West*, edited by F. Lynch and C. Burgess, pp. 107–17. Bath: Adams and Dart.

Bailey, G. N. 1983 Concepts of Time in Quaternary Prehistory. *Annual Review of Anthropology* 12: 165–92.

Barrett, J. 1987 Contextual Archaeology. *Antiquity* 61: 468–73.

Binford, S. R. and L. R. Binford (eds.) 1968 *New Perspectives in Archaeology*. Chicago: Aldine.

Bintliff, J. (ed.) 1991a *The Annales School and Archaeology*. Leicester: Leicester University Press.

1991b Post-modernism, Rhetoric and Scholasticism at TAG: The Current State of British Archaeological Theory. *Antiquity* 65: 274–8.

1992 Comment, in Thomas and Tilley 1992: 111–14.

Childe, V. G. 1925 *The Dawn of European Civilization*. London: Kegan Paul, Trench, Trubner.

1936 *Man Makes Himself*. London: Watts.

1942 *What Happened in History*. Harmondsworth: Penguin Books.

Chippindale, C. 1990 An Intellectual History of Stonehenge Studies. In *Critical Traditions in Contemporary Archaeology*, edited by V. Pinsky and A. Wylie, pp. 68–79. Cambridge: Cambridge University Press.

Clarke, D. L. 1968 *Analytical Archaeology*. London: Methuen.

1972 A Provisional Model of an Iron Age Society and its Settlement System. In *Models in Archaeology*, edited by D. L. Clarke, pp. 801–69. London: Methuen.

Clarke, D. V., T. G. Cowie, and A. Foxon 1985 *Symbols of Power at the Time of Stonehenge*. Edinburgh: HMSO for National Museum of Antiquities of Scotland.

Coles, J. M. and E. S. Higgs 1968 *The Archaeology of Early Man*. London: Faber.

Darvill, T. 1987 *Prehistoric Britain*. London: Batsford.

Delano Smith, C. 1992 The *Annales* for Archaeology? [review of Bintliff 1991], *Antiquity* 66: 539–41.

Earle, T. K. and R. W. Preucel 1987 Processual Archaeology and the Radical Critique. *Current Anthropology* 28: 501–38.

Embree, L. 1987 Archaeology: The Most Basic Science of All. *Antiquity* 61: 75–8.

Gardin, J.-C. 1987 Review of Hodder (1986). *Antiquity* 61: 322–3.

Garton Ash, T. 1990 *We the People: The Revolutions of 1989 in Eastern Europe*. Cambridge: Granta Books.

Giddens, A. 1977 *Studies in Social and Political Theory*. London: Hutchinson.
  1979 *Central Problems in Social Theory: Action, Structure and Contradiction in Social Analysis*. London: Macmillan.

Higgs, E. S. (ed.) 1975 *Palaeoeconomy, Being the Second Volume of Papers of the British Academy Research Project in the Early History of Agriculture*. London: Cambridge University Press.

Higgs, E. S. and M. R. Jarman 1969 The Origins of Agriculture: A Reconsideration. *Antiquity* 43: 31–41.

Hodder, I. 1978a Preface in 1978b: vii–viii.
  1987b (ed.) *Simulation Studies in Archaeology*. Cambridge: Cambridge University Press.
  1982a *Symbols in Action*. Cambridge: Cambridge University Press.
  1982b (ed.) *Symbolic and Structural Archaeology*. Cambridge: Cambridge University Press.
  1982c *The Present Past*. London: Batsford.
  1986 *Reading the Past*. Cambridge: Cambridge University Press.
  1987a (ed.) *Archaeology as Long-term History*. Cambridge: Cambridge University Press.
  1987b (ed.) *The Archaeology of Contextual Meaning*. Cambridge: Cambridge University Press.
  1987c Bow Ties and Pet Foods: Material Culture and the Negotiation of Change in British Industry, in Hodder 1987b: 11–19.
  1987d The Contribution of the Long Term, in Hodder 1987a: 1–8.

Knapp, B. (ed.) 1992 *Archaeology and Annales*. Cambridge: Cambridge University Press.

Leone, M. P. and P. B. Potter (eds.) 1988 *The Recovery of Meaning in Historical Archaeology*. Washington: Smithsonian Institution Press.

Leone, M. P., P. B. Potter, and P. A. Shackel 1987 Toward a Critical Archaeology. *Current Anthropology* 28: 283–302.

Lewis, J. 1969 *Printed Ephemera*. London: Faber and Faber.

Opie, R. 1980 *The Pack-age*. London: HMSO.

Patrik, L. E. 1985 Is There an Archaeological Record? *Advances in Archaeological Method and Theory* 8: 27–61.

Preucel, R. W. (ed.) 1991 *Processual and Postprocessual Archaeologies: Multiple Ways of Knowing the Past*. Carbondale (IL): Center for Archaeological Investigations, Southern Illinois University at Carbondale. Occasional Paper 10.

Shanks, M. and C. Tilley 1987a. *Re-constructing Archaeology: Theory and Practice*. Cambridge: Cambridge University Press.
  1987b *Social Theory and Archaeology*. Cambridge: Polity Press.

Sharples, N. 1991 *Maiden Castle*. London: Batsford.

Sherratt, A. 1988 Breton Megaliths. Unpublished seminar paper.

Thomas, J. and C. Tilley 1992 TAG and 'Post-Modernism': A Reply to John Bintliff, *Antiquity* 66: 106–14.

Turner, E. S. 1959 *The Shocking History of Advertising*. London: Michael Joseph.

Wheeler, R. E. M. 1954 *Archaeology from the Earth*. London: John Murray.

Wynne-Edwards, V. E. 1962 *Animal Dispersion in Relation to Social Behaviour*. Edinburgh: Aberdeen University Press.

PART II

Archaeological theory from the Palaeolithic to the State

4
Ancestors and agendas

CLIVE GAMBLE

Introduction

Palaeolithic archaeologists do not often reflect on the history of their subject beyond examining the heroes who established human antiquity (Grayson 1983). In this paper I want to consider how the questions on today's palaeolithic agenda have been set. To do this I will need to go beyond the familiar accounts of the founding fathers of the subject and attempt to set them and the questions they posed in a broader cultural, political, and scientific context.

Disembedding concepts such as those relating to human origins is difficult but necessary if we are to advance our chosen subject. Historicizing the contexts of discovery and interpretation are all important, as many historians of science are now aware (Bowler 1986; Desmond 1982; Stocking 1987). This involves tracing both the overt and subtle undercurrents in the growth, acceptance, and rejection of ideas. The aim is to overturn what Gould (1988) has referred to as "cardboard histories" (of which archaeology has many examples) by recognizing the social, cultural, and political contexts within which science operates.

The risk is that many archaeologists will not accept such an endeavor. As hostile reaction to the World Archaeological Congress in 1986 showed, many palaeolithic specialists object to what they see as the politicization of the subject. They refer instead to the neutrality of scientific enquiry and the independence of academic thought about human origins. I had better warn them at the outset that they might find much of what follows equally suspicious to their belief systems about deep time, human origins, and the way they should be presented.

What is at issue in tackling who sets, or set, the questions in the palaeolithic agenda, is the future development of a world prehistory. The palaeolithic is of course the one obvious world history. Hunters and gatherers, the economic invention of the seventeenth century Enlightenment, did once inhabit a world without agriculture. Lubbock in 1865 provided us with one view of their world prehistory dominated by progress. But other questions, such as how global colonization occurred, were dismissed by influential contemporaries such as Wallace. In this paper I investigate why this happened. Migration and biogeography provide the means of examining some of the political and cultural contexts. Biogeography in particular provided a metaphor for conceiving processes affecting humans which operated at a world scale. However, the concepts which were borrowed were not entirely scientific. They came as much from the politics of imperialism as from the discoveries of science. Biogeographers have recognized this and proposed alternatives which, although sometimes idiosyncratic, nonetheless jolt us out of our complacency that we are indeed following a neutral agenda, asking the only questions about our origins at the global scale which either can, or should, be asked.

In this paper I will examine why such agendas have been slavishly followed as well as ask what other questions could have been put. My alternative is to focus on the process of world colonization (Gamble in press), asking how and why our global humanity arose *in prehistory*. My aim is to consider variation and variability in past human behavior as a central part of any future world prehistory. But while it is comparatively simple to insist on new scales of analysis for world prehistory, I believe a satisfactory, fresh agenda will only emerge by retracing some intellectual steps. We need to understand why the rediscovery by the West of the global prehistoric process of colonization was downplayed when a prehistoric agenda was created. Why was this aspect of our humanity excluded from any serious investigation? To provide an answer we need to examine the theoretical content of the two competing concepts of time (as a cycle and as an arrow) which were used to structure research into the palaeolithic period.

The results, I believe, of digging into our history indicate that it is now time to loosen the hold of the ancestors over research into human origins. The prospect is a redefinition of world prehistory to those sister disciplines which nurtured nineteenth-century prehistory but which have now largely forgotten about it. And where better to start the exercise of disinterring the history of our subject than at a graveside?

Darwin's funeral (and the death of prehistory?)

On 26 April 1882, Charles Darwin was buried in Westminster Abbey, a few feet from the grave of Newton, and in the company of many other ·intellectual and political ancestors of the new age. Among the pall-bearers were Wallace, Hooker, and Huxley, as might be expected, as well as a senior cleric and several Dukes. The principal pall-bearer, however, was Sir John Lubbock M.P. (later Lord Avebury), author of the bestselling *Pre-historic Times*, published in 1865 with the enthusiastic approval of Darwin, who was his neighbor; Lubbock was also the son-in-law of General Pitt-Rivers and sponsor of the private members' bill which, when passed in 1882, became the first Ancient Monuments Act.

The principals around Darwin's grave were typical of the diverse, but close-knit community of Victorian science in which prehistory played an important and sometimes central role; as shown, for example, by the arguments over a monogenic or polygenic origin for the living races. In the fifty years from the first edition of Lyell's *Principles of Geology* to Darwin's funeral and the legalization of the past in 1882, prehistory, as we now know it, was created. During this critical period the subject absorbed much of its intellectual content and defined its future contribution to wider issues. Those gathered around Darwin's coffin on that spring day not only set the prehistoric agenda, they were about to bury it.

Nowhere has this been felt more than in the study of human origins and its implications for a world prehistory. Thirty years before the funeral, Latham, in *Man and His Migrations* (1851: 49), identified the three great problems facing ethnology and, by implication, prehistory as,

1. The unity or non-unity of the human species
2. Its antiquity
3. Its geographical origin

This agenda has been followed ever since. The first item has received the greatest attention and the results of scientific research are now enshrined in the *Universal Declaration of Human Rights* (1948) and UNESCO's *First Statements on Race* (1950), if not in global political practice.

The other two items on the agenda have, in the intervening period, proved highly contentious. The age and location of the earliest humans has fluctuated widely and continues to do so, even though Darwin's choice of Africa now commands the majority view and science-based dating has replaced educated guesses. Detailed research into human origins now operates within these well-defined frameworks.

But why should the major questions remain those on Latham's brief agenda of almost one hundred and fifty years ago? Why are others excluded and why should the field of human origins be so predictable in outline, if not in the details of discovery and interpretation?

Darwin/Wallace biogeography

At the heart of traditional-origins research lies the Darwin/Wallace system of biogeography. Dubbed the *imperial tradition* by Nelson (1983; Patterson 1983; Nelson and Rosen eds. 1981; Nelson and Platnick 1981; Humphries and Parenti 1986) its main proposition is that species arise in centers and then disperse. The distribution of plants and animals therefore depends upon the location of these centers and the opportunities for dispersal. In practice this means reconstructing centers from present and past distributions. Before plate tectonics solved some of the anomalies in plant and animal distributions, it was common to explain them by landbridges, drifting logs, and icebergs carrying biotic cargoes from one continent to another (Simpson 1940).

There are two aspects of these centers which need considering. First, there is the general model that some areas acted as centers for most, if not all, of creation. In *The Origin of Species* Darwin regarded the northern latitudes as having larger and more efficient "workshops" when it came to speciation (1859: 371). This became the cornerstone of Matthew's influential survey on *Climate and Evolution* (1915) (see also Wallace 1876; Lydekker 1896; Stratz den Haag 1904; Black 1925; Taylor 1927) which had all life dispersing from the roof of the world in Tibet (Fig. 4.1). Much later Darlington (1957) shifted the "workshops" south, around the equator in the Old World. This central position allowed the route for dispersal to move from larger to smaller areas and into ever less favorable climates.

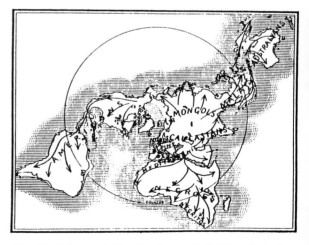

Fig. 4.1 Asian model for the dispersal of all life, including humans (Matthew 1915).

The essence of this *imperial tradition* is a competitive model. In its most extreme formulation we learn from Thistelton-Dyer in the *Darwin Centenary* (1909: 308) that

> If we accept the general configuration of the earth's surface as permanent a continuous and progressive dispersal of species from the centre to the circumference, i.e., southwards, seems inevitable. If an observer were placed above a point in St. George's Channel . . . he would see the greatest possible quantity of land spread out in a sort of stellate figure. The maritime supremacy of the English race has perhaps flowed from the central position of its home. That such a disposition would facilitate a centrifugal migration of land organisms is at any rate obvious, and fluctuating conditions of climate operating from the pole would supply an effective means of propulsion.

Such views are well known to archaeologists since they underlay Elliot Smith's well publicized studies on diffusion and migration (1929, 1933, 1934). At its most extreme this imperial tradition, when applied to civilization, located the center in Egypt where the diffusion of culture to the rest of the world then took place (1934: Fig. 67). His study of fossil apes and extinct human genera was more restrained but still shows the same principle at work. The Siwalik Hills of Pakistan formed his best-guess center (*ibid.*: Fig. 12), although he was careful to leave the possibility open that better data might relocate it anywhere between the Himalayas and the heart of Africa (*ibid.*: 68).

The outcome of these exercises which defined a center and its edge was to deny history to many areas of the globe. The worlds of either the Miocene or the Middle Kingdom would have few active centers and a great passive hinterland. The parallel with the colonial worlds run from London, Paris, and Washington is obvious. Darlington (1957: 553) expressed the same general principle in the vocabulary of social darwinism:

> Ability to spread is one of the attributes of dominance . . . Dominant animals spread . . . and replace other animals . . . animals spread to obtain advantages, not to escape disadvantages.

The second aspect relates more directly to the location of the human cradle within the general model of biological regions as either active, i.e., where speciation occurs, or passive, where new forms disperse.

Matthew was very clear on this point since he identified the roof of the world as the human cradle using this simple proposition:

> At any one time . . . the most advanced stages should be nearest the center of dispersal, the most conservative stages farthest from it. It is not in Australia that we should look for the ancestry of man, but in Asia (1915: 180).

The same area had been championed by Quatrefages (1879) and, in both cases, the proximity of the cradle to the early civilizations of the Middle East, India, and China outweighed the present sparse populations and non-existent fossil records from the roof of the world itself.

In the period between the publication of these two influential works there had been the sensational discovery by Dubois in 1891 of "*Pithecanthropus*" (*Homo erectus*) along the Solo River of Java. His search was apparently inspired by Haeckel's hypothesis that humans were of Asian origin, even though the great German biologist had changed the location of the cradle from the sunken continent of Lemuria in the Indian Ocean to Pakistan between the first and fourth English editions of his *History of Creation* (1876, 1909). It seemed to matter little that Java lies some five and a half thousand kilometers from these Asian cradles. Most recently the claims for Asia have been resuscitated by Mochanov (*et al.* 1983) and by Larichev (*et al.* 1988) in their claims from scant artifactual evidence for early humans on the Lena River in Siberia.

Of course these and other claims for the human cradle in Australia (Schötensack 1901) and the Americas (Laing 1895) now seem quaint and as ill informed as a belief in Lemuria, although disconcerting evidence such as early stone tools in Pakistan (Dennell *et al.* 1988) and refutations of the *imperial tradition* by vicariance biogeographers continue to nibble away at the current intellectual edifice of African origins.

The tipping over of the Asian cradle in the last 40 years and the triumph of research in Africa (Clark 1976) seems to have answered Latham's third question. Speculations, as they now appear, by Matthew (1915) and by Taylor (1927), which ranked the races and civilizations of the world to provide a geographical chronology that could be used to identify the cradle, have been replaced by an arsenal of scientific dates and fossil evidence. Shifts in the cradles were also accompanied, as Campbell and Bernor have commented (1976), by a reassessment of how a key feature such as bipedalism evolved. When Asia held the cradle, upright walking evolved from brachiation using the gibbon and orang-utan as models. Once positioned in Africa, the same trait was derived instead from knuckle-walking, as suggested by chimpanzee and gorilla locomotion.

The case for an African cradle is therefore based on very different reasons than those put forward for Asia. But is the underlying agenda still similar? Why bother with trying to locate the human cradle at all?

I ask this question since opinions, formed within the *imperial biogeographical tradition*, about the position of the human cradle will probably be strongly shaped by current political perceptions of the relations between nations. In this respect it is worth noting that amongst the shifting cradles of the last two hundred years (Gamble in press), Europe has rarely figured, even though for many years it had the only significant fossil evidence, genuine or forged. I shall discuss below the other role this continent played in the biogeography of human origins, but simply note here that like the Garden of Eden the human home lay outside its borders. Europe received and transformed the human raw material that entered its space. It did not create. Europeans have usually looked outside their continent for evidence of the human cradle and therefore within their Old World colonies. It is interesting to see that as the latter's relationship to the European centers changed, due to Independence, so we find a shift in the location of human origins from Asia to Africa (Fig. 4.2). The timescale may be short but it is significant that the sub-Saharan center for human origins research is located within the most recently independent nations of that continent.

Many of course would argue that the shift was due to the inspired fieldwork of the Leakeys at Olduvai Gorge, now in Tanzania, which produced evidence to prove Darwin right, especially in two remarkable seasons for fossil discoveries in 1959 and 1960 (Day 1977: 152). However, the scientific indifference meted out to Dart's much earlier discoveries of *Australopithecus* (1923) in the Union of South Africa (independent since 1910) rather than the colony of Tanganyika (independent in 1961 and becoming Tanzania in 1964) should serve as a warning that the automatic acceptance of scientific evidence for the position of the cradle does not always follow in this political game of center and periphery.

The lesson is quite clear. Whatever data are accumulated, the contemporary political and economic circumstances of those nations which set the scientific agendas are all important in defining the human cradle. Whether it will always be in a country with a third-world economy is an interesting point. Predicting where it may move next is also germane to such an argument and I believe that it will change in the future. Just as fossil bones and absolute dates identified Africa as the cradle in the post-war period, there will no doubt be changes in the next 50 years backed, of course, by "irrefutable" scientific evidence, including perhaps more accurate genetic clocks.

If the world continues to be ordered asymmetrically in terms of power, then the poorer and dependent nations will continue to receive the accolade of custodians of the human cradle. Should equality be established then human origins could happen, as Croizat argued (1962), anywhere along a track (Fig. 4.3) where the conditions for *in situ* speciation, by vicariance, rather than by allopatry (in another place) followed by dispersal, pertain. Alternatively, the question could fade from the scientific agenda as its political rationale disappears.[1]

Tinkering with such speculative agendas may seem far-fetched until we recall the good faith of earlier attempts to reconcile such universal history with political reality. The world and its peoples have always provided a rich source of material for the West to reflect on its uniqueness and peculiar global position. This is brought home with great clarity in the transfer during the last century of remoteness from Paris and London into remoteness in time. The substitution of age for distance is present in one of the foundation texts of anthropology when Dégerando, from his armchair, advised the Pacific explorer Baudin in 1800 that on his voyage

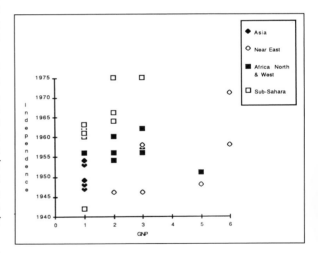

Fig. 4.2 The timing of the post-colonial era and the shift of the human origins cradle from Asia to Africa. This was finally sealed with the discoveries at Olduvai in 1959/60. GNP, as measured in 1975, is ranked as follows: 1 = <$200, 2 = $200–500, 3 = $500–1500, 4 = $1501–3000, 5 = $3001–5000, 6 = >$5000 per capita.

The cradle is usually found in countries with the lowest (1) GNP ratings and the diagram shows how the shift follows the earlier movement to independence in Asia. Since there are no further major colonies waiting to gain political independence the cradle has remained in sub-Saharan Africa as the finds at Koobi Fora, beginning in 1970, confirm.

We shall in a way be taken back to the first periods of our own history; we shall be able to set up secure experiments on the origin and generation of ideas, on the formation and development of language, and on the relations between these two processes. *The philosophical traveller, sailing to the ends of the earth, is in fact travelling in time; he is exploring the past; every step he makes is the passage of an age. Those unknown islands that he reaches are for him the cradle of human society* (Moore 1969: 63; my emphasis).

As the world has shrunk, so other measures have been devised and the concept of living prehistory discarded. However, the imperial tradition of biogeography still continues with its assumption that by identifying the cradle through whatever means – racial, scientific, geographical – the problem of human origins is being adequately addressed. On the contrary, the gift of the human cradle to the developing world is a continuing symbol of the developed world's assessment of their political and economic immaturity. As children grow, so cradles are loaned to neighbors starting a family. As the world moves, so the cradle rocks.

Time concepts

During the foundation of prehistory in the nineteenth century, remoteness in space became synonymous with remoteness in time. In the interim the world has shrunk in scale and such absolute distance is hard to find. The Tasaday and other lost tribes enjoy ever briefer moments as living prehistory before the reality of their circumstances is uncovered. The advent of absolute dating appears to have

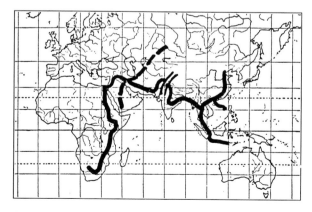

Fig. 4.3 The track for vicariant human origins (Croizat 1962: Fig. 78), constructed by joining up fossil findspots. Its merit is to suggest a wider perspective on the location of human origins than one tied to narrow political agendas.

provided an unbiased, objective means of ordering the remote past. However, the scientific infrastructure now needed for absolute dating still places the authorization and legitimation of human origins by these means in familiar power centers dedicated to the production of the past (Dennell 1990). Furthermore, the proliferation of books about paleoanthropologists (Lewin 1989; Willis 1989) continue to make the same geographical distinctions in terms of an active core of powerful, industrial, scientific nations surrounded by a passive global hinterland. The energies of the former tease out universal history, in the form of human origins, from the buried landscapes of the latter.

One of the scientific gifts in this continuing relationship is the measurement of time, since this provides a yardstick for evaluating importance on the basis of age and antiquity. But as Bailey has pointed out (1983: 102), for a subject which commits so much of its resources to dates and a chronological framework, archaeology has very little to say about the time concepts it employs. All too frequently it is expected that the dates will speak for themselves.

The fallacy of this position is well brought out in the recent resurgence of a particular time concept as environmental issues have crept up the contemporary political agenda. This is the cyclical notion of time as developed by Hutton (1795) and employed later, but with important additions, by Lyell (1830–2, 1862). This time concept helped set the human origins agenda by facilitating the establishment of human antiquity (Grayson 1983) and hence the definition of earliest prehistory.

At the moment the wider focus is more on Hutton than on Lyell. This is mostly due to the interest generated by so-called Gaia theory (Lovelock 1982, 1989) which in many ways is a restatement of Hutton's vision of the earth as a single organism. Accordingly, there is no vestige of a beginning or prospect of an end as the cycles of decay, sedimentation, and rebuilding repeat their inexorable roll. For both Hutton and Lovelock, earth and life are one.

Leon Croizat expressed similar sentiments when he argued that "earth and life evolve together" (1962: 605). In his panbiogeographical synthesis, published privately in 1958, he set out in considerable detail his case against the imperial biogeographical tradition. His alternative was speciation as a vicariant event, the result of *in situ* replacement rather than dispersal. Hence earth history leads to the isolation of population and so to the possibility of allopatric speciation by *in situ* replacement. The obvious splitting processes are the separation of land masses through continental drift and the formation of regions by mountain building. Once created, these features are not barriers to dispersal but are integral to speciation through separation.

Updating Hutton by adding plate tectonics to his cyclical

model of time means that Croizat's tracks complement the plate margins and focus attention on the ocean basins as the areas for speciation as these shift and change (Patterson 1983; Humphreys and Parenti 1986). These paleogeographical rims are not barriers – ditches to be crossed – but regions where different taxa, hominids included, are repeatedly reproduced, *as the earth evolves*. Darwinian procedures, where reproductive isolation occurs through niche adaptation, and speciation by dispersal then follows, are therefore contradicted. Indeed, hardline vicariance biogeographers such as Croizat deny any importance at all for dispersal (1962: 579). Early humans never left Africa but were repeatedly created along the track (Fig. 4.3) where, due to the circumstances of earth history, many other species were also continually being formed (Croizat 1958: Fig. 259). Others, understandably, have dismissed this as latter-day polygenism (Bowler 1986: 146).

While there is much to disagree with, and be baffled by, in Croizat's thesis, it has to be admitted that his track is no less nonsensical than the cradle-shifting that attends the imperial biogeography he castigates. Indeed, until we have an adequate model for the location of hominid evolution, rather than explanations tailored to discovery, then adopting a track makes equal sense to isolating a cradle.[2]

But there are other issues than centers of origins which a consideration of vicariance biogeography highlights. These matters relate to the concept of time's cycle and the portrayal of history. As Gould (1988) has comprehensively argued, Hutton's cycles ran to a timeless set of causes. This no doubt explains the enthusiastic endorsement today from Lovelock and his Gaia theory where life makes the world go round (1989). Here in fact is a recycling of Croizat's phrase, "nature forever repeats" (1962), which in turn can be traced back to Hutton and his repeated cycles of uplift and erosion (1795). Prehistory benefited directly from this concept of time as a cycle since Hutton opened the way to the concept of *deep time* which found its prehistoric expression in the work of Boucher de Perthes (1847) and Prestwich (1860).

It is at this point for the setting of the prehistoric agenda in the last century that the role of Sir Charles Lyell becomes critical. He also embraced the cyclical model of time in the early editions of his *Principles of Geology* (1830–3) by presenting the world in constant motion, always the same in substance and condition but changing bit by bit in a stately dance towards nowhere (Gould 1988). The lesson of the rocks for Lyell in his early works was not an unfolding history of progress with humans eventually discovered sitting on top of time's mountain. Fossils were simply markers of historical uniqueness. They distinguished the epochs, but passed no comment on the direction of history. As the cycles repeated, so their contents changed. The time

required to achieve this demonstrated great antiquity. But this was far from the concept of time as an arrow, proceeding down a set historical path and where changing fossils marked the precise passage of time in the form of genealogical connections. Such arrows could speed through the past for only 4004 or for 4 billion years. Each fossil passed was a signpost on the road to the present rather than a recurrent, cyclical statement, of an immanent process.

Lyell's conversion to a more progessionist stance and one which the definers of prehistory, in the form of Lubbock (1865) and others, embraced, came in 1862 with his publication *On the Geological Evidences for the Antiquity of Man*. By accepting the mechanics of evolution contained in darwinian theory, Lyell made what seemed to him to have been an uneasy compromise between the opposed timeless principles of time's cycle and the narrative power, seized by the Victorians as a metaphor for progress, that came from viewing the development of life through time's arrow.

The importance of these twin concepts, time's cycle and time's arrow, should need little emphasis for archaeologists. Neither, as Gould points out (1988: 191) is both or either "right." It is instead the variable emphasis they enjoy that directs a historical discipline. The irreversibility of history, time's arrow, subverted into the notion of unstoppable progress, has dominated human origins since the agenda was set in the last century.

As a result Lyell, rather than Hutton, is the ancestor feted in our archaeological "cardboard histories" (e.g. Daniel 1962) because he gave us "scientific" proof about antiquity and the ammunition to rout creationists and polygenists alike. The answers to Latham's first two questions (1851) had therefore been adequately answered. But at the same time the subject had been tied into the agenda of progress and its temporal metaphor would very soon be confirmed by Pleistocene geology.[3]

In this regard the case can be made that the importance of science-based dating in the last fifty years has been over-emphasized in archaeology at the expense of considering the time concepts the dates illuminate. Belief in long-term processes, akin to time's cycles, as an explanation for change and variation in the patterns of the archaeological record, is currently about as numinous as Darwin's icebergs (1859: 372) floating between biotic provinces in the south Atlantic. Evolutionary diagrams are shot instead from the bow as typified by the marching hominids who with each pace become progressively more human (Johanson and Edey 1981: 286–7).

Set beside this depiction are the recent discussions of evolutionary time (Butzer 1982: Table 2.2; Foley 1984: Fig. 1.2; Vrba 1985; Gamble 1987: Fig. 1) and the distinction that is drawn with time at an ecological scale. These are important developments but still are rarely discussed and applied (see Bailey 1983). Instead we continue to find echoes of G. G. Simpson's famous dictum that elegantly argued away the unimaginable for the imperial tradition of biogeography,

> Any event that is not absolutely impossible (and absolute impossibility is surely rare in problems of dispersal) becomes probable *if enough time elapses* (1952: 174, my emphasis).

Since time is what the palaeolithic has in spades, there seems little need to many people to develop time concepts any further but instead simply to build chronology.

The mechanics of the human drift

While no one pretends that speciation is a simple matter of sufficient, elapsed time, this is not the case when it comes to the question of dispersal. It is here that the agenda on human origins is most firmly set, not just in the nineteenth century, but far back into Western history and literature.

The essence of the problem is very simple. The people of the West rediscovered the world in the past 500 years and, as they did, so they found other humans everywhere (Gamble in press). The singular fact is that this raised little surprise, as shown in captains' logs and travellers' diaries. The lack of surprise was echoed by scientific explorers, among them Wallace and Darwin. A succinct summary of the unimportance to them of the "discovery" of global humanity was provided by the architect of biogeography, Alfred Wallace, in his preface to *Island Life* (1880: viii). He wrote that there was a great deal to understand and describe about the geographical distribution of all species except *Homo*. All that could be said for us was "the bare statement – 'universally distributed' . . . and this would inevitably have provoked the criticism that it conveyed no information." As a result one of the main properties of humans – that we are globally distributed – was consigned to a non-question. This agenda-setting had an important consequence since prehistory concentrated instead upon technology, as it differentiated races in the present and the past, while progress provided a vehicle for understanding change and writing history. The process and timing by which global humanity had been achieved was less considered.

One reason for Wallace's rejection of prehistoric human biogeography was that humans had *enough* time to get everywhere, even though by his standards many of the extant races lay at the bottom of the moral and technological ladder. It is easy to see how such a concept was, and still is, embedded in Western culture. The slowness of the "primitive" world was not a scientific discovery but rather an idea of gradualism rooted in literature and common knowledge, borrowed rather than demonstrated by a new science such as prehistory.

This pattern is best described as the *human drift* (after the short story by Jack London 1919) since it conjures up the aimless movement of people driven by hostile forces of nature that included hunger, cold, disease, and population numbers.

In one of the earliest ethnographies of the Americas written in 1589, José de Acosta suggested that "men came to the [West] Indies driven unwittingly by the wind" (Fagan 1987: 28). He also believed that they took the overland route through Asia, driven by starvation and other hardships. There is little difference to be seen three hundred years later when T. H. Huxley (1863: 251) proposed hunger as an adequate reason for dispersing primitive families around the world. At the same time, Quatrefages settled for the other favorite explanation for the human drift, population pressure, with this cup-floweth-over model from the roof of the world:

> The first human beings appeared and multiplied till the populations overflowed as from a bowl and spread themselves in human waves in every direction (1879: 177).

It is not difficult to find these examples of imperial biogeography expressed in a pre-scientific age. These opinions, partly because of the form by which they were expressed, have had more impact on the foundations of science than many normally give credit. Terms like Industrial Revolution imply a break with the pre-scientific past, a fresh, scientific start, which among other things saw the foundation of prehistoric science. But much was inherited rather than invented. Consider, for example, the closing lines to Paradise Lost (1667) where Milton wrote of the expulsion of Adam and Even from the Garden of Eden, the original cradle for human origins.

> The World was all before them, where to choose
> Their place of rest, and Providence their guide:
> They hand in hand *with wandring steps and slow*,
> Through Eden took their solitarie way [my emphasis].

Contrast this with the scientific gloss provided by Sir John Lubbock two hundred years later in *Pre-historic Times* (1865: 476)

> There can be no doubt that man originally crept over the earth's surface, little by little, year by year, just for instance as the weeds of Europe are now gradually but surely creeping over the surface of Australia.

Therefore we can trace the historical embeddedness of the concept of drift. Milton may not have been a scientist, but it would be unwise to underestimate his ability posthumously to shape opinion about a process which even in 1865 could not be measured in absolute terms. Consequently for Lubbock there was nothing to explain, since the human drift and global colonization was an inevitable process which, if it could be achieved by savages, obviously had little to tell us about the rise to civilization of the societies which mattered in the world and its history. For example, Morgan (1877) identified his stage of middle savagery, when fire and fishing were introduced, as the time when migration from an original habitat to the greater part of the globe took place. These were not historical, purposeful migrations like those of the Angles and Saxons, but rather, as Ratzel called them, "dim impulses" (1896: 10), either by boat or on foot, inspired by nothing more than the trite observation that "restless movement is the stamp of mankind."

Belief in the human drift is deeply ingrained. Milton still sets the pace. For example, *The National Geographic Magazine* in an issue on Peopling the Earth (1988: 434–7) recorded that mankind has continually migrated due to fear, hunger, curiosity, and a sense of destiny, and this was achieved by drifting north and then east from Africa.

Umberto Eco, hypnotized by Foucault's Pendulum, again rocks Haeckel's cradle of 1876. As the copper sphere of the pendulum grazes the sand beneath, it leaves

> . . . a tale, recorded on an expanse of desert, in tracks left by countless caravans of nomads, a story of slow millennial migrations, like those of the people of Atlantis when they left the continent of Mu and roamed, stubbornly, compactly, from Tasmania to Greenland, from Capricorn to Cancer, from Prince Edward's Island to the Svalbards. The tip retraced, narrated anew in compressed time what they had done between one ice age and another, and perhaps were doing still, those couriers of the Masters. Perhaps the tip grazed Agarttha, the Centre of the World, as it journeyed from Samoa to Novaya Zemlya. And I sensed that a single pattern united Avalon, beyond the north wind, to the southern desert where lies the enigma of Ayers Rock (1989).

Compared to this mystical nonsense, the diffusion of Elliot Smith's ragbag heliolithic culture (1929) seems mild-mannered, although the essentials of the drift are common to both.

Literature or science, the result is the same. By stressing the mechanics of the drift as enough time pushed by simple causal factors from the environment, we reach the unavoidable conclusion that global colonization took place without any evolutionary change. The inevitability of global humanity denies a history to those peoples who pioneered

our global distribution and, instead, returns that honor to the explorers of the West. The "purpose" of Columbus, and others who followed, is still contrasted with the "instinctive" responses of prehistoric migrations. The political conquest of the world after 1492 provided a metaphor to build a biogeographical model for the investigation of variation, as we have already seen expressed by Thistelton-Dyer (1909). Although anthropology is using 1992 to reflect on the definitions of other cultures and humanity that have been constructed in the past five hundred years (Fowler and Fowler 1991), it remains to be seen if such an exercise will be observed everywhere as we seek to disembed our prehistoric science from its historical contexts.

The evolution of humanity

The final part of our ancestral agenda involves the continent of Europe. As already remarked, this is rarely put forward as a candidate for the human cradle. Palaeolithic people reached Europe, as Breuil put it (1912), in waves and left their flints behind like seaweed on the beach.

Europe's role has been to provide the great marinade for such human raw material. Lubbock put this well when he stressed the interplay between environment and "national character" which gave rise to cultural diversity due to the effect of external conditions on previous generations (1865: 446). With this argument he could put some distance between contemporary hunters such as the Tasmanians and Fuegians – examples of living prehistory – and those of his continent's stone age, where climatic conditions differed greatly and so produced in its prehistory a unique and more advanced "European" palaeolithic culture.

This special pleading for our ancestors draws on the frequent use of differences in global climate as responsible for morals and history. Montesquieu in *De l'Esprit des Lois* (1748) made the link that has been repeated ever since between temperate climates and progress, and the climatically easy life and stagnation. A typical example of this comes from E. B. Tylor (1881: 113) who regarded the northern white races, on account of the climates they endured, to be "gifted with the powers of knowing and ruling which gave them sway over the world."

Coon expressed the "marinade theory" very forcefully when he declared that Africa "was only an indifferent kindergarten. Europe and Asia were our principal schools" (1962: 656).

Forty years earlier Hrdlicka (1922: 540) pointed out that the evidence was too sparse to identify the human cradle. He redefined the agenda so that he could achieve a result from the fossil and archaeological record by concentrating on the origin of *humanity* as the main issue. He singled out South-western Europe as the cradle where the long gestation that produced humanity (*ibid.*: 545 and Plate VIII) took place. From here, he argued, the peopling of the rest of the earth had taken place comparatively recently. He put this late date down to the "insufficient effectiveness" of stone age peoples who only expanded after mental and cultural thresholds had been passed. This process, in his view, led to control of the environment and larger populations so that humans were forced to people the earth under the inevitability of the laws of drift.

As might be expected, a strong case for Europe as the cradle for humanity, the truly efficient northern "workshop," was put by Elliot Smith. He identified the Mediterranean race as the occupants of the original home of modern humans (1934: 155). This was a big cradle since his Mediterranean race not only circled both shores but also the Levant, Eastern Africa, and Western Europe including parts of the British Isles, notably Wales and the Celtic fringe. This race coalesced its creative energies into the civilization of Egypt and led him to the conclusion

> that the building up of civilization of the world at large began amongst members of one race – and from them was diffused abroad (1934: 179).[4]

The question of the origins of modern humans is currently one of the central issues in Pleistocene archaeology (Mellars and Stringer eds. 1989). Here, too, the lists are drawn between regional continuity and replacement using anatomical, behavioral, and genetic evidence to reach a definition of what is a modern human. Dispersal and vicariance both provide claims to particular geographical territories at vastly different scales and containing highly varied cultural products. As a result the situation is very volatile with new scientific analyses (e.g., mitochondrial DNA or TL dating of the Middle Palaeolithic) and discoveries (e.g., the St. Césaire Neanderthal burial or Pleistocene colonization of the Pacific) leading to claims and counterclaims reminiscent of earlier debates over Africa or Asia as the human cradle.

This activity may be a reaction to the apparent sewing up of human origins in sub-Saharan Africa. It is also linked to the current interest in complex hunters and gatherers (Gamble 1991). As presented in Price and Brown (eds. 1985) hunters and gatherers, past and present, can be separated into complex, and by default, simple categories (Keeley 1988). This division only refers to cultures and societies which have passed the modern human threshold. Neanderthalers and other archaic forms of *Homo sapiens* are not considered.

The interest in complex hunters is that they are judged to

have the potential for change. They will transfer, through intensification, to agriculture and consequently they will have history. The "cold" counterparts to these "hot" societies, will not (Bender 1985).

This denial of history to some prehistoric groups provides an interesting twist to those political agendas, camouflaged by biogeographical principles, which I have identified as essential to human origins research. While the papers in Price and Brown (1985) provide many case studies from around the world, the oldest examples which are discussed are in Europe (Conkey 1985; Mellars 1985; Soffer 1985). The next oldest comes from the Levant (Henry 1985) and so falls within Elliot Smith's cradle. Elsewhere in this important volume, complexity is presented as a later, post-glacial phenomenon in the Americas and Australia, while Africa and Asia are not considered.

Europe stakes out its claim, in the tradition started by Lubbock and continued by Hrdlicka, in no uncertain terms

> If the Upper Palaeolithic is regarded as representing a phase of generally "advanced" or "complex" hunter–gatherers – as most of the textbooks imply – then the Upper Palaeolithic communities of the classic Franco-Cantabrian region of southwestern France and north-western Spain *must surely be ranked among the most impressive representatives of this stage* (Mellars 1985: 271; my emphasis).

Moreover,

> the Franco-Cantabrian region does represent some form of *unusually* "complex" behaviour (*ibid.*: 273; my emphasis).

The European evidence appears to be setting the standard again in the form of economy, art, burials, and other paraphernalia judged to represent complex behavior. Its Pleistocene age means that it can readily be exported to the rest of the world. According to Elliot Smith (1934: 106), the early history of Europe becomes intelligible if we appreciate that "European civilization is the achievement of men who have woven the heritage of the world into a new fabric (*ibid.*: 496). For all the sophistication of our current studies into the Upper Palaeolithic, are we doing any more than reiterating anew the familiar political and scientific agenda? Are not all societies "complex," although in different dimensions (Gamble 1991), and is not understanding this variation a more worthwhile goal? The recent challenge (Cosgrove *et al.* 1990) to the idea of Holocene complexity in Australia (Lourandos 1985) is a healthy sign that politically dictated agendas are now being put into their proper perspective.

Any other business?

My discussion of the human origins agenda can be summarized as shown in Table 4.1.

Table 4.1 may seem to dichotomize the agenda to the extent that no one working on human origins could be found who scrupulously observed such rigid paths. Consequently, it should not be read as a list of what distinguishes researchers, but rather as an indication of where we derive our ideas, and why these are often contradictory as we continue to pursue the questions laid down in the last century when prehistory was created. If a world prehistory is to emerge, then archaeologists will have to reflect on the history of the subject and tease out the undercurrents of politics and society which informed scientific activity and resulted in theory-laden concepts of time, humanity, colonization, and centers of origin.

Understanding how this agenda arose is a step towards loosening the hold of the ancestors by embarking on fresh questions. The four elements listed in the Table 4.1 will continue to be the infrastructure upon which interpretation, informed by analysis of new and old data, will continue to be built. At the moment this is still largely an investigation of the contents of the cradle as described in terms of hominid lifeways reconstructed from evidence for technology, diet, landscape, and living space.

My alternative is to grant at least equal weight to the investigation of colonization. Since a pan-global distribution is a characteristic of modern humans, then the possibility of another route to the study of the past is presented. We need to reject Wallace's (1880) proposition that there would be nothing to say about the prehistory of our global distribution. Instead we can now recognize that the creation of our global humanity was a punctuated process, rather than a temporal pattern of progressive drift. The ecology and behavior involved in such a massive extension of range has never been adequately considered. As a result fieldwork techniques, designed to identify the signposts on the route to civilization, are presently too coarse to pick up information at the resolution needed to measure the subtlety of the colonization process at local and regional scales of enquiry.

A start, however, has been made to define the problems for the next research agendas. The recent "World at 18,000 BP" project (Soffer and Gamble eds. 1990) compiled global data on the archaeology of the last glacial maximum. Concentrating on a time spike is a first step towards global comparisons of complete climatic cycles and their recurrent selective impact on population at times of either refugia or expansion. Vrba (1985, 1988) has provided an evolutionary model contrasting range occupancy between gracile and robust lineages of early hominids in sub-Saharan Africa and

Table 4.1

Biogeography	
Dispersal	Vicariance
active, imperial, cradle	passive, autonomous, track
Time concepts	
Time's arrow	Time's cycle
irreversibility of history	immanent processes
Colonization	
Migration	Drift
purposive, calculated	passive, externally forced
Humanity	
Complex	Simple
"hot" societies engaged in history	"cold" societies, living prehistory, timeless, unchanging

where the former persist through climatic cycles due to their generalist diets. The test of such a model will depend on sampling regions for their settlement histories, for example, recording the variable ebb and flow of regional hominid population at a resolution of less than 41,000 years, the standard duration of a full climatic cycle in the Lower Pleistocene. At the last count there were some twenty-seven such cycles. Existing analytical techniques are clearly not up to such demands, but neither were those of Boucher de Perthes over a century ago to the investigation of modern questions about living areas or microstratigraphy. New techniques require the stimulus of fresh questions. From this perspective the continuing value of science-based dating would be to investigate these climatic cycles. For example, what selection pressure, if any, did their changing rhythms have for anatomical and behavioral change? How can climatic cycles and the concept of time's cycle (Gould 1988) be integrated to investigate variation and change among past human populations? Building chronologies to document genealogy, through the concept of time's arrow, will no longer be our only goal.

The focus on the timing and pattern of global colonization presents an alternative set of measures for the investigation of variation and difference in past human behavior. This route to a truly world prehistory interweaves the twin time concepts of arrow and cycle to replace the existing, asymmetrical, view of world prehistory as a salute to civilization. Instead, world prehistory becomes the study of unity through the celebration of historical diversity within an expanding tradition of how humanity is, and has been, constructed. Since evolutionary theory, it is often claimed, was developed to answer questions about variation and variability, this seems a sensible return to first principles.

Therefore, one hundred and forty years after Latham posed his three big questions for prehistory, I would replace them with only two:

1. Why were humans everywhere in prehistory?
2. What is the purpose of a world prehistory?

There is no answer to one without the other. In the "World at 18,000 BP" project we concluded that world prehistory was both a simple narrative justifying our present condition, as well as a metaphor to reflect upon our universal humanity (Gamble and Soffer 1990: 20). The purpose in demystifying the context of our present research paradigms, as I have done here by tackling the inherited, historically embedded agenda, will, I hope, allow us to consider the second question more closely. Examining global colonization provides a means to establish the essential parameters of an evolving humanity. Darwin made his voyage of discovery to these questions aboard the Beagle, and never forgot that day in 1832 in Tierra del Fuego, and

> the astonishment which I felt on first seeing a party of [natives] on a wild and broken shore . . . , for the reflection at once rushed into my mind – such were our ancestors (1871: 404).

We can now make our voyage by broadening such horizons to include not only those on the shore but also those on the ship.

Acknowledgments

Thanks are due to Tim Murray and Norman Yoffee for many helpful suggestions on earlier drafts. Any editorializing and digressions remain mine.

Notes

1 But neither would I be surprised if the cradle went extraterrestrial if space, and any Star Wars races it may contain, becomes a colony and has to be incorporated into the scheme of human history. On the other hand we will be able to judge our galactic rank if our world holds the "honor" of being identified as some interplanetary cradle for intelligent life!

2 Whether vicariant biogeography is more suited to the scientific politics of the post-colonial era remains to be seen. In common with the imperial tradition it seeks to replace, it too is firmly tied to a global political agenda of fragmentation and intellectual hegemony. It is certainly not neutral in the political metaphors for explaining change and understanding variability which it employs.

3 Penck and Bruckner (1909), the fathers of the four-ice-age system, produced a chronological framework that gave ascendancy to time's arrow and which sidelined for many years the repetition of time's cycle as originally proposed by Croll (1865) for the study of the ice ages (Imbrie and Imbrie 1979; Gamble in press).

4 Elliot Smith's great theme was the principle of continuity (1934: 133) which reiterated the imperial tradition of biogeographical dispersal, to which he supplied a cultural gloss.

References

Bailey, G. N. 1983 Concepts of Time in Quaternary Prehistory. *Annual Review of Anthropology* 12: 165–92.

Bender, B. 1985 Prehistoric Developments in the American Midcontinent and in Brittany, Northwest France. In *Prehistoric Hunter–gatherers: the Emergence of Cultural Complexity*, edited by T. D. Price and J. A. Brown, pp. 21–57. New York: Academic Press.

Black, D. 1925 Asia and the Dispersal of Primates, *Bulletin of the Geological Society of China* 4: 133–83.

Boucher de Perthes, J. 1847 *Antiquités Celtiques et antédiluviennes. Mémoire sur l'industrie primitive et les arts, leur origine*. Vol. I. Paris: Treuttel & Wurtz.

Bowler, P. J. 1986 *Theories of Human Evolution: a Century of Debate 1844–1944*. Oxford: Blackwell.

Breuil, H. 1912 Les subdivisions du Paléolithique supérieur et leur signification. *Comptes Rendus de 14e Congrès International d'Anthropologie et d'Archéologie Préhistorique*, Genève 165–238.

Butzer, K. W. 1982 *Archaeology as Human Ecology*. Cambridge: Cambridge University Press.

Campbell, B. G. and R. L. Bernor 1976 The Origin of the Hominidae: Africa or Asia? *Journal of Human Evolution* 5: 441–54.

Clark, J. D. 1976 Africa in Prehistory: Peripheral or Paramount? *Man* 10: 175–90.

Conkey, M. W. 1985 Ritual Communication, Social Elaboration, and the Variable Trajectories of Palaeolithic Material Culture. In *Prehistoric Hunter–gatherers: The Emergence of Cultural Complexity*, edited by T. D. Price and J. A. Brown, pp. 299–323. Orlando: Academic Press

Coon, C. S. 1962 *The Origin of Races*. London: Cape.

Cosgrove, R., J. Allen and B. Marshall 1990 Palaeo-ecology and Pleistocene Human Occupation in South Central Tasmania, *Antiquity* 64: 59–78.

Croizat, L. 1958 *Panbiogeography or an Introductory Synthesis of Zoogeography, Phytogeography, and Geology; with Notes on Evolution, Systematics, Ecology, Anthropology, etc.* 2 vols. Caracas: Published by the author.

1962 *Space, Time, Form: the Biological Synthesis*. Caracas: Published by the author.

Croll, J. 1865 *Climate and Time in their Geological Relations: a Theory of Secular Changes of the Earth's Climate*. Edinburgh: Black.

Daniel, G. 1962 *The Idea of Prehistory*. Harmondsworth: Penguin Books.

Darlington, P. J. 1957 *Zoogeography: The Geographical Distribution of Animals*. New York: Wiley.

Darwin, C. 1859 *On the Origin of Species by means of Natural Selection, or the preservation of favoured races in the struggle for life*. Harmondsworth: Penguin Books 1968 edition.

1871 *The Descent of Man, and Selection in Relation to Sex*. London: John Murray.

Day, M. 1977 *Guide to Fossil Man*. Cassel: London.

Dennell, R. W. 1990 Progressive Gradualism, Imperialism and Academic Fashion: Lower Palaeolithic archaeology in the 20th century, *Antiquity* 64: 549–58.

Dennell, R. W., H. Rendell and E. Hailwood 1988 Early Tool Making in Asia: Two Million Year Old Artefacts in Pakistan, *Antiquity* 62: 98–106.

Desmond, A. 1982 *Archetypes and Ancestors*. London: Blond & Briggs.

Eco, U. 1989 *Foucault's Pendulum*.

Fagan, B. M. 1987 *The Great Journey: The Peopling of Ancient America*. London: Thames and Hudson.

Foley, R. A. 1984 Putting People into Perspective: an Introduction to Community Evolution and Ecology. In *Hominid Evolution and Community Ecology*, edited by R. A. Foley, pp. 1–24. London: Academic Press.

Fowler, D. D. and C. S. Fowler, 1991 The Uses of Natural Man in Natural History, in D. H. Thomas (ed.) *Columbian Consequences: Retrospective on a Century of Borderland Scholarship*. Washington: Smithsonian Institution Press, 37–71.

Gamble, C. S. and O. Soffer (eds.) 1990 *The World at 18,000 B.P. Volume 2 Low Latitudes*. London: Unwin Hayman.

Gamble, C. S. and O. Soffer 1990 Pleistocene Polyphony: The Diversity of Human Adaptations at the Last Glacial Maximum. In *The World at 18,000 B.P. Volume 1 High Latitudes*, edited by O. Soffer and C. Gamble, pp. 1–23. London: Unwin Hayman.

Gamble, C. S. 1987 Man the Shoveller: Alternative Models for Middle Pleistocene Colonization and Occupation in Northern Latitudes. In *The Pleistocene World: Regional Perspectives*, edited by O. Soffer, pp. 81–98. New York: Plenum.

1991 The Social Context for European Palaeolithic Art. *Proceedings of the Prehistoric Society*, 57: 3-15.

in press *Timewalkers: The Prehistory of Global Colonization*. New York: John Wiley.

Gould, S. J. 1988 *Time's Arrow, Time's Cycle: Myth and Metaphor in the Discovery of Geological Time*. London: Penguin Books.

Grayson, D. K. 1983 *The Establishment of Human Antiquity*. New York: Academic Press.

Haeckel, E. 1876 *The History of Creation: or the Development of the Earth and its Inhabitants by the Action of Natural Causes*. 2 Vols. London: H. S. King.

Henry, D. O. 1985 Preagricultural Sedentism: the Naufian Example. In *Prehistoric Hunter–gatherers: The Emergence of Cultural Complexity*, edited by T. D. Price and J. A. Brown, pp. 365–84. Orlando: Academic Press.

Hrdlicka, A. 1922 The People of Asia. *Proceedings of the American Philosophical Society* 60: 535–45.

Humphries, C. J. and L. R. Parenti 1986 *Cladistic Biogeography*. Oxford: Clarendon Press.

Hutton, J. 1795 *Theory of the Earth with Proofs and Illustrations*. Edinburgh: William Creech.

Huxley, T. H. 1863 *Man's Place in Nature and Other Anthropological Essays*. London: Macmillan.

Imbrie, J. and K. P. Imbrie 1979 *Ice Ages: Solving the Mystery*. London: Macmillan.

Johanson, D. C. and M. Edey 1981 *Lucy: the Beginnings of Mankind*. New York: Simon and Schuster.

Keeley, L. H. 1988 Hunter–gatherer Economic Complexity and "Population Pressure": a Cross-cultural Analysis, *Journal of Anthropological Archaeology* 7: 373–411.

Laing, S. 1895 *Human Origins*. London: Chapman and Hall.

Larichev, V., U. Khol'ushkin and I. Laricheva 1988 Lower and Middle Palaeolithic of Northern Asia: Achievements, Problems, and Perspectives, *Journal of World Prehistory* 1: 415–64.

Latham, R. G. 1851 *Man and His Migrations*. London: John van Voorst.

Lewin R. 1989 *Bones of Contention: Controversies in the Search for Human Origins*. London: Penguin Books.

London, J. 1919 *The Human Drift*. London: Mills and Boon.

Lourandos, H. 1985 Intensification and Australian Prehistory. In *Prehistoric Hunters and Gatherers: the*

Emergence of Cultural Complexity, edited by T. D. Prince and J. A. Brown, pp. 385–423. New York: Academic Press.

Lovelock, J. 1982 *Gaia: a New Look at Life on Earth*. Oxford: Oxford University Press.

1989 *The Ages of Gaia: a Biography of our Living Earth*. Oxford: Oxford University Press.

Lubbock, J. 1865 *Pre-Historic Times, as Illustrated by Ancient Remains and the Manners and Customs of Modern Savages*. London: Williams and Norgate.

Lydekker, R. 1896 *A Geographical History of Mammals*. Cambridge: Cambridge University Press.

Lyell, C. 1830–3 *Principles of Geology, being an attempt to explain the former changes of the earth's surface by reference to causes now in operation*. 3 Vols. London: Murray.

1862 *On the Geological Evidences of The Antiquity of Man with remarks on Theories of the origin of Species by Variation*. London: Murray.

Matthew, W. D. 1915 *Climate and Evolution, Annals of the New York Academy of Science* 24: 171–318.

Mellars, P. A. and C. B. Stringer (eds.) 1989 *The Human Revolution*. Edinburgh: Edinburgh University Press.

Mellars, P. A. 1985 The Ecological Basis of Social Complexity in the Upper Palaeolithic of Southwestern France. In *Prehistoric Hunter–gatherers: the Emergence of cultural Complexity*, edited by T. D. Price and J. A. Brown, pp. 271–98. Orlando: Academic Press.

Mochanov, U. A., S. A. Fedoseeva and V. P. Alexeev 1983 *Archaeological Sites of Yakut. The Adlan and Ol'okma basins*. Novosibirsk: Nauka.

Montesquieu, C. L. S. Baron de 1748 *De l'esprit des lois*. Paris.

Moore, F. C. T. (translator) 1969 *The Observation of Savage Peoples by Joseph-Marie Degérando (1800)*. London: Routledge & Kegan Paul.

Morgan, L. H. 1877 *Ancient Society*. New York: World Publishing.

Nelson, G. and D. E. Rosen (eds.) 1981 *Vicariance Biogeography: a Critique*. New York: Columbia University Press.

Nelson, G. and N. Platnick 1981 *Systematics and Biogeography: Cladistics and Vicariance*. New York: Columbia University Press.

Nelson, G. 1983 Vicariance and Cladistics: Historical Perspectives with Implications for the Future. In *Evolution, Time and Space: the Emergence of the Biosphere*. edited by R. W. Sims, J. H. Price and P. E. S. Whalley, pp. 469–92. London: Academic Press.

Patterson, C. 1983 Aims and Methods in Biogeography. In *Evolution, Time and Space: the Emergence of the Biosphere*, edited by R. W. Sims, J. H. Price and P. E. S. Whalley, pp. 1–28. London: Academic Press.

Penck, A. and E. Brückner 1909 *Die Alpen in Eiszeitalter*. Leipzig.

Prestwich, J. 1860 On the Occurrence of Flint Implements, Associated with the Remains of Animals of Extinct Species in Beds of a Late Geological Period, in France at Amiens and Abbeville, and in England at Hoxne. *Philosophical Transactions of the Royal Society of London* 150: 277–317.

Price, T. D. and J. A. Brown (eds.) 1985 *Prehistoric Hunter–gatherers: the Emergence of Cultural Complexity*. New York: Academic Press.

Quatrefages, A. de 1879 *The Human Species*. London: C. Kegan Paul.

Ratzel, F. 1896 *The History of Mankind*. 3 Vols., translated by A. J. Butler. London: Macmillan.

Schötensack, O. 1901 Die Bedeutung Australiens für die Heranbildung des Menschens aus einer niederen Form. *Zeitschrift für Ethnologie* 33: 127.

Simpson, G. G. 1940 Mammals and Land Bridges, *Journal of the Washington Academy of Sciences* 30: 137–63.

1952 Probabilities of Dispersal in Geologic Time, *Bulletin of the American Museum of Natural History* 99: 163–76.

Smith, G. E. 1929 *The Migrations of Early Culture*. Manchester: Manchester University Press.

1933 *The Diffusion of Culture*. London: Watts.

1934 *Human History*. 2nd edn. London: Jonathan Cape.

Soffer, O. and C. S. Gamble (eds.) 1990 *The World at 18,000 B.P. Volume 1: High Latitudes*. London: Unwin Hayman.

Soffer, O. 1985 Patterns of Intensification as seen from the Upper Palaeolithic of the Central Russian Plain. In *Prehistoric Hunter–gatherers: the Emergence of Cultural Complexity*, edited by T. D. Price and J. A. Brown, pp. 235–70. New York: Academic Press.

Stocking, G. W. 1987 *Victorian Anthropology*. New York: Free Press.

Stratz den Haag, C. H. 1904 The Problem of Classifying Mankind into Races. In *This is Race*, edited by E. W. Count (1950), pp. 230–8. New York: Hen Schuman.

Taylor, G. 1927 *Environment and Race: a Study of the Evolution, Migration, Settlement, and Status of the Races of Man*. London: Oxford University Press.

Thistelton-Dyer, W. 1909 Geographical Distribution of Plants. In *Darwin and Modern Science*, edited by A. C. Seward, pp. 298–318. Cambridge: Cambridge University Press.

Tylor, E. B. 1881 *Anthropology: an Introduction to the Study of Man and Civilization*. London: Macmillan.

Vrba, E. S. 1985 Ecological and Adaptive Changes Associated with Early Hominid Evolution. In *Ancestors: the Hard Evidence*, edited by E. Delson, pp. 63–71. New York: Alan R. Liss.

1988 Late Pliocene Climatic Events and Hominid Evolution. In *Evolutionary History of the "Robust" Australopithecines*, edited by F. E. Grine, pp. 405–26. New York: Aldine de Gruyter.

Wallace, A. R. 1876 *The Geographical Distribution of Animals, with a study of the relations of living and extinct faunas as elucidating the past changes of the earth's surface*. London: Macmillan.

1880. *Island Life: or the phenomena and causes of insular faunas and floras, including a revision and attempted solution of the problem of geological climates*. London: Macmillan.

Willis 1989 *The Hominid Gang*. New York: Viking.

5

After social evolution: a new archaeological agenda?

STEPHEN SHENNAN

Introduction

The social archaeology of non-state agrarian societies emerged in the 1960s and 1970s as a concern with the growth and differentiation of social institutions within a neo-evolutionary framework. Such societies were characterized as tribes or chiefdoms; or as ranked societies, a category which largely obviated the need for distinguishing between the other two. Criticisms of this approach have been of various kinds. "Processual" attacks criticized typologies in general for a failure to recognize that there is a continuum of social complexity and for bundling together a variety of different social attributes, regarded as characterizing particular social types, instead of explaining the contingent social relations between them. Other attacks have been more radical, in both substance and political intent. It has been suggested that the discourse of social complexity in which recent discussions of social evolution have been framed is merely a re-expression of the ethnocentric emphasis on progress which characterized the nineteenth century, and which Rowlands (1989) suggests is typical of the Judaeo-Christian tradition. The view may be summed up in the statement by Giddens (1984: 236) that "Human history does not have an evolutionary 'shape' and positive harm can be done by attempting to compress it into one." Giddens intends this statement in both an empirical and an evaluative sense. First, there is no reason to consider the vast majority of human history as a "world growth story"; our tendency to think in these terms is a product of the last four hundred years of history in the West. Second, there is a tendency to see particular paths of historically specific change as general and universal. Third, there is a tendency to see "a homology between the stages of social evolution and the development of the individual personality" (1984: 239), in which members of non-western cultures are seen as "children of nature" in contrast to the mature, rational adult individuals of western society. This is in turn associated with the fourth tendency which Giddens identifies in evolutionism, "the inclination to identify superior power, economic, political or military, with moral superiority on an evolutionary scale" (1984: 242).

Acceptance of the view that social evolutionary approaches are fundamentally ideological has considerable implications, which extend as much to the marxist version of evolutionism as to the neo-evolutionary one. In the specific case of non-state societies it helps us to escape from the deeply ingrained view that they are evolutionary stepping stones, and from the associated tendency to look at them from an unsatisfactory teleological point of view as containing the seeds of future states.

The theoretical tools to cope with the vacuum left by the rejection of evolutionism have begun to emerge from recent work on the nature of power deriving from a variety of theoretical perspectives, including marxist and feminist ones. The tenor of these is that patterns of inequality, power differentials, and situations of domination and resistance arise in all societies, including those conventionally regarded as (relatively) egalitarian. The characteristic insistence on looking for centralized hierarchies and control within non-state societies is one of the teleological aspects of seeing them in terms of their potential as the ancestors of future states; and even in the case of states the "myth of control" can be overdone (see Yoffee, this volume).

The thrust of the argument to be developed below is that these new approaches are not only theoretically more satisfactory but also, *contra* the numerous opponents of so-called "post-processualism," are methodologically more convincing for archaeology. The point may be made by an analysis of the methodological problems raised by attempts to use archaeological data for the purposes of neo-evolutionary reconstruction.

Evolutionary reconstruction and archaeological method

The basis of the social evolutionary approach in its various guises has been the reconstruction of social institutions from archaeological evidence. With the appearance of literate civilizations, the link between the archaeological record and social institutions is often fairly clear cut, not least because it is now corroborated by documentary sources and because social institutions are greatly differentiated. However, the possibility of making this link between the archaeological record and social institutions in developed states, especially those with documentary records, combined with the social evolutionary emphasis on the importance of tracing the progressive development of such institutions, has had the unfortunate effect of leading archaeologists studying agricultural societies on a dubious quest to link the archaeological record with social institutions in order to trace the history of social evolution. As a result, archaeologists in this sub-field of the discipline, unlike those concerned, for example, with hunter–gatherers, have never managed to take Marvin Harris's advice (1968) and "shrive themselves of anthropological categories." Among other things, a consequence has been that they have remained wedded to what Binford has called "unrealistic identification approaches" to the archaeological record, which usually involve developing checklists of archaeological characteristics believed to be associated with supposed evolutionary stages.

To infer directly from the archaeological record to social institutions breaches the requirements of what Runciman (1983) calls "reportage," in the context of a set of distinctions he makes between reportage, explanation, description, and evaluation in the social sciences. Reportage corresponds in certain respects to the concerns of "middle range theory." It refers to the process of reporting an event, process, or state of affair as having occurred. Such reports are not, of course, presuppositionless, but they should as far as possible be theory-neutral, in the sense that holders of rival theories should be able to agree on them; reports should not imply or pre-empt particular theoretical positions at the level of explanation (compare Wylie 1992: 27).

To make this point is not to assert some kind of radical inductivism, or to suggest that data are not theory-laden; rather, it is a generalized prescription for avoiding the fallacy of affirming the consequent characteristic of so much social archaeology. Obviously, archaeological data are always selected with problems in mind, but the theoretical basis for making what we may call "reconstruction inferences" should not depend on our initial assumptions about, for example, the existence of tribes or chiefdoms, but on at least semi-autonomous lines of argument (Wylie 1992).

It is in this matter of failing to avoid pre-emption at the reporting stage that much social archaeology has proved guilty. Thus, for example, Creamer and Haas (1985) postulate the existence of tribes and chiefdoms, list a series of archaeological correlates, and then check them off for the two areas they are comparing. There are clearly interesting archaeological differences between the two areas, but the conclusion that one area represents a chiefdom form of organization and the other a tribe is a classic example of the fallacy of affirming the consequent, since the existence of tribes and chiefdoms is an unsubstantiated starting assumption which is not subject to testing, while the archaeological

patterns could be accommodated to a range of different models.

Postulating/constructing the existence of certain social institutions can never simply be a matter of constructing an appropriate indicator variable, because the institutions cited are invariably abstractions of a complex nature which, more often than not, are themselves contested in a different literature. Thus, for example, on the basis of an examination of the social anthropological literature, an archaeologist may decide that he should look for the presence of "segmentary lineages" in the archaeological record and devise some supposed test implications for their existence which turn out to be fulfilled. However, his position will be undermined if a subsequent anthropologist re-examines the original sources for segmentary lineages and demonstrates that they did not actually exist but were constructs arising from misinterpretations, and incomplete knowledge of what people said and did, on the part of the original ethnographers (see for example Kuper 1988, and the discussion of chiefdoms in Knight 1990, also Yoffee, this volume). The postulation of social institutions then belongs to the stage of explanation, not reportage, in Runciman's terms, and is certainly not a straightforward matter of "middle range theory." It arises in response to "why" questions, as part of claims to explain the links between reconstructed phenomena. The criterion for accepting such phenomena is the justification of the claim that they belong to the sphere of reportage, where the construction of indicator variables can be demonstrably more convincing. This will be at the level of specific practices, not of abstract social institutions, as Francfort (1989, 1990) demonstrates, and will involve the use of (semi-)autonomous lines of argument and evidence, as suggested above.

Social archaeology and social evolution

The reasons why social archaeology became oriented around the problems of social evolution conceived as institutional differentiation are two-fold. First, this provided the only available theoretical framework for a subject whose declared concern was *long-term* change; recent social anthropology and traditional history had little to offer to the study of long-term change, and for different reasons had an attitude to archaeology best described as contemptuous. Second, a concern with broad questions of institutional differentiation seemed to be appropriate for the widely agreed coarse-grained nature of the archaeological record, since it seemed to provide an appropriate macro-scale for the study of process. However, although archaeological evidence may be coarse-grained in comparison with the information in the ethnographer's diary, the idea of coarseness is to some extent misleading. Most of the archaeological record is a record of "moments in time" from the perspective of the enormous spaces, spatial and temporal, in which it is scattered. Furthermore, the record is extremely particular in its specific instances, just as historical documents are. The fact that a distribution of artifacts and bones in a cave is not the product of a single event but may have accumulated over a long period of time should not be taken as a justification for resorting to misleading abstractions at an altogether different level of supposed "description," but rather as a challenge to our understanding of the archaeological record as the residue of *practices*: the aim must not be to make statements of the type, "this represents a band society," but rather, for example, "there seem consistently to have been three beds up against the cave wall, with hearths in between them."

In summary then, one of the problems with much existing social archaeology is that it has tried to write a history of very generalized social institutions, made up of vague roles, when it has evidence in general not of roles but of practices. The fact that burials sometimes appear to provide a record of roles has been their key attraction to social archaeology and the fact that this record is mediated through a very special kind of practice has been the biggest problem in realizing the attraction. Written records tend to have the opposite virtues: weak as a record of practice but strong as a record of roles and institutions and the normative expectations associated with them.

The practices of which archaeology provides a record are at two extremes: on the one hand, important "events" which affected the way social space was structured, for example the construction of Stonehenge; on the other, and much more frequent, at least in non-state societies, the routinized activity of individuals going about their daily round, repetitive everyday happenings – in other words a micro-scale record of micro-scale activities. Unlike sociologists, who can decide to work at the level of social institutions rather than individual interactions because they can obtain information at both these levels (Turner 1987), archaeologists do not have the option of "bracketing out" the micro-level of analysis as many have attempted to do. Nevertheless, this requirement to address the micro-scale need in no sense be a bar to the declared aim of studying long-term change. To identify long-term patterns in terms of the repetition of micro-scale activities is both more informative than the usual generalized social abstractions and more suited to the nature of archaeological evidence; moreover, it is not only archaeologists who see its relevance:

If we reduce the length of the time observed, we either have the event or the everyday happening. The event is, or is taken to be, unique; the everyday happening is repeated, and the more often it is repeated the more likely

it is to become a generality or rather a structure. It pervades society at all levels and characterises ways of being and behaving which are perpetuated through endless ages. Sometimes a few anecdotes are enough to set up a signal which points to a way of life (Braudel 1981: 29).

It is these same everyday happenings – practices – of which archaeological material provides a record. Similarly, the patchy nature of the archaeological record is not necessarily any more of a problem than it is for more traditional historical sources in terms of setting up "a signal which points to a way of life." Braudel's structures, although they may last a long time, are not abstractions of the nature of, for example, "chiefdom society," but the continuity of specific sets of practices which have to be (re)constructed.

As we have seen, an emphasis on the importance of practices has considerable advantages for archaeologists because of its compatibility with the nature of the archaeological record. However, it has also come to play an increasing role in sociology and anthropology more generally, especially, of course, as represented in the work of Bourdieu (e.g. 1977, 1984). Bourdieu's theory of practice is again grounded in the micro-scale, concerned with day-to-day activities. Thus, his analysis of the distinctions present in modern French society is based among other things on the quantitative analysis of household expenditure patterns, of household inventories and domestic spaces, data analogous to that seen in the archaeological record.

The patterned actions which make up practices are performed by motivated individuals with intentions, beliefs, and particular social resources. This does not necessarily imply a *reduction* of all social phenomena or explanations of them to a concern with individuals and their motivation, but it does imply a *dependence* of the higher levels on the level of the individual and a satisfactory model of this level (Runciman 1983: 29–32). Reportage and explanation in archaeology, as in any other social science, presuppose an account of what individual people were doing. In archaeology not only is it not possible to "bracket out" this account and take it as understood, but providing the basis for such micro-level accounts is what archaeology is good at.

A recent example of this approach is Mithen's (1990) work on modelling Mesolithic hunter–gatherer activity. A central part of the work is the modelling of day-to-day individual hunting decisions. Different hunting priorities lead to different kill-off patterns which lead to different outputs in terms of bone frequencies at archaeological sites (subject to the usual preservational qualifications). That individual Mesolithic hunters thought in the terms specified by Mithen's models is highly unlikely to say the least, and he is certainly not claiming to reconstruct their thought processes. Nevertheless, the outcomes of their actions point to certain priorities being more important to them than others, however they were actually conceived and even if they did not follow them every day. We are dealing with distributions of outcomes, not mechanistic determinism, and have the statistical tools to analyze them just as the rest of the social sciences do. In other words, we can investigate the outcomes of individuals' decisions using the evidence of archaeology, in this case via the evidence of bone frequencies.

To say that such individuals are not real individuals at all, but a collective mentality, is to miss the point; first, because no claim is being made to reconstruct thought processes; second, because if the majority of individuals did not in fact act in accord with one set of priorities rather than another, the patterned outcome would be different, and if there were no patterned priorities in terms of decision-making this too would be apparent. Case studies such as Mithen's are not claiming to reconstruct a universal mesolithic mentality but the practices of particular people, places, and times. All this is, or should be, commonplace.

Social archaeology and social actors

The argument so far has emphasized that archaeology provides a record of social practices rather than abstracted/ generalized social roles, and certainly not institutions, and that these practices are the outcomes of decisions by individuals which we can therefore reasonably hope to understand. In addition, it has been argued more briefly that assumptions about individuals are in fact behind any attempts at understanding past socio-economic change, or indeed social evolution. The basic ingredients required are social actors with intentions, who may or may not stand for more than themselves; conditions of action, acknowledged and unacknowledged; and consequences, intended and unintended. Without a starting point at the level of individuals, for example, there is no possibility of understanding such phenomena as the disasters that can arise as a result of the aggregate effect of individually rational behavior. Furthermore, *real actors* of some kind are a prerequisite for any approach to social interactions which involves the evaluation of costs and benefits.

While the analysis of people interacting with the environment in terms of costs and benefits has a pedigree within archaeology going back thirty years, the same is not true for the evaluation of costs and benefits in terms of the interactions between people. This has not been done explicitly at all, and insofar as it has been done implicitly it has been done in the social evolutionary and institutional terms outlined

above, where the neo-evolutionists assume the largely beneficial impact of new social institutions and the marxists assume that for most people they will be deleterious. However, within the neo-marxist framework at least, the importance of the emergence of social institutions which are not the conscious design of the people who produce them has been recognized, even if not adequately described or explained (Terray 1977).

Of course, game theory provides an important basis for theorizing such situations, not least with the concept of the Nash equilibrium, but also in showing that some games are unpredictable in their outcomes, and even micro-regularities can lead to chaotic and unpredictable long-term outcomes. Similarly, it is now a well-established point in the dynamical-systems literature that interactions between people and between processes can have emergent properties for a variety of reasons, including imperfect information held by social actors and the potential effects of time delays which lead to different processes becoming de-synchronized from one another, with unpredictable results (e.g. McGlade and Allen 1986).

The social evolution approach has nothing to offer in the analysis of such processes. On the theoretical side within archaeology it continues to be concerned with the development of conceptual frameworks based on social typologies (cf. Kristiansen 1991), albeit more sophisticated than those of Fried and Service, and largely oriented towards understanding the "rise of the state." Empirically it is based on the production of dubious synthetic "factoids" (Chippindale, this volume) concerning social institutions, in which the process of synthesis which creates them is carried out on the basis of assumptions rather than any investigation of the contingent relations between the different practices through which people live their lives. The fact that, in addition, the existing approach is not appropriate to the nature of the material with which archaeologists work only confirms this diagnosis.

Such skepticism about social evolutionary approaches is also coming to be shared in sociology. Mann's framework for the evolution of social power (Mann 1986) was criticized recently for its failure to address micro-level social mechanisms at the level of specific social actors and their intentions and interests (Kiser and Hechter 1991). It was argued that at the abstracted level at which he deals with social and political processes, causal mechanisms and causal relations could not be specified and therefore could not be investigated; abstractions cannot enter directly into social relations.

At present perhaps the best that can be said about social-evolution case studies is that they can provide useful outline scenarios of social and economic processes which can then be further developed with the micro-scale approaches argued for here; the worst is that they may be totally misleading, because of the way they define their problems and collect and describe their data. On the other hand, what the micro approaches described so far can be accused of is over-simplifying the real issues out of existence, especially questions of differential power relations, and of losing the richness of description of the prehistoric past which is characteristic of the best recent work within the social evolutionary tradition.

Decision-making in a cultural context

What is missing at the moment? Clearly, the micro-economic decision-making framework outlined above cannot assume that decisions are taken in a context where everyone has equal power, nor can it neglect the ideological framework within which decisions take place. However, more generally than this, some idea of culture has to be introduced, for without it there is little basis, or at least only a very generalized one, for understanding rational choices and why they should change through time. If, as seems reasonable, they are affected by individual preference structures, we have to investigate the factors that influence those structures, and potentially important among them is the process of cultural transmission.

This topic is of especial significance in examining patterns of inequality, domination, and resistance in societies which do not have a powerful coercive apparatus, for here, as anthropologists of all persuasions have long recognized, the reproduction of social order is based on the reproduction of the ideological conditions in terms of which it makes sense. The post-processualists have seen this largely from a structuralist point of view, in which it is envisaged that societies have deep structuring principles determining their organization, which endure for greater or lesser periods before giving way to different principles by processes which are rarely clear. Such supposed principles are, however, abstractions and thus in themselves have no causal power (Sperber 1985); moreover, there are good reasons to regard them as *post hoc* rationalizations, a mere exegesis of reality.

A more satisfactory framework derives from recent work on the subject of social reproduction which deals with real social actors and processes, and does so in terms relating directly to the micro-scale approach advocated above. The argument may be illustrated by the example of Toren's ethnographic work on the social construction of hierarchy in Fiji (Toren 1990). Like Bloch (1991), Toren sees cognitive development as domain specific and as varying between individuals, not as some kind of blanket imposition of

structuring principles. She shows how children's notions of gender, space, and hierarchy are constructed over time through daily experience of relative seniority in respect to their own activities and in relation to the adult rituals which they observe.

In this construction, Toren shows, material objects have a particular significance:

> The continuity between a child's and an adult's conception of the hierarchy inscribed in people's disposition in space rests on the material stability of ritual, on the fact that certain highly salient material elements are *always* disposed in the same way (1990: 228).

In the Fijian case, people's relation to the cloth at meals and the drink container at drinking rituals is what matters, so there is, in effect, an awareness that status is more "concrete" in certain ritual situations. But whereas for the child a certain person is higher in status *because* they are sitting in a certain place, for the adult, at least when called upon to address the subject explicitly, the fact that someone is sitting in a certain place is a mark of their position in terms of an abstract notion of hierarchy: "what is constitutive for children is, for adults, expressive" (1990: 228). On the basis of this argument, Toren draws some important general conclusions concerning the nature of the "symbolic." Far from it being some kind of distinct domain, archetypically seen in ritual, as it is usually regarded, the "symbolic" is "the product of a process of cognitive construction in persons over time" (1990: 229): signs *become* symbols, propositions *become* metaphors.

The key cognitive scheme that Toren refers to as "above/below" is created/manifest in people's behavior, which affects the behavior of others, while children imitate the posture and manners of adults in increasingly complex ways as they get older. Children's behavior is "objectively adapted to the expression of hierarchy" even though this is not as such an end in view or a rule being followed. Clearly, this closely parallels Bourdieu's (1977) rejection of the "fallacies of the rule," but the implications are actually stronger than that. They point to the conclusion that it is highly misleading to think of culture as communication in the structuralist fashion, or to think of cultural phenomena, and rituals in particular, as representations of something else. Like the "fallacies of the rule," the "fallacy of representations" is encouraged by the role of the anthropologist as observer, but it derives even more directly from the basic (and erroneous) presupposition that cultural practices follow the sentential logic of language, which is quintessentially representational (Bloch 1991).

In my view, and very much in keeping with Durham (1990), the conclusion to draw from this is that what matters about cultural practices is not so much any communicative aspect but their *genealogy*. The argument seems to me to be supported by Boyer's work on tradition as truth and communication (Boyer 1990). In Boyer's view, to construe the traditional discourse seen in rituals as the expression of world views is to focus on irrelevant aspects of these rituals and ignore the key aspects:

> One could still claim that some "meanings" are transmitted despite the ritual language . . . As it happens, however, the people concerned take the formalisation to speech to be, not a contextual or secondary property, but a crucial feature, so much so that a translation in ordinary language is not supposed to convey a truth at all. By taking the expression or transmission of information as the main point of the ritual we . . . consider irrelevant what the actors take to be essential, what they try to transmit from generation to generation (1990: 108).

In other words, as far as the process of cultural transmission is concerned, what are transmitted are not mental models but "specific recipes, words, gestures and other such 'surface' phenomena" (1990: 117). In effect, what we see is an inversion of the principles of structuralism and the idea of deep structure: what matters is the surface and everything is secondary rationalization. The surface *is* the genealogy.

The Fijian example just mentioned provides an indication of what is involved in a specific cultural genealogy and its transmission. Such genealogies may be considered as having their own "historical logic" and any attempt to understand change in such contexts has to take this into account because it will inevitably condition the kinds of changes which can take place, as well as the manner in which they occur. However, this certainly does not imply a teleology; the process is *coming from* somewhere, *not going* somewhere.

As noted above, in the absence of large-scale coercion, which does not occur in non-state societies, the reproduction of cultural genealogies is central to the distribution and use of social power. Furthermore, archaeology is extremely well placed to trace such genealogies over long periods of time.

Conclusion

The social evolutionary approach to social change is unsatisfactory, for the reasons outlined at the beginning of this paper and many more (see Yoffee, this volume). Much of the criticism which has led to this view has derived from a "post-processualist" perspective. However, that perspective has not itself come up with any very satisfactory alternative, for a variety of reasons; its radically relativist epistemology; its keenness to eschew any methods, such as mathematical modelling, which might be regarded as anti-humanist and "scientistic"; and its Durkheimian insistence on explaining the social in terms of the social, which has led to the exclusion of ecology on the one hand and cognitive psychology on the other.

The approach presented here advocates first of all the micro-scale analysis of the costs and benefits of alternative courses of action, using such tools as game theory. The reasons for this are as follows:

(i) We must deal at the level of real social actors, interacting with one another; only these have interests and only these have causal powers (see Sperber 1985 for this argument in a different context).

(ii) Without such micro-scale approaches it is almost inevitable that anthropological and archaeological accounts will be shot through with functionalist fallacies.

(iii) Only by starting at this level can we understand the unintended consequences and unstable dynamic behavior which can emerge over the long term and which are certainly a key part of the complexity of history. If our attempted explanations of the large-scale patterns we observe are at the level of these patterns we will never understand them. They can arise as a result of the intrinsic properties of small-scale processes (e.g. Glance and Huberman, in press), as well as through imperfect information and lags and leads between different processes.

Such micro-scale analyses have to be situated in a cultural context which must also be relevant at that level. Once again, we should forego the abstractions of structural principles and develop models based on studies of the cognitive psychology of individual development in specific contexts; the micro-scale is the real level of social and cultural reproduction.

Finally, and in keeping with this program, our archaeological work has to be at the level of reconstructing specific social practices, rather than generalized social institutions. Adopting this goal will have the additional and highly desirable virtue of avoiding the production of pre-emptive explanatory packages masquerading as reports of prehistoric situations.

References

Bloch, M. 1991 Language, Anthropology and Cognitive Science. *Man* 26: 183–98.

Bourdieu, P. 1977 *Outline of a Theory of Practice.* Cambridge University Press, Cambridge.

1984 *Distinction.* Routledge and Kegan Paul, London.

Boyer, P. 1990 *Tradition as Truth and Communication.* Cambridge University Press, Cambridge.

Braudel, F. 1981 *Civilisation and Capitalism 15th–18th Century.* Vol. I: *The Structure of Everyday Life.* Fontana, London.

Creamer, W. and J. Haas 1985 Tribes vs. Chiefdoms in Lower Central America. *American Antiquity* 50: 738–54.

Durham, W. 1990 Advances in Evolutionary Culture Theory. *Annual review of Anthropology* 19: 187–210.

Francfort, H. P., M. S. Lagrange, and M. Renaud 1989 *Palamède: application des systèmes experts à l'archéologie des civilisations urbaines préhistoriques.* LISH/UPR No. 315. C.N.R.S., Paris.

1990 Modelling Interpretive Reasoning in Archaeology with the Aid of Expert Systems: consequences of a critique of the foundation of inferences. In *Interpretation in the Humanities: Perspectives from Artificial Intelligence*, edited by R. Ennals and J. C. Gardin, pp. 101–29. Library and Information Research Report 71. The British Library, London.

Giddens, A. 1984 *The Constitution of Society.* Polity Press, Cambridge.

Glance, N. S. and B. Huberman in press The Outbreak of Cooperation. *Journal of Mathematical Sociology.*

Harris, M. 1968 Comments. In *New Perspectives in Archaeology*, edited by L. R. and S. R. Binford, pp. 359–61. Aldine, Chicago.

Kiser, E. and M. Hechter 1991 The Role of General Theory in Comparative-historical Sociology. *American Journal of Sociology* 97: 1–30.

Knight, V. R. 1990 Social Organization and the Evolution of Hierarchy in South-eastern Chiefdoms. *Journal of Anthropological Research* 46: 1–23.

Kristiansen, K. 1991 Chiefdoms, States and Systems of Social Evolution. In *Chiefdoms: Power, Economy and Ideology*, edited by T. K. Earle, pp. 16–43. Cambridge University Press, Cambridge.

Kuper, A. 1988 *The Invention of Primitive Society.* Routledge and Kegan Paul, London.

Mann, M. 1986 *The Sources of Social Power*, Vol. I: *A History of Power from The Beginning to A.D. 1760.* Cambridge University Press, Cambridge.

McGlade, J. and P. M. Allen 1986 Fluctuation, Instability and Stress: Understanding the Evolution of a Swidden Horticultural System. *Science and Archaeology* 28: 44–50.

Mithen, S. 1990 *Thoughtful Foragers.* Cambridge University Press, Cambridge.

Rowlands, M. J. 1989 A Question of Complexity. In *Domination and Resistance*, edited by D. Miller, M. J. Rowland, and C. Tilley, pp. 29–40. Unwin Hyman, London.

Runciman, W. G. 1983 *A Treatise on Social Theory*, Vol. I: *The Methodology of Social Theory.* Cambridge University Press, Cambridge.

Sperber, D. 1985 Towards an Epidemiology of Representations. *Man* 20: 73–89.

Terray, E. 1977 Event, Structure and History: the Formation of the Abron Kingdom of Gyaman (1700–1780). In *The Evolution of Social Systems*, edited by J. Friedman and M. J. Rowlands, pp. 279–301. Duckworth, London.

Toren, C. 1990 *The Social Construction of Hierarchy in Fiji.* Athlone Press, London.

Turner, J. 1987 Analytical Theorizing. In *Social Theory Today*, edited by A. Giddens and J. Turner, pp. 156–94. Polity Press, Cambridge.

Wylie, A. 1992 The Interplay of Evidential Constraints and Political Interests: Recent Archaeological Research on Gender. *American Antiquity* 57: 15–35.

6

Too many chiefs? (or, Safe texts for the '90s)

NORMAN YOFFEE

For the past three decades, the prevailing "model" that has been used by archaeologists to investigate the rise of the earliest states is that of "neoevolutionism" – the stepladder model of bands becoming tribes, then chiefdoms, and finally states (Fig. 6.1). In the late 1970s and the 1980s, however, some – but not by any means all – archaeologists (see below for references) questioned the utility of the received model, leaving the situation unresolved for the 1990s. For example:

> The neoevolutionist perspective in anthropology . . . is neither dead nor seriously ailing; with appropriate modifications it can continue to enhance our understanding of the development of complex human societies (Spencer 1990: 23).

> The data from sequences of early state formation do not neatly fit neoevolutionary expectations (Paynter 1989: 387).

> Such obvious and irreconcilable beliefs as to what a state (or, indeed, a chiefdom) is arise from the intellectual exercise inherent in classificatory theory . . . (I)t is time for us to reject typological theory in favor of a perspective that more closely conforms to observable evolutionary reality (Bawden 1989: 330).

In this essay I briefly review the arguments that have been made both for and against the typological stage-level neoevolutionary model; I further consider the social and intellectual contexts that help us understand why many archaeologists who once accepted the model now seem ready to jettison it. This discussion in social evolutionary theory can serve as a case study, I submit, for a larger range of issues concerning the building of archaeological theory. As has been argued in this volume (see Introduction), most archaeological theory comes from outside archaeology itself, and the neoevolutionary model is a prime example of such borrowing. Although such finding of theory from outside archaeology does not preclude the possibility of appropriately bridging or operationalizing that theory into archaeological practice, the stage-level model used by archaeological neoevolutionists constitutes a "paradigmatic" dead-end that prevents empirical analysis of the evolution of ancient states. A new, archaeological theory must be designed to explain social evolutionary change in late prehistoric and early historic states and civilizations and it must be "contextually appropriate" by linking archaeological problems to the archaeological data available for their investigation. In this essay I center the discussion of evolutionary model-building on the concept/stage of "chief" and "chiefdom" because in the so-called transition from chiefdom to state one confronts very clearly the nature of neoevolutionary logic and its shortcomings.

Why archaeologists find chiefdoms

While Braun and Plog (1984) represent one of the few attempts to demarcate the archaeological correlates of "tribes," a mighty company of archaeological wallahs has pursued the wily chiefdom. Renfrew (1973) isolated twenty features of chiefdoms that might qualify the builders of European megaliths as chiefs; Sanders (1974) and colleagues (e.g., Michels 1979) have identified chiefdoms in prehistoric highland Mayaland, while Creamer and Haas (1985) have found them in lower Central America; Drennan and Uribe (1987) find them everywhere in the Americas; Knight (1990) has chiefdoms in the Southeast U.S.A. and Doyel (1979) has them in the Southwest U.S.A.; Fairservis sees the Harappan culture as a chiefdom (1989: 217); Earle thinks Ubaid and Uruk Mesopotamia were both chiefdoms (1987), although Watson holds that in the preceding Halaf there were chiefdoms (1983); for Henry (1989), even the Natufian of the Northern Levant was a "matrilineal chiefdom."

There's no great secret, of course, why the chiefdom is so ubiquitous. First, something must precede states that is not even crypto-egalitarian, yet is not exactly state-like, and it requires a name. Second, anthropological archaeologists need a frame for cross-cultural comparison. Pristine states arose independently in various parts of the world and so similar pre-state entities must be identified in order to measure their distances from statehood. And third, the received anthropological wisdom has directed archaeologists to flesh out the fragmentary material record of an extinct social organization by means of an appropriate ethnographic analogy. The "archaeological" procedure is to correlate one or more central features of a favorite ethnographic type with some excavated material; then the archaeologist can extrapolate all the rest of the characteristics of the type and so bring the not-directly-observable dimensions of ancient reality into view.

What archaeologists find in chiefdoms

The history of social evolutionary theory in archaeology, as a number of commentators have noted (e.g., Yoffee 1979, Dunnell 1980, McGuire 1983, Willey and Sabloff 1980, Trigger 1989), began as a renaissance within social anthropology led by Leslie White and Julian Steward in the 1950s. Such trends towards evolutionary studies reflect the prestige of scientific inquiry within anthropology as a whole. "New archaeologists," as is well known, were particularly eager first to be anthropologists (which such titles as "Archaeology and Anthropology" [Willey and Phillips 1958: 2] unambiguously show [cf. Binford 1962, Longacre 1964]) and scientific (as the subtitle "An Explicitly Scientific Approach" to Watson, LeBlanc, and Redman 1971 indicates). It was logical then, when Sahlins declared that

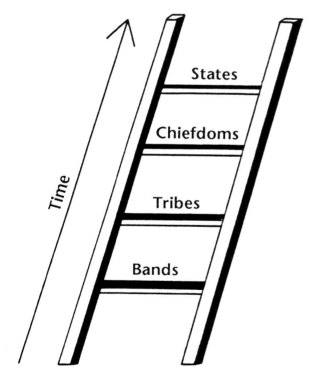

Fig. 6.1 Evolutionary Stepladder (drawn by B. Montgomery)

"any representative of a given cultural stage is inherently as good as any other, whether the representative be contemporaneous and ethnographic or only archaeological" (1960: 33), that archaeologists should adopt the general evolutionary model espoused within social anthropology.

In the canonical version of that neoevolutionist model (though Leslie White rejected any "neo-" prefix to it: his model was just that of Tylor and Morgan), the chiefdom was the stage that preceded the state and that which followed bands and tribes. Although there were variants on the theme, notably Fried's coercion model which opposed Service's benefits (or voluntarism) model (see Fried 1978; Yoffee 1979), most archaeologists were comfortable with the concept of chiefdom. Some, like William Sanders, conducted student seminars with the view to identifying chiefdoms in the material world (1974) and gatherings of professionals still meet today to sort out the chiefdom (Earle, ed. 1991).

That task hasn't been easy for archaeologists for the good reason that the essential criteria of the chiefdom have changed significantly over the years from the classical description of Service (1962 and subsequently 1975; for a genealogy of the concept of chiefdom, see Carneiro 1981). The chiefdom began life in anthropology with several defining attributes: social organization consisted of branching kinship structures called ramages or conical clans, wherein all members are ranked pyramidally in terms of distance from real or putative founding ancestors. Chiefdoms are "kinship societies" (Service 1962: 171) because status is largely determined through place in the generational hierarchy of groups and of individuals within the groups. In political terms, chiefdoms contain hereditary and usually endogamous leaders (sometimes called a nobility) and centralized direction, but have no formal machinery of forceful repression. As Netting has put it,

> The general pattern of the rights, duties, role, and status of the priest–chief is numbingly familiar to anthropological students of society. He is the famous *primus inter pares*, the essentially powerless figure who does not make independent decisions but voices the sense of the meeting. He leads by example or by persuasion. As chief he may have a title and an office, but his authority is circumscribed; he *is* something, but he *does* very little. As Sahlins (1968: 21) remarks, "the Chieftain is usually spokesman of his group and master of its ceremonies, with otherwise little influence, few functions, and no privileges. One word from him and everyone does as he pleases" (Netting 1972: 221).

Such chiefly authority in the classical view is universally correlated with religious authority (Service 1975: 16).

Therefore, chiefdoms are "theocracies" with authority distributed as of a religious congregation to a priest–chief. Economically, for Service, who strongly contested the view that chiefdoms contained any roots for economic differentiation, matters of production and consumption were governed by sumptuary rules. The redistribution of goods is one of the main responsibilities and perquisites of centralized chiefly leadership. Finally, according to Service, these characteristics of chiefdoms become incorporated in the successive evolutionary stage of states, since each new stage includes many aspects of the previous stages.

To archaeologists the most appealing aspect of these classical attributes of chiefdoms was redistribution. Sanders (1974), for example, was able to "operationalize" redistribution by finding storehouses in a society that at the same time lacked palaces. A chief, so the idea went, had the power to effect the construction of a storehouse, because it was a public facility, but not the right to order the construction of his own residence. Unfortunately, Timothy Earle (1977, 1978) effectively questioned whether redistribution, that is, the collection of goods from specialized producers into a center and the circulation of those goods to members of an organically integrated society (see Service 1962: 144), really occurred in prehistoric Hawaii, a *locus classicus* of the chiefdom. In Earle's latest account (Earle 1987, Johnson and Earle 1987), he argues that local communities were in fact self-sufficient in staple goods (also strongly declared by Peebles and Kus 1977), and such imports of staples to chiefs were mobilized mainly in order to support the chiefly-led public feasts and to feed the chief's attendants.

If redistribution has now been all but eliminated as a characteristic of the "chiefdom," so have considerations of economically egalitarian communities and powerless chiefs. For Earle, chiefly elites control strategic resources, mainly by achieving ownership of the best land and directing the labor of commoners who worked it as dependents. In short, the most important social characteristics of chiefdoms to social anthropologists, that of conical clans, the sumptuary rules accompanying chiefly authority, the loose control of chiefs, and the function of the chief as a beneficent priest–king, have completely disappeared from the archaeological literature. What has replaced them is a conception of chiefly political organization.

In influential articles written by a confederation of scholars associated with the Department of Anthropology, University of Michigan (Earle 1987, Peebles and Kus 1977, Steponaitis 1978, 1981, Wright 1977, 1984, Spencer 1987, 1990) and joined significantly by Carneiro (1981 – Carneiro is a graduate of an earlier generation at Michigan), the basic point of the chiefdom is that it is a political unit. That is, a chiefdom represents a breakthrough in social evolution in which local autonomy – which constituted 99% of all the societies that have existed (according to Carneiro 1981: 37) – now gives way to a form of authority in which a paramount controls a number of villages. Chiefdoms thus organize regional populations in the thousands or tens of thousands, control the production of staples and/or the acquisition of preciosities, and are surely early stages in the rise of civilizations (Earle 1987). For Carneiro (1981), states are only quantitatively different than chiefdoms.

Although there may still be *simple* chiefdoms, which are of the classically ascriptive sort, with ranks determined according to the distance from common ancestors, there is also the *complex* chiefdom (Wright 1984). The complex chiefdom consists of a regional hierarchy, with a paramount chief and subsidiary chiefs. These paramount chiefs have centralized decision-making authority in which they mobilize resources, but they leave local communities and sub-chiefs more or less in place. That is, as Wright puts it, complex chiefdoms are *externally* specialized (in order to get the goods from their regions to the chief's control) but are not *internally* specialized (i.e., with a specialized bureaucracy) to accomplish the task. There is a rank difference between chiefs and commoners, with the chiefs forming a sort of "class" and competing with each other for leadership and control of ritual institutions that could legitimize their status. However, such attempts at control of goods without a coercive machinery at hand meant that rebellions, breakdowns, destructions of centers, and changes in symbolic orientation are part of what complex chiefdoms are about (Wright 1984).

Charles Spencer, in one of the latest of the Michigan school's exegeses on the chiefdom (1990), has detected one point of schism in the analysis of complex chiefdoms and so of neoevolutionary theory. According to Spencer, the single inconsistency in the position of the evolutionary typologists and their view of the chiefdom as a stage that precedes the state, is the mistaken idea that social change is gradual (Earle 1987: 221) and continuous (Wright 1984). Such a notion of change would reduce the distinction between chiefdom and state only to a quantitative difference (*à la* Carneiro) and so render the neoevolutionist stage model of little utility. For Spencer, the distinction between chiefdom and state must be emphasized: chiefs, lacking internally specialized enforcement machinery, avoid delegating central authority and rely on the local power of sub-chiefs, while kings (in states) systematize and segment their power so as to undermine local authority. Thus, the transition from chiefdom to state proceeds transformationally (when it does occur – chiefdoms could also collapse). The key conditions leading to transformation are growth in population and increase in surplus mobilization that require an alteration in "regulatory strategies" (p. 10) which transcend "the limitations of chiefly efficiency" (p. 11). The evolution of states, for Spencer, is not gradualistic but punctuational. It lies in the creation of new administrative technology, new administrative facilities, and an altogether new kind of administrative system from that of chiefdoms.

Now for Spencer, as well as for the others cited, the overwhelming interest in chiefdoms is in their political structure. Indeed, having stripped the chiefdom of its character as a kind of kinship network, and with a redistributive economic base, it is only the political nature of the chiefdom as a supra-local entity that is emphasized. As Spencer puts it, "before an administration can be centralized and also internally specialized, it must first be centralized" (p. 10). As chiefdoms are concerned with centralized administration, it is to them that we must look as predecessors of states.

This emphasis on administration can be criticized precisely for diverting attention from evolutionary trends such as how institutionalized social and economic dependencies are created outside the kinship system. By de-emphasizing or simply ignoring the economic and social structures of chiefdoms, one can only conclude that political centralization must precede differentiation and stratification. But, even assuming that chiefdoms are "centralized," we are left with the dilemma that Service never quite resolved: how do beneficent, redistributive, relatively authorityless, and non-economically stratified chiefly societies become socially and economically riven states with kings and their bureaucracies attempting to exercise repressive force? (Anderson [1990] notes that "internal contradictions in the kin based structure of chiefdom societies . . . sow the seeds of repeated organizational collapse" [p. 630]. The cycling between complex and simple chiefdoms in the southeastern U.S.A. might lead to "primary states" [if given enough time, p. 633], although "environmental deterioration and administrative failures" [p. 631] resulted in their collapses.) If an answer was not apparent to Service, much empirical archaeological work indicates that – contrary to Spencer's argument – trends towards economic and social differentiation were characteristic developments in the *early* phases of evolutionary trajectories leading to ancient states.

Archaeologists who originally embraced the neo-evolutionary model of "our contemporary ancestors" (Fig. 6.2) did so because it strongly allied ethnology to archaeology in one big happy family of anthropologists. The Old Timer, as quoted by Flannery (1982: 269), declared, "There is no 'archaeological' theory. There's only *anthropological* theory." Neoevolutionism, by "arbitrarily rip[ping] cultures out of context of time and history and plac[ing] them, just as arbitrarily, in categories of lower and higher

development" (Sahlins 1960: 32), provided archaeologists with a series of ready ethnographic analogies that could be introduced into the past. Such neoevolutionary trees of "our contemporary ancestors" were constructed, curiously, without any reservation that the ethnographic societies themselves did not lead one to the other, but were, indeed, contemporary. As Flannery notes (in contradicting the Old Timer), the neoevolutionary model was made by ethnologists, not archaeologists; while evolutionary theory is a proper subject of archaeological investigation, ethnographic stages are merely metaphysical constructions (1983: 362). No processes of long-term changes in the past can be adequately modeled on the basis of short-term observations in the present.

Even with much of the original defining characteristics of chiefdoms eliminated, and the ethnologically-derived model for social change in empirical disrepute, the need to have some anthropologically familiar form of society to precede the state continues as an article of faith to atavists: "chiefdoms" must be part of the "Bauplan" (construction plan) through which the state had to pass (Spencer 1990).

Criticisms of neoevolutionism

Having reviewed the history of neoevolutionist thought in archaeology and some of the internal difficulties inherent in introducing an artificial sequence of ethnographic societies into archaeological time-depth, I now turn to a broader range of critiques of the model and especially the concept of the chiefdom within it.

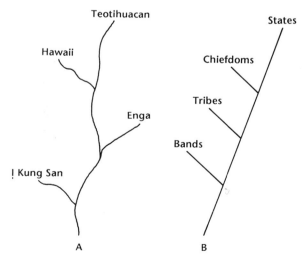

Fig. 6.2 "Our Contemporary Ancestors" (drawn by B. Montgomery)

The first published argument that chiefdoms might lie outside the evolutionary trajectory towards the state was the essay by Sanders and Webster (1978). In correlating environmental variables of climatic "risk" and "diversity" of resources, Sanders and Webster considered that chiefdoms, which occurred in low risk/high diversity situations, were alternatives to state development. There could be a transition from chiefdom to state, but the process was one of contact from already developed states, which effected a drastic change in the social and economic organization in chiefdoms.

Yoffee (1979) and McGuire (1983) rejected neoevolutionism as a model of holistic change. For McGuire, the variables of "inequality" and "heterogeneity" needed to be kept separate and not subsumed one by the other. His point was that a society could be very unequal vertically (as he considered the earliest states to be) but with a corresponding small degree of heterogeneity, that is, with few horizontally differentiated economic and social groups. As societies grew more complex, the amount of heterogeneity tended to increase. My criticism of holistic change was that it inevitably tied all social institutions – politics, economics, and social organization – in a bundle such that change had to occur in all institutions at the same time, at the same pace, and in the same direction. In the neoevolutionist view, systems theory embraced substantivism: a particular kind of economy was embedded in a corresponding kind of society. Thus, egalitarian bands and tribes had reciprocal forms of exchange, while chiefdoms were characterized by redistribution. Although there is obviously some relation between forms of exchange and social organization, these simple correlations were challenged by critics (e.g., Pryor 1977, Allen 1985) who pointed out that market principles operated in societies that were not highly stratified, and that reciprocity and redistribution are found in modern states. In studies of the "collapse" of states (see Yoffee and Cowgill, eds. 1988), it is especially apparent that the political systems (governments) of states could fall while other social institutions continued to survive and even thrive. The continued existence of certain social corporations (as in the especially clear example of Chinese literati) provided the political ideology and bureaucratic infrastructure so that the state (i.e., the political system) could re-emerge. Also criticizing the neoevolutionist scheme, Feinman and Neitzel (1984) observed that since prehistoric change was continuous (see also Plog 1974, Upham 1987), it was wholly arbitrary to break the sequence into discrete and distinct blocks.

In the two articles cited in the introduction to this paper, Paynter (1989) and Bawden (1989) represent the current dissatisfaction with neoevolutionary theory. Paynter notes that the stages of neoevolutionism imply a set of stable social

formations which, beset by certain problems (like population growth), move to the next higher stage. Complex society, in Paynter's view of the neoevolutionist position, is a "problem solver, not a problem creator" (1989: 374), with hierarchies emerging as responses to the need to produce and monitor information. For Paynter a large number of evolutionary concerns for modern archaeologists cannot be accommodated in the neoevolutionism scheme: culture is not a machine for processing energy, individuals are not culture bearers but "agents," and cultures are not distinct, bounded entities. Rather, social evolution must consider the nature of the cores, peripheries, and semi-peripheries; coercive powers of the state are often just attempted mechanisms of legitimization of the social order; ideas have institutional, not epiphenomenal status; and culture is partitive rather than holistic (with intra-elite struggle as well as inter-class tension).

For Bawden, neoevolutionist typologies are, if anything, in worse shape than they are for Paynter: the types are all states of mind. Commenting on a recent volume on the "Andean state" (the subject of Bawden's review article), he notes that everything from late preceramic horizons on up (in time) have been called states. In Bawden's view, however, the state itself is only "a general catchall description of complex society in its most highly evolved forms" (1989: 330). Stages, thus, are only failed intellectual exercises at identifying sets of diagnostic features. Unfortunately, these features tend to be accumulative rather than discretely transformational since, for example, in Andean societies one finds "mixtures of characteristics that have been used to identify chiefdoms and states, ranked and stratified societies" (p. 331). Both Paynter and Bawden conclude that the trends towards inequality, stratification, and (partial) social integration – trends that rightly can be considered at the heart of social evolutionary theory – must be broken down into institutional units that can combine and sunder in various patterns. There is no invariable "Bauplan" that links institutions in discrete stages.

It may be churlish to remind an archaeological audience considering the utility of borrowing the concept of chiefdom into the archaeological record, and worrying about what the real essence of the ethnographic chiefdom is, that the subject of "chiefdoms" is light-years away from anything that modern anthropologists study. This neglect of the chiefdom, on the one hand, may be ascribed to changing fashions in anthropological research but, on the other hand, it reflects an agreement that the typological effort to identify a chiefdom was and is useless. In Melanesia and Polynesia, the original example for Sahlins' famous distinction (1963) between bigman (or tribal) societies and chiefdoms, critics were quick to point out that some societies have the annoying habit of possessing traits of both types (Chowning 1979, Douglas 1979). The absurdest of situations occurs when Melanesian chiefs, so defined according to their kin-ranking and inheritance of position, have as their foremost goal to become big-men (by achieving super-trader status [Lilley 1985]). Indeed, Sahlins' discussion on big-men and chiefs is basically a description of the types; readers are left to imagine the unspecified evolutionary forces that would have transformed a big-man society into a chiefdom. In Kirch's archaeological study of the evolution of the Polynesian chiefdoms (1984), there is no such transition from any putatively prior big-man society to a chiefdom, since chiefs existed before migrations to Polynesia. The only "evolution" is that dependent on island geography – how the availability of land, resources, and other islands affected the size and structure of various sorts of Polynesian chiefdoms.

In the neoevolutionist movement from big-man societies to chiefdoms and then to states, there is something profoundly illogical: big-man societies are classically those in which rank, wealth, and status hinge on achievement, but in which such rank cannot be inherited; in chiefdoms, classically, rank and status are ascribed (through the kinship system) and passed along intergenerationally; in states, it is achievement – through control of resources, for example – that is again the hallmark of social organization, while kin groups and ascription play less important roles in social life. It would make far more sense, perhaps, to derive states from achievement-oriented big-man societies than it would from ascriptively-determined chiefdoms. In this essay, however, a rather more complex skein of evolutionary trajectories is developed.

Mesopotamian states and their evolutionary trajectories

In rejecting the classificatory exercise of neoevolutionism, I offer here an outline for a new social evolutionary theory. Before doing so, however, I am conscious that I have already indulged in the very un-archaeological luxury of presenting a lengthy theoretical discussion in the absence of any specific case studies. I intend to remedy this deficiency in this section by discussing several facets of Mesopotamian social and political organization, specifically identifying the major institutional players in the struggle for power in Mesopotamian states. If neoevolutionists have stressed the "centralized" nature of chiefdoms, they have also (necessarily) regarded states as efficient information-processing machines that integrated and monopolistically controlled spheres of law, production, and distribution.

In this section, I tack freely between historic and prehistoric periods in an analytical procedure that is particularly appropriate in Mesopotamian studies. While writing is the trait that technically separates history from prehistory in Mesopotamia, it is the most inconsequential of traits for purposes of evolutionary periodization. Mesopotamian writing is restricted to an exceedingly small group, whose members do not themselves normally possess high status, but are in service to the increasingly routinized bureaucracies of temple and palace estates in the early third millennium BC. Although writing does signify the existence of, and plays an important role in, the hierarchical organization of these great estates, control of the production of written tablets has relatively little impact on the formation of social boundaries, on the flow of information between groups, or on the creation of new status and dependency.

Studying the social configuration of Mesopotamian states
The turning point in the story of Mesopotamian social organization and political history – or so I believe – occurred in the year 1969 with the appearance of critically important essays by I. J. Gelb and I. M. D'jakonov (conventionally spelled Diakonoff). While differing considerably on some specific issues (for example, Gelb 1979 as against Diakonoff 1982), both agreed that only from the concatenation of data contained in economic and administrative archives, not from royal inscriptions, scribal *belles lettres*, and date formulas, could history be written. In short, they regarded basic economic and social processes as the keys to understanding change. Mesopotamian societies were composed of partly overlapping and partly opposing fields of behavior – especially as represented in the competition between temple and palace estates and the interests of the "community," i.e., those traditional kin groups and non-traditional economic corporations (for example, traders) that were not strictly dependent on temple or palace. Rather than view different Mesopotamian social systems as "phenotypic" expressions of respective ethnic "genotypes" (such as Sumerian or Akkadian or Amorite institutions), the task became to investigate the networks of endemic social conflicts and organizational compromises in given segments of time and space. The flow of history concerns the nature of power struggles, the opportunities and constraints on economic and social mobility, and the overarching, inherently fragile political institutions which both reflect and legitimize the hierarchical and ethnically diverse nature of Mesopotamian social systems (for examples of political fragility, see Yoffee 1988).

The implications of this perspective have very direct relevance for my critique of the stage of chiefdom as an evolutionary type and for the analysis of evolutionary trends in Mesopotamian prehistory. Perhaps the most striking lack of fit between the evolutionary concept of chiefdom and

Mesopotamian data lies in the claim that the chiefdom is an autonomous regional unit under a paramount chief (Carneiro 1981: 45) and that it is "externally specialized" with central decision-making activity but without internal specialization (Spencer 1990 after Wright 1977, 1984). What is an "autonomous regional unit" in Mesopotamia and what is the nature of authority and specialization in it?

First, it must be realized, perhaps surprisingly to non-Mesopotamianists, that there is no "Mesopotamia," at least in the political sense of the term. Rather, there is a congeries of independent city-states and ephemeral confederations of them. Only in a "cultural" sense, can one refer to "Mesopotamian" languages, including literary languages (Cooper 1989, Larsen 1987, 1988, 1989, Michalowski 1987, 1990), a "Mesopotamian stream of tradition" (Oppenheim 1964, Machinist 1985), "Mesopotamian" belief systems, and "Mesopotamian art styles." A "Mesopotamian great tradition" (Yoffee 1993b) is thus palpable and over-arches the independent city states and regional empires that characterize aspects of Mesopotamian history.

These central characteristics of Mesopotamian *civilization*, however, were not carried by any semi-autonomous group of literate elites, as was in fact the case in ancient China (Hsu 1988, Schwartz 1985). Furthermore, the Mesopotamian "great tradition" did not function to legitimize (in any important way) political power in the manner in which artistic and literary display are said to do in the Egyptian and Maya "great traditions" (for Egypt, see Baines 1983; for Maya, see Schele and Miller 1986; compare these with Winter's studies of Mesopotamian art as communication essentially to subject peoples and as statements of power [1981, 1983]). Important questions for understanding the prehistoric evolution of this *cultural* boundary of Mesopotamia cannot be answered by means of analogy with any chiefly notion of "autonomous regional units."

City-seals and the Mesopotamian great tradition

Let me point to a particularly interesting domain of material evidence that may be considered to indicate the formation of such cultural ties among the first city-states of the early third millennium BC (see Yoffee 1993b). So-called "city-seals," really the clay impressions of cylinder seals, found mainly at Ur (Legrain 1936), are "decorated" with the names of city-states (Fig. 6.3), and have long ago been interpreted by Jacobsen (1957) as evidence for his putative Kengir League, an early political unity of Sumerian cities with Nippur as the amphictyonic center. Since no such unity is likely, however, before Sargon's era, before which conflict among city-states was the name of the game, Nissen (1983; see Cooper 1983) has considered that such seals reflect economic transactions among city-states (see Michalowski n.d., Smith 1984 for

similar views). Without claiming to explain the exact purpose of these city-seals, I do wish to raise the possibility that they may reflect neither political nor economic patterns of behavior. Indeed, it may make perfectly adequate sense to regard these seals, which record the names of various cities, as presenting an idea, specifically the idea of a common cultural structure among city-states that were politically independent. I reckon, further, that such an *idea* of "Mesopotamia" begins much before the third millennium BC (see Oates 1983 and the essays in Henrickson and Thuesen, eds. 1989, also Yoffee 1993a for discussions of cultural uniformity in the Ubaid). If the notion of chiefdom is unhelpful in explaining the formation of the "civilizational" boundary within which Mesopotamian city-states are embedded, it also fails to account for the kind of political struggle one observes *within* Mesopotamian city-states. Modern Mesopotamianists have moved very far, indeed, from the claim that the earliest city-states were first organized by temples and only subsequently by secular

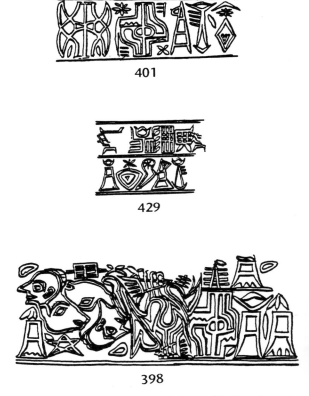

401

429

398

Fig. 6.3 Examples of Sumerian "city-seals" (from Legrain 1936)

establishments (this was one of the breakthroughs in analysis led by D'jakonov and Gelb). The first city-state from which we have any evidence is Warka (see, conveniently, Nissen 1983). In the late Uruk period, we witness an enormous urban implosion, which is hardly predictable from the antecedent Ubaid. The acropolis at Gawra or the series of temples at Eridu in the Ubaid, themselves representing an impressive break from previous public architecture, are dwarfed by the Eanna precinct at Warka (Fig. 6.4). In this comparison, change certainly looks abrupt and qualitatively "transformational" rather than gradual. Furthermore, in the late Uruk, attendant to this process of urbanization, we see an interregional expansion in which southern Mesopotamians, perhaps from Warka itself, established colonies far up the Euphrates (Fig. 6.5) in order to secure distant resources required by the new urban elites (Algaze 1989, Sürenhagen 1986). Not only did specialized military prowess and new economic demand flow from the concentration and restructuring of social relationships within Wark (and other city-states), but the countryside itself was "ruralized" in response to, or accompanying, those urban processes. Adams has calculated that by the mid third millennium, nearly 80% of all settlements are cities (1981). This twin process of urbanization and ruralization resulted in profoundly new divisions of labor and opportunities for creating both wealth and misery. Evidence of this process also renders incredible the neoevolutionist idea that antecedent stages of social integration became included in later stages. Although not everything changes utterly when cities appear in Mesopotamia, it is certainly not the case that cities simply sit atop whatever the previous social order is imagined to be.

In the third millennium, at cities like Kish (see Charvat 1976, Moorey 1978, Gibson 1972), there is no architectural record of a temple-estate preceding royal estates. At Lagash, texts depict the on-going competition for power between temple and palace, most clearly delineated in the priestly usurpation of UruKAgina at the end of the Early Dynastic period (ca. 2400 BC, see Cooper 1983). Mesopotamian priests certainly enjoyed the economic fruits of ritual prerogative, but they were not chiefly directors of Mesopotamian states.

In addition to the theoretical problems concerning civilizational boundaries and political integration that make it difficult to get from chiefdom to state, we must consider the nature of social organization with Mesopotamian city-states. In early second millennium examples, councils of elders, sometimes led by "mayors," exercised large degrees of power. These councils typically functioned as legal bodies, deciding cases of personal wrongs and family disputes. The crown's decision-making apparatus only entered into such legal matters when there was a royal officer involved (Yoffee 1988, Westbrook 1988). For the early third millennium, the critical period of city-state formation, less is known about local community authority, since texts are almost exclusively artifacts of temple and palace bureaucracies. Still, epic tales referring to these times do imply the existence of councils; also terms for councils and community leaders occupy prominent positions in some of the earliest texts that we can read, which are the lists of occupations (Nissen 1986). Thus, the evolution of *community* power structures, and their relationship to developing temple and royal institutions, must be part of the trajectory to Mesopotamian states and civilization.

The point of the foregoing, obviously selected view of aspects of the Mesopotamian historic past is that none of the supposed characteristics of ethnographic chiefdoms can "predict" the form of Mesopotamian historic states. The kinds of institutional differentiation and the several foci of social integration and inherent political struggle in Mesopotamia preclude this trajectory. Mesopotamian rulers are normatively non-regional, are never well functioning and "systemic," and do not even attempt to control all facets of production, information, or authority. The picture, rather, is one of several kinds of institutionalized power, resting on different bases of social incorporation. If Mesopotamian states look like this, we cannot expect that pre-state Mesopotamia will be redistributively (or otherwise) centralized, grouped according to ascribed kinship relations, externally specialized in terms of social control processes, or will exist as a regional entity with a paramount chief – as Polynesian, Central American, and/or African chiefdoms are or are not accounted to be. In fact, from just about any kind of chiefdom to a Mesopotamian state you cannot get – either gradualistically or with an evolutionary punctuation mark. A heterodox claim might be that ethnographic chiefdoms lie in a different evolutionary line from states altogether.

To investigate evolutionary phenomena in prehistoric Mesopotamia, it seems to me, it is far more useful to see what happened in historic times than to rely on an abstracted (and disputed) ethnographic stage of chiefdom or to study some distant chiefdom that never would become a state. The vast expanse of Halaf, with local centers of nascent elites (Watson 1983), the cultural boundary of a "Mesopotamian" Ubaid, or the logic of the urban implosion and subsequent political explosion in Uruk cannot begin to be accounted for through a series of ethnographic analogies masquerading as social evolutionary theory. What is needed is archaeological analyses of these archaeological data and the confidence that appropriate theory can be constructed by archaeologists to do the job.

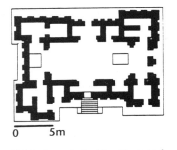

Eridu temple in Ubaid period

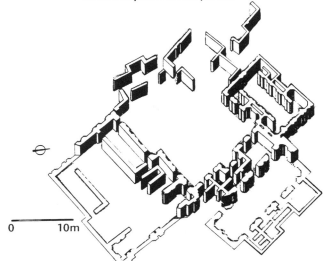

Gawra acropolis—3 temples in Ubaid period

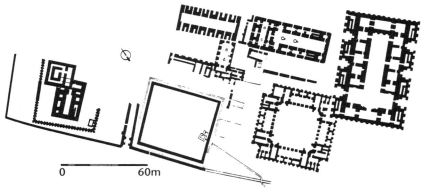

Temple complex at Warka—Uruk period

Fig. 6.4 Comparison of Ubaid and Uruk sacred architecture (from Heinrich 1982): Eridu temple in Ubaid period; Gawra acropolis – 3 temples in Ubaid period; Temple complex at Warka – Uruk period.

The dimensions of power: towards a new social evolutionary theory

Varieties of power

In order to construct a social evolutionary theory adequate to explain trends towards the formation of, by anyone's definition, those highly stratified and politically organized societies we call states and civilizations (herewith Yoffee's Rule: if you can argue whether a society is a state or isn't, then it isn't), we must first identify the distinctive and empirically evident features of evolutionary change.

Closely following Runciman (1982, and ultimately Weber), I suggest (see also Yoffee 1985; compare – and contrast – Mann 1986) that the most important necessary and jointly sufficient condition that separates states from non-states is the emergence of certain socioeconomic and governmental roles that are emancipated from real or fictive kinship; that is, the basis of relations between the occupants of governmental offices and those who are governed is not ascription. The social corporation of such governmental roles, usually denominated the state, includes the quality of paramount and enforceable authority, and more than ephemeral stability. It is further asserted that the process by which states develop depends on the cumulative accretion of power available to incumbents of prospective governmental roles.

For purposes of tracing archaeologically the evolution of

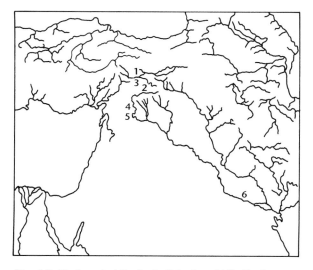

Fig. 6.5 Uruk period "colonies" in the middle Euphrates (after Sürenhagen 1986; drawn by K. Lasko) Key: 1, Tepecik; 2, Norşuntepe; 3, Arslantepe; 4, Jebel Aruda; 5, Habuba Kabira South; 6, Warka.

these state societies, it is held that power can be subdivided into three, and perhaps only into three, dimensions: economic power, societal (including ideological) power, and political power. It must be stressed that these three dimensions of power reinforce one another and the state does not rest on only one dimension. It is the combination of economic productivity – the control over the sources and distribution of subsistence and wealth, the segregation and maintenance of the symbols of community boundary, and the ability to impose obedience by force, that together mark the essential qualities of states. All these trends must be considered integral to an evolutionary trajectory that includes state development. Although each of these dimensions (or sources) of power is overlapping and interpenetrating (see below), they are not only analytically separable but also represent different possibilities of gaining power over people and resources. In evolutionary terms, we must now ask whence come these varieties of power and what constrains them into social coexistence?

First, economic power is created through a process of horizontal specialization in the production of subsistence and a diversification of tasks in the storage and distribution of reliable surplus. The means from agricultural production to economic power lies in the conversion of stored wealth to a system of dependencies arising from differential access to land and labor. Organizations consist of elites, managers, and dependents, including both craft specialists and laborers who have been attracted by or forced into the security provided by the land-owning and surplus-producing estate. These estates may belong to temples and palaces, but they also might be those of cadet royalty, lineage heads, or entrepreneurially successful persons. All states contain such economic elites and all trajectories towards the earliest states include processes of agricultural differentiation and organization into non-kin-based estates (although in some states kin-based estates remain important).

The second major source of economic power is through mercantile activity. Long-distance, regular networks of exchange are generally found to accompany the first inequalities in economic access to basic productive means. Not only does the acquisition of preciosities represent burgeoning economic status, but the process of acquisition becomes an institution requiring organization and thus a means through which status is produced. Long-distance trade, when coupled with other institutions of economic (and other forms of) inequality becomes a particularly important (and visible) institution in ancient societies, precisely because economic "action at a distance" (Renfrew 1975) produces wealth and status outside the moral economy (of sharing) usually imposed by kinship systems.

In Mesopotamia, the data are clear that economic

entrepreneurs form their own organizations, wield political power, and are only minimally supervised by the state (Larsen 1976). The importance of mercantile groups in organizing trade, however, varies greatly: Aztec pochtecas seem relatively independent (Hassig 1985); specialized traders (*mindalaes* and Chincha) were used by Inka (Rostoworowski 1970, Salomon 1986; references courtesy of H. Silverman); Teotihuacan obsidian producers seem closely monitored by the state (Spence 1981); and in China the state attempted to monopolize bronze technology (Chang 1983). Let me conclude this brief discussion of economic power with the reminder that trends towards economic inequality in production and exchange are normally measured by archaeologists in differing sizes of residences, accompanying features and artifacts, and in mortuary furniture. No prehistoric trajectory to any state fails to contain indications of significant economic inequality well before the appearance of anything that might be called a state.

Societal or ideological power refers initially to the horizontal segmentation of social structures and thus entails a consideration of numbers of people and population growth. This vital horizontal component of societal power can be ascertained from both material and ethnohistoric records – of Aztec calpulli, Inka ayllu, Mesopotamian ethnic groups, barrios at Teotihuacan or Huari.

Societal power also denotes the establishment of territorial interactions, nucleation into urban complexes, and, perhaps most saliently, the creation/adaptation of certain symbols of cultural and political commonality and a cadre of people to interpret and maintain them. Ceremonial buildings and artistic and literary representation not only link diverse peoples (and their diverse orientations) and settlements beyond factors of kinship, but confer honor and prestige on those maintaining those symbols. The people who have unequal access to these items that legitimize social life beyond face-to-face interactions, and who are thus able to command goods ostensibly on behalf of the community, but especially for their own ends, exercise societal power. Archaeological study of the institutions of ideology, from great monuments to ceramic horizon-styles, is a growth industry in modern archaeology.

In a comparison between Mesopotamia and the Maya (Yoffee 1990a), it is noted that neither area can be defined in any political sense, but only in an ideological one, since both areas were comprised of autonomous, rival city-states. If in Mesopotamia it has been noted (above) that there was endemic conflict between temples and palaces for political power, Cowgill has argued similarly that Teotihuacan seems a lot less theocratic than it once was thought to be (1983). His analysis of the Ciudadela as a state ceremonial complex and the Street-of-the-Dead complex as a palace provides a fuller perspective through which the great cultic structures at Teotihuacan, as well as the enormous apartment complexes and barrios, can be investigated. All state-level societies have large and wealthy institutions that owe their existence precisely to the management of supernatural affairs. At least part of their function is to legitimize rulers as agents of the cosmic plan, who reign under divine protection (or/and are themselves considered divine), and who perform the required ceremonies that ensure the perpetuation of the universe.

Finally, political power refers to the ability to impose force throughout a community through specialized permanent administrators, including a differentiated military organization. The administrators and other clients of the dominant estate occupy their offices through means of recruitment beyond the co-existing system of kinship in a society. This system of political differentiation is seen perhaps most clearly in ancient China where the well-known literati served as state bureaucrats but were not kinsmen of the rulers themselves. While political power is exercised in administrative decision-making, including settling disputes in which the parties are of differing social groups, and defending the society in times of war and defense, it is important to note that local (societal) powers also maintain their traditional roles of decision-making in areas (e.g., of family law) that do not directly affect the ruling estate.

In some societies it is important to disembed the political from societal power by founding new capitals, not because better access to land or water is needed, but because a formal separation from other elites allows for new policies to be implemented and new dependents to be recruited for the new enterprises. Blanton, thus, has identified the founding of Monte Albán as a "disembedded capital" (1983); King David transformed Jerusalem as a means to create a new political system, Sargon built Agade, and neo-Assyrian kings were continually founding new capitals in their attempts to disenfranchise the old landed aristocracy.

To summarize this section on the sources of power in evolutionary trajectories, it is worth reiterating that all three sources need to be co-evolving for states to emerge since these three sources of power all reinforce each other. Landowners and traders seek political power (or at least freedom from political power and taxation), while political leaders own much land, manage personnel, and commission traders with goods produced on palace estates. Religious leaders also own land and sometimes seek political power, usually in opposition to oppressive political leaders, while political leaders require legitimation from the cultic establishment.

From this interplay among various sources of power, I argue, comes the evolution of new society-wide institutions, especially of supreme political leadership, and new symbols of community boundary – in short of states and civilizations. The process obviously does not happen overnight and any attempt to find the exact date of the creation of the state is quixotic. Finally, it should be noted that social evolution does not end with the rise of states. Nothing is more normal for an ancient state than for it to "collapse," for the same inherent struggle for supremacy among various types of elites that resulted in the formation of states could also lead to their failure. Ancient states (no less than modern ones) function with a good deal of bungling and generating of conflict within themselves as well as with their neighbors (Kaufman 1988). States were (and are) "at best half-understood by the various people who made them, maintained them, coped with them, and struggled against them" (Cowgill 1988: 253–4).

Social evolutionary theory for archaeologists

New social evolutionary theory (as opposed to neo-evolutionism) is archaeological theory because it does not rest on an assumption that ethnological "types" of societies, in which relations are fixed within a type, represent macrosocietal processes of change in the past. It attempts, furthermore, to investigate social change, both gradualistic and transformational, in particular archaeological sequences and by means of a controlled, cross-cultural, intra-archaeological frame of comparison.

New social evolutionary theory is concerned with the following archaeological domains: (1) the probability of growth of states; (2) the constraints on growth of social complexity; (3) the range of variability of ancient states; (4) the relation between the earliest states, secondary states, and societies peripheral to states; (5) the collapse of states. New social evolutionary theory expands the range of anthropological, sociological, and economic inquiry, but it firmly rejects many of the preconceptions in those disciplines about the nature of late prehistoric and early historic change.

(1) In new social evolutionary theory it is considered that states are not rare and precious entities in the evolution of human societies and do not require special explanations (e.g., "prime causes") for their development. This old neoevolutionist view was based on two quantitative fallacies. The first is a fallacy of time: because most of human (pre)history consists of a variety of hunter–gatherer societies, states, which rest on agricultural surpluses, have been reckoned "atypical." In new social evolutionary theory, it is held, to the contrary, that trends towards state formation are probable. Given specific biological evolution in the Pleistocene, climatic change at the end of the Pleistocene, and with long-term knowledge of flora and fauna, sedentism,

domestication, population growth, and social differentiation are exactly what one expects. Indeed, states emerged in every part of the world and they did so independently. What needs to be explained, therefore, is not only the emergence of new constellations of power and the range of variation in complex societies, but also why some societies did not develop states (see below).

The second quantitative fallacy is sociological: because most social anthropologists (the majority in American departments of anthropology and in the American Anthropological Association) and the majority of archaeologists study non-stratified societies, archaeologists investigating the origin of states are in a distinct minority in their profession. The study of state societies is again considered to represent "atypical" professional concerns, while ethnographic and ethnoarchaeological studies are normative. In new social evolutionary theory, however, it is held that social anthropologists who investigate "traditionally organized" societies of the present are studying alternatives to the rule of probable growth in social evolutionary theory.

(2) Constraints on growth is an especially significant – and difficult – topic in new social evolutionary theory. Many archaeological data, of course, are the residues not only of extinct but of collapsed societies. Similarly, much ethnoarchaeological and ethnographic work is done in societies that have not (yet) become completely integrated into modern states. In new social evolutionary theory such societies are not simply to be regarded as fossilized stages, the "Neolithic" or "formative" levels, as it were, of ancient states (see Fig. 6.2). Rather, it is held that these societies may have lacked one of the crucial sources of power (outlined above), the interplay among which is required for the formation of states. Brief examples of the absence of, or constraint on, a source of economic power can be cited: lack of domesticable flora and fauna (e.g., in Australia); the inability to store surplus foods and so lead to specializations in distribution (as seems the case in Polynesia); and, controversially, the difficulty of getting reliable surpluses in areas in which poor soils and harsh climatic fluctuations predominate (and in which social aggregations would not have been "adaptive," as may have been the case in the American Southwest). Constraints on growth also include political factors, especially the marginalization of societies into "peripheries" of already developed "cores."

Figure 6.6 attempts to diagram a new social evolutionary model in which constraints on kinds of power can result in very different evolutionary trajectories. This diagram is *not* meant as a four-part "epigenesis," that is, one with four teleologies instead of the one that is well known in Friedman and Rowlands' model (1977). Rather, one must imagine that many different evolutionary trajectories can exist and that not all known human societies fall on the progressive steps of a social evolutionary ladder (contrast Fig. 6.1. Figure 6.6 does not intend to exclude the possibility of societies in one trajectory [e.g., chiefdoms] moving to another trajectory [as presumably occurs in numerous cases of secondary state formation, see also Anderson 1990] and it only guesses at the possibly different "bases" and/or common ancestor ["bandishness"] from which different evolutionary trajectories might arise. Rather, this diagram seeks to inspire research into the nature and roots of inequality and power: at what point and why can one "trajectory" be differentiated from another? Can a trajectory be arrested or a society transformed so that it may be said to lie in a different "trajectory"? The logical outcome of this depiction of evolutionary trajectories may be an abandonment of the taxonomic quest to "type" societies [which requires that social institutions fall into only one of the discrete types; see Bawden 1989, "Yoffee's Rule," above p. 69]. This figure is meant to imply, however inadequately, that the taxonomic labels of neo-evolutionism have falsely ranked the diversity of human societies, both past and present. These labels have also been wrongly used by archaeologists who seek to "type" a prehistoric society as a "state" or a "chiefdom" as if such a categorization might elevate their empirical research into the realm of higher evolutionary thought – and as if they actually know something more about a prehistoric society having so stuck a label on it).

(3) Collateral to the topic of constraints on growth is the consideration of cores and peripheries, world-systems, interaction spheres, and secondary state formation. These topics have been the subject of recent archaeological work (Rowlands et al. 1987, Kohl 1986, Falconer 1987) and will continue to be investigated in new social evolutionary theory. Trigger's various essays on the need to "historicize" archaeology (1984a, 1984b) and the renewed commitment to considering "extra-systemic" modes of change (Schortman and Urban 1987, Rouse 1986, Yoffee 1990b) represent a needed openness for explaining the varying paces and scales of state formation through inter-societal contact.

(4) The archaeological concern with variability in ancient states can be approached in new social evolutionary theory by *weighting* the dimensions of power in evolutionary trajectories. In ancient China, for example, Chang (1983) has observed that in the later Shang dynasty, rulers attempted to control the production of bronze vessels, which were the magical vehicles of communication to the ancestors. In his analysis, differential access to the gods was one of the most important resources in manipulating kin allegiances and was what made the Shang a state. In the process of controlling such symbolic communication and so redefining the ideology of power, the Shang dynasty may also have reorganized the literate diviners into a quasi-professional cadre of officials. To simplify the process greatly, in the subsequent Zhou periods, a group of ideologically differentiated specialists was transformed into a routinized, professionalized literati class and became the "carriers" of the idea of the Chinese state. This situation contrasts markedly with Mesopotamia, in which literati held almost no power independent from their sacral or secular employers. If all states emerge along a similar trajectory towards social and economic differentiation and political integration, it is critical to investigate both the specific nature and the "weight" of the dimensions of power in those states.

(5) Finally, in this agenda of new social evolutionary concerns is that of the collapse of ancient states and civilizations. Two significant publications have appeared recently (Yoffee and Cowgill, eds. 1988, Tainter 1988), with very different emphases on this subject but which in common demonstrate that social evolution did not end with the appearance of ancient states. Furthermore, the concern with "rise," to the near exclusion of collapse, in neoevolutionist theory, has had important theoretical implications: social change was perceived as a process of irreversible, "emergent" levels of sociocultural integration. Collapse, on the other hand, requires that societies be conceived in terms of institutional groupings of partly overlapping and partly opposing fields of action that lend the possibility of instability, as well as stability, to overarching social institutions (Adams 1988).

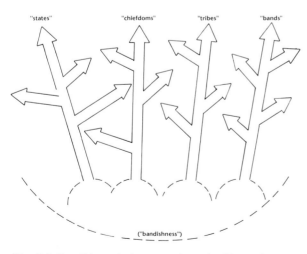

Fig. 6.6 Possible evolutionary trajectories (drawn by K. Lasko)

Conclusion

In Fig. 6.7, degrees of stratification in chiefdoms and states are depicted to show the relation between two evolutionary trajectories. "Hawaii" stands for "chiefdom" (C), that is, a society in which inequality is determined according to ascription and paramount chiefs controlled a region in which local authority was vested in sub-chiefs (Earle 1987, Withrow 1990). "Teotihuacan" represents a "state" (S), a society in which inequality is significantly based on access to certain resources and the power accruing therefrom. "Formative Teotihuacan" refers to an early period in the evolution of the "Teotihuacan state" when relatively little inequality existed: let us assume a society in which agricultural specialization is just beginning and long-distance trade is of little significance. It is important to recognize, however, that the production and storage of maize and the exploitation of obsidian sources were already in their beginning stages in "Formative Teotihuacan."

In Fig. 6.7a, "real" inequality refers to a comparison between "Formative Teotihuacan" and the fully developed "Hawaii chiefdom." The comparison shows that the amount of inequality in the former is much less than in the latter. In Fig. 6.7b, however, trends towards vast levels of inequality (in scales measuring economic, ideological, and political institutions) are *potentially much greater* in "Formative Teotihuacan" than they are in the "Hawaii chiefdom." In the latter, constraints on growth, specifically the difficulties of storing surplus and establishing power on the basis of specializations in distribution, place a hypothesized ceiling on the evolutionary trajectory.

The imputed significance of Fig. 6.7 is that *no formative stage of a state-level society can be modeled according to any whole ethnographic example* because the trajectories of their development are completely different (contrast Fig. 6.6 and Fig. 6.1). If chiefdoms exist in the ethnographic record, they do not precede the development of the state, but are alternate trajectories to it. In new social evolutionary theory, the basis for cross-cultural comparison consists in trajectories of past social change, not the projection into the archaeological record of (questionable) ethnographic analogies jerked out of time, place, and developmental sequence.

The old rules of neoevolutionism used to explain the rise of the earliest states haven't worked. Indeed, the model developed by anthropologists in the late 1950s and the 1960s, and employed by archaeologists ever since, now actively hinders modern research on state formation. This is both unfortunate and clear given the enormous, worldwide expansion of empirical data – discovery of new sites, recovery of artifacts, execution of regional surveys,

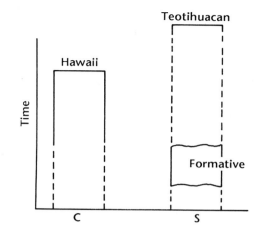

Stratification (distance between leaders and led)

A "Real inequality"

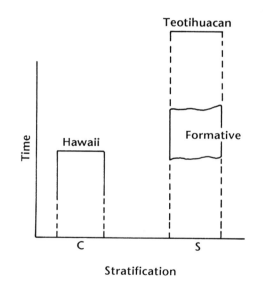

Stratification

B "Potential inequality"
(Kinds of inequality, e.g., in fundamental processes of production, storage, and distribution)

Fig. 6.7 "Real" and "potential" inequality (chiefdom v. state) (drawn by B. Montgomery): a. "real inequality"; b. "potential inequality"

establishment of temporal controls, and advances in analytical skills. The neoevolutionist studies, further, were seldom linked to the critical evidence produced by ancient historical sources (from Mesopotamian cuneiform tablets to New World *relaciones* and *visitas*), dramatic glyphic decipherment (from Maya stelas to Chinese oracle bones), and art historical remains (from Egypt to Teotihuacan).

A new social evolutionary theory represents new opportunities for archaeological analysis. It is contextually appropriate, for it insists that archaeologists develop their own standards of cross-cultural investigation as they finally become unshackled from the bonds of inappropriate theory borrowed from other fields. The heady possibility is, in short, that archaeologists will become important contributors to social evolutionary theory, not just adaptors or low-brow acolytes of their fellow social scientists. So, new social evolutionary theorists unite! You have nothing to lose but your chiefs.

Acknowledgments

Many thanks to the last generation of readers who have suggested improvements to this essay: Helaine Silverman, Joyce Marcus, Susan Pollock, Peter Brown, and Steve Lekson.

References

Adams, Robert McC. 1981 *The Heartland of Cities.* Chicago: University of Chicago Press.

1988 Contexts of Civilizational Collapse: A Meso-potamian View. In *The Collapse of Ancient States and Civilizations*, edited by N. Yoffee and G. L. Cowgill, pp. 20-43. Tucson: University of Arizona Press.

Algaze, Guillermo 1989 The Uruk Expansion: Cross-Cultural Exchange in Early Mesopotamian Civiliz-ation. *Current Anthropology* 30: 571–608.

Allen, Jim 1985 Pots and Poor Princes: A Multidimensional Approach to the Role of Pottery Trading in Coastal Papua. In *The Many Dimensions of Pottery*, edited by S. van der Leeuw and J. C. Pritchard, pp. 409–63. Amsterdam: Institute of Archaeology.

Anderson, David George 1990 Political Change in Chief-dom Societies: Cycling in the Late Prehistoric South-eastern United States. Unpublished Ph.D. dissertation, University of Michigan, Ann Arbor.

Baines, John R. 1983 Literacy and Ancient Egyptian Society. *Man* 18: 572–99.

Bawden, Garth 1989 The Andean State as a State of Mind. *Journal of Anthropological Research* 45: 327–32.

Binford, Lewis 1962 Archaeology as Anthropology. *American Antiquity* 28: 217–25.

Blanton, Richard 1983 The Founding of Monte Alban. In *The Cloud People*, edited by Kent Flannery and Joyce Marcus, pp. 83–7; see also editors' notes, pp. 79–83. New York: Academic Press.

Braun, David and Steve Plog 1984 Evolution of "Tribal" Social Networks: Theory and Prehistoric North American Evidence. *American Antiquity* 47: 504–25.

Carneiro, Robert 1981 The Chiefdom as Precursor of the State. In *The Transition to Statehood in the New World*, edited by Grant Jones and Robert Kautz, pp. 37–79. Cambridge: Cambridge University Press.

Chang, K. C. 1983 *Art, Myth, and Ritual: The Path to Political Authority in Ancient China.* New Haven: Yale University Press.

Charvat, Petr 1976 The Oldest Royal Dynasty of Ancient Mesopotamia. *Archiv für Orientforschung* 44: 346–52.

Chowning, A. 1979 Leadership in Melanesia. *Journal of Pacific History* 14: 66–84.

Cooper, Jerrold 1983 *Reconstructing History from Inscrip-tions.* Malibu: Undena Publications.

1989 Writing. *International Encyclopedia of Communi-cation*, vol. 4: 321–31.

Cowgill, George L. 1983 Rulership and the Ciudadela: Political Inferences from Teotihuacan Architecture. In *Civilization in the Ancient Americas*, edited by Richard Leventhal and Alan Kolata, pp. 313–44. Albuquerque: University of New Mexico Press.

1988 Onward and Upwards with Collapse. In *The Collapse of Ancient States and Civilizations*, edited by N. Yoffee and G. L. Cowgill, pp. 244–76. Tucson: University of Arizona Press.

Creamer, Winifred and Jonathan Haas 1985 Tribe Versus Chiefdom in Lower Central America. *American Antiquity* 50: 738–54.

D'jakonov (Diakonoff), Igor' M. 1969 The Rise of the Despotic State in Ancient Mesopotamia. In *Ancient Mesopotamia*, edited by I. M. Diakonoff, pp. 173–97. Moscow: Akademija Nauk SSSR.

1982 The Structure of Near Eastern Society Before the Middle of the Second Millennium B.C. *Oikumene* 3: 7–100.

Douglas, Bronwyn 1979 Rank, Power, Authority: A Reassessment of Traditional Leadership in South Pacific Societies. *Journal of Pacific History* 14: 2–27.

Doyel, David 1979 The Prehistoric Hohokam of the Arizona Desert. *American Scientist* 67/5: 544–54.

Drennan, Robert D. and Carlos A. Uribe, eds. 1987 *Chief-doms in the Americas.* Boston: University Presses of America.

Dunnell, Robert 1980 Evolutionary Theory and Archaeology. *Advances in Archaeological Method and Theory* 3: 35–99.

Earle, Timothy 1977 A Reappraisal of Redistribution: Complex Hawaiian Chiefdoms. In *Exchange Systems in Prehistory*, edited by T. K. Earle and J. E. Ericson, pp. 213–29. New York: Academic Press.

1978 *Economic and Social Organization of a Complex Chiefdom: The Halelea District, Kauai, Hawaii*. Ann Arbor: Museum of Anthropology.

1987 Chiefdoms in Archaeological and Ethnohistorical Perspective. *Annual Review of Anthropology* 16: 279–308.

1991 *Chiefdoms: Power, Economy, and Ideology*, edited by T. Earle. A School of American Research Book. Cambridge: Cambridge University Press.

Fairservis, Walter 1989 An Epigenetic View of the Harappan Culture. In *Archaeological Thought in America*, edited by C. C. Lamberg-Karlovsky, pp. 205–17. Cambridge: Cambridge University Press.

Falconer, Steven 1987 The Heartland of Villages. Unpublished Ph.D. Dissertation, Dept. of Anthropology, University of Arizona, Tucson.

Feinman, Gary and Jill Neitzel 1984 Too Many Types: An Overview of Sedentary Prestate Societies in the Americas. *Advances in Archaeological Method and Theory* 7: 39–102.

Flannery, Kent 1982 The Golden Marshalltown: A Parable for the Archaeology of the 1980s. *American Anthropologist* 84: 265–78.

1983 Archaeology and Ethnology in the Context of Divergent Evolution. In *The Cloud People: Divergent Evolution of the Zapotec and Mixtec Civilizations*, edited by Kent Flannery and Joyce Marcus, pp. 361–2. New York: Academic Press.

Fried, Morton 1978 The State, the Chicken, and the Egg: or, What Came First? In *Origins of the State*, edited by Ronald Cohen and Elman Service, pp. 35–48. Philadelphia: ISHI.

Friedman, Jonathan and Michael Rowlands 1977 Notes Toward an Epigenetic Model of the Evolution of Civilisation. In *The Evolution of Social Systems*, edited by Jonathan Friedman and Michael Rowlands, pp. 201–76. London: Duckworth.

Gelb, Ignace J. 1969 On the Alleged Temple and State Economies in Ancient Mesopotamia. In *Studi in Onore de Edoardo Volterra* Vol. 6: 137–54.

1979 Household and Family in Early Mesopotamia. In *State and Temple Economy in the Ancient Near East*, edited by E. Lipinski, vol. 1: 1–97. Louvain.

Gibson, McGuire 1972 *The City and Area of Kish*. Coconut Grove, FL: Field Research Projects.

Hassig, Ross 1985 *Trade, Tribute, and Transportation*. Norman: University of Oklahoma Press.

Heinrich, Ernst 1982 *Tempel und Heiligtümer im alten Mesopotamien*. Berlin: Walther de Gruyter.

Henrickson, Elizabeth and Ingolf Thuesen, eds. 1989 *Upon this Foundation: The 'Ubaid Reconsidered*. Copenhagen: The Carsten Niebuhr Institut of Ancient Near Eastern Studies, University of Copenhagen.

Henry, Donald 1989 *From Foraging to Agriculture: The Levant at the End of the Ice Age*. Philadelphia: University of Pennsylvania Press.

Hsu, Cho-yun 1988 The Roles of the Literati and of Regionalism in the Fall of the Han Dynasty. In *The Collapse of Ancient States and Civilizations*, edited by Norman Yoffee and George Cowgill, pp. 176–95. Tucson: University of Arizona Press.

Jacobsen, Thorkild 1957 Early Political Development in Mesopotamia. *Zeitschrift für Assyriologie* 52: 91–140.

Johnson, Allen and Timothy Earle 1987 *The Evolution of Human Societies*. Stanford: Stanford University Press.

Kaufman, Herbert 1988 The Collapse of Ancient States and Civilizations as an Organizational Problem. In *The Collapse of Ancient States and Civilizations*, edited by Norman Yoffee and George Cowgill, pp. 219–35. Tucson: University of Arizona Press.

Kirch, Patrick 1984 *The Evolution of Polynesian Chiefdoms*. Cambridge: Cambridge University Press.

Knight, Jr., Vernon J. 1990 Social Organization and the Evolution of Hierarchy in Southeastern Chiefdoms. *Journal of Anthropological Research* 46: 1–23.

Kohl, Philip 1986 The Use and Abuse of World Systems Theory: The Case of the "Pristine" West Asian State. *Advances in Archaeological Method and Theory* 11: 1–35.

Larsen, Mogens Trolle 1976 *The Old Assyrian City-State and its colonies*. Copenhagen: Akademisk Forlag.

1987 The Mesopotamian Lukewarm Mind: Reflections on Science, Divination, and Literacy. In *Language, Literacy, and History: Philological and Historical Studies Presented to Erica Reiner*, edited by Francesca Rochberg-Halton, pp. 203–25. New Haven: American Oriental Society.

1988 Literacy and Social Complexity. In *State and Society*, edited by John Gledhill, Barbara Bender, and Mogens Trolle Larsen, pp. 173–91. London: Unwin Hyman.

1989 What They Wrote on Clay. In *Literacy and Society*, edited by Karen Schousboe and Mogens Trolle Larsen, pp. 149–70. Copenhagen: Akademisk Forlag.

Legrain, Leon 1936 *Archaic Seal Impressions*. Ur Excavations Vol. 3. Philadelphia and London.

Lilley, Ian 1985 Chiefs Without Chiefdoms. *Archaeology in Oceania* 20: 6–65.

Longacre, William 1964 *Archaeology as Anthropology: A Case Study*. Tucson: University of Arizona Press.

Machinist, Peter 1985 On Self-Consciousness in Mesopotamia. In *Origins and Diversity of Axial Age Civilizations*, edited by S. N. Eisenstadt, pp. 183–202. Albany: State University of New York Press.

Mann, Michael 1986 *The Sources of Social Power*. Cambridge: Cambridge University Press.

McGuire, Randall 1983 Breaking Down Cultural Complexity: Inequality and Heterogeneity. *Advances in Archaeological Method and Theory* 6: 91-142.

Michaelowski, Piotr 1987 Language, Literature, and Writing at Ebla. In *Ebla 1975–1985. Dieci Anni di Studi Linguistici e Filologici*, edited by Luigi Cagni, pp. 165–76. Naples.

1990 Early Mesopotamian Communicative Systems: Art, Literature, and Writing. In *Investigating Artistic Environments in the Ancient Near East*, edited by Ann Gunter, pp. 53–69. Washington: Smithsonian Institution Press.

n.d. On the Early Toponymy of Sumer. Unpublished manuscript.

Michels, J. W. 1979 *The Kaminaljuyu Chiefdom*. College Park: Pennsylvania State University Press.

Moorey, P. R. W. 1978 *Kish Excavations 1923-33*. Oxford: Oxford University Press.

Netting, Robert 1972 Sacred Power and Centralization: Aspects of Political Adaptation in Africa. In *Population Growth: Anthropological Implications*, edited by Brian Spooner, pp. 219-44. Cambridge: MIT Press.

Nissen, Hans J. 1983 *Grundzüge einer Geschichte der Früehzeit des vorderen Orients*. Darmstadt: Wissenschaftliche Bibliothek (Translated as *The Early History of the Ancient Near East*. Chicago: University of Chicago Press, 1988).

1986 The Archaic Texts from Uruk. *World Archaeology* 17: 317–35.

Oates, Joan 1983 Ubaid Mesopotamia Reconsidered. In *The Hilly Flanks and Beyond*, edited by T. C. Young, Jr., Philip E. L. Smith and Peder Mortensen, pp. 251–82. Chicago: The Oriental Institute of the University of Chicago.

Oppenheim, A. Leo 1964 *Ancient Mesopotamia*. Chicago: University of Chicago Press.

Paynter, Robert 1989 The Archaeology of Equality and Inequality. *Annual Review of Anthropology* 18: 369–99.

Peebles, Christopher and Susan Kus 1977 Some Archaeological Correlates of Ranked Societies. *American Antiquity* 42: 421–8.

Plog, Fred 1974 *The Study of Prehistoric Change*. New York: Academic Press.

Pryor, Frederic 1977 *The Evolution of the Economy*. New York: Academic Press.

Renfrew, Colin 1973 *Before Civilization*. London: Jonathan Cape.

1975 Trade as Action at a Distance: Questions of Integration and Communication. In *Ancient Civilization and Trade*, edited by J. A. Sabloff and C. C. Lamberg-Karlovsky, pp. 3–59. A School of American Research Book. Albuquerque: University of New Mexico Press.

Rostoworowski, Maria 1970 Mercaderes del valle de Chincha en la época prehispánica: un documento y unos comentarios. *Revista Española de Antropología Americana* 5: 135–78.

Rouse, Irving 1986 *Migrations in Prehistory*. New Haven: Yale University Press.

Rowlands, Michael, Mogens Trolle Larsen, and Kristian Kristiansen, eds. 1987 *Centre and Periphery in the Ancient World*. Cambridge: Cambridge University Press.

Runciman, W. G. 1982 Origins of States: The Case of Archaic Greece. *Comparative Studies in Society and History* 24: 351–77.

Sahlins, Marshall 1960 Evolution: Specific and General. In *Evolution and Culture*, edited by Marshall Sahlins and Elman Service, pp. 12–44. Ann Arbor: University of Michigan Press.

1963 Poor Man, Rich Man, Big Man, Chief: Political Types in Melanesia and Polynesia. *Comparative Studies in Society and History* 5: 285–303.

Salomon, Frank 1986 *Native Lords of Quito in the Age of the Incas: The Political Economy of North Andean Chiefdoms*. Cambridge: Cambridge University Press.

Sanders, William 1974 Chiefdom to State: Political Evolution at Kaminaljuyu, Guatemala. In *Reconstructing Complex Societies*, edited by Charlotte B. Moore, pp. 97–121. Supplement to the *Bulletin of the American Schools of Oriental Research* No. 20.

Sanders, William and David Webster 1978 Unilinealism, Multilinealism, and the Evolution of Complex Societies. In *Social Archaeology: Beyond Subsistence and Dating*, edited by C. L. Redman, M. J. Berman, E. V. Curtin, W. T. Langhorne, N. M. Versaggi, and J. C. Wanser. New York: Academic Press.

Schele, Linda and Mary Ellen Miller 1986 *The Blood of Kings*. New York: Braziller.

Schortman, Edward and Patricia Urban 1987 Modelling Interregional Interaction in Prehistory. *Advances in Archaeological Method and Theory* 11: 37–95.

Schwartz, Benjamin 1985 *The World of Thought in Ancient China*. Cambridge: Harvard University Press.

Service, Elman 1962 *Primitive Social Organization*. New York: Random House.

1975 *The Origins of the State and Civilization*. New York: W. W. Norton.

Smith, Colin 1984 The "Kengir League" Seals: An Essay into Speculation. Unpublished paper.

Spence, Michael 1981 Obsidian Production and the State in Teotihuacan, Mexico. *American Antiquity* 46: 769–88.

Spencer, Charles 1987 Rethinking the Chiefdom. In *Chiefdoms in the Americas*, edited by Robert Drennan and Carlos Uribe, pp. 369–89. Boston: University Presses of America.

1990 On the Tempo and Mode of State Formation: Neoevolutionism Reconsidered. *Journal of Anthropological Archaeology* 9: 1–30.

Steponaitis, Vincas 1978 Location Theory and Complex Chiefdoms. In *Mississippian Settlement Patterns*, edited by Bruce Smith, pp. 417–53. New York: Academic Press.

1981 Settlement Hierarchies and Political Complexity in Non-Market Societies: The Formative Period in the Valley of Mexico. *American Anthropologist* 83: 320–63.

Sürenhagen, Dietrick 1986 The Dry-Farming Belt: The Uruk Period and Subsequent Developments. In *The Origins of Cities in Dry-Farming Syria and Mesopotamia in the Third Millennium B.C.*, edited by Harvey Weiss, pp. 7–44. Guilford: Four Quarters Publishing.

Tainter, Joseph 1988 *The Collapse of Complex Societies*. Cambridge: Cambridge University Press.

Trigger, Bruce 1984a Alternative Archaeologies: Nationalist, Colonialist, Imperialist. *Man* 19: 335–70.

1984b Archaeology at the Crossroads: What's New? *Annual Review of Anthropology* 13: 275–300.

1989 *A History of Archaeological Thought*. Cambridge: Cambridge University Press.

Upham, Steadman 1987 Theoretical Consideration of Middle Range Societies. In *Chiefdoms in the Americas*, edited by Robert Drennan and Carlos Uribe, pp. 343–67. Boston: University Presses of America.

Watson, Patty Jo 1983 The Halafian Culture: A Review and Synthesis. In *The Hilly Flanks: Essays on the Prehistory of Southwestern Asia presented to Robert J. Braidwood*, edited by T. C. Young, Jr., P. E. L. Smith, and P. Mortensen, pp. 231–50. Chicago: Oriental Institute.

Watson, Patty Jo, Steven LeBlanc, and Charles Redman 1971 *Explanation in Archaeology: An Explicitly Scientific Approach*. New York: Academic Press.

Westbrook, Raymond 1988 *Old Babylonian Family Law*. Graz: Archiv für Orientforschung Beiheft.

Willey, Gordon and Philip Phillips 1985 *Method and Theory in American Archaeology*. Chicago: University of Chicago Press.

Willey, Gordon and Jeremy Sabloff 1980 *A History of American Archaeology*, 2nd edn. San Francisco: Freeman.

Winter, Irene 1981 Royal Rhetoric and the Development of Historical Narrative in Neo-Assyrian Reliefs. *Visual Communication* 7/2: 2–38.

1983 The Program of the Throne Room of Assurnasirpal II. In *Essays in Near Eastern Art and Archaeology in Honor of C. K. Wilkinson*, edited by Prudence Harper and Holly Pittman, pp. 15–31. New York: Metropolitan Museum of Art.

Withrow, Barbara M. 1990 Prehistoric Distribution of Stone Adzes on Hawai'i Island: Implications for the Development of Hawaiian Chiefdoms. *Asian Perspectives* 29: 235–50.

Wright, Henry 1977 Recent Research on the Origin of the State. *Annual Review of Anthropology* 6: 379–97.

1984 Prestate Political Formations. In *On the Evolution of Complex Societies: Essays in Honor of Harry Hoijer*, edited by Timothy Earle, pp. 41–77. Malibu: Undena Publications.

Yoffee, Norman 1979 The Decline and Rise of Mesopotamian Civilization: An Ethnoarchaeological Perspective on the Evolution of Social Complexity. *American Antiquity* 44: 1–35.

1985 Perspectives on "Trends Towards Complex Societies in Prehistoric Australia and Papua New Guinea." *Archaeology in Oceania* 20: 40–9.

1988 Context and Authority in Early Mesopotamian Law. In *State Formation and Political Legitimacy*, edited by Ronald Cohen and Judith Toland, pp. 95–113. New Brunswick: Transaction Books.

1990a Maya Elite Interaction: Through a Glass, Sideways. In *Classic Maya Political History*, edited by T. P. Culbert, pp. 285–310. Cambridge: Cambridge University Press.

1990b Before Babel. *Proceedings of the Prehistoric Society* 56: 299–313.

1993a Mesopotamian Interaction Spheres. Forthcoming in *Early Stages in the Evolution of Mesopotamian Civilization: Soviet Excavations in the Sinjar Plain, Northern Iraq*, edited by N. Yoffee with J. Clark. Tucson: University of Arizona Press.

1993b The Late Great Tradition in Ancient Mesopotamia. Forthcoming in Festschrift for W. W. Hallo.

Yoffee, Norman, and George Cowgill, eds. 1988 *The Collapse of Ancient States and Civilizations*. Tucson: University of Arizona Press.

PART III

Case studies in archaeological theory and practice

7

When is a symbol archaeologically meaningful?: meaning, function, and prehistoric visual arts

KELLEY ANN HAYS

Background and goals

Post-processual archaeology[1] has demanded that attention be directed to the symbolic systems that played important roles in prehistoric lives, but few methods of accessing symbolic systems have been developed. Certain aspects of symbolic systems are available to archaeological study, notably visual arts.[2] This paper examines one kind of role that symbolic systems played in prehistory in order to address an on-going discussion in the archaeology of the proto-historic period in the American Southwest.

Most of those now working at large, late Pueblo sites in Arizona, such as Grasshopper, Homol'ovi, Awatovi, and Chavez Pass, are addressing the problem of what happens to social organization of village farming communities during the process of population aggregation and agricultural intensification. Controversy arose between those who think fourteenth century Puebloans had complex social organization, that is, social differentiation based on wealth and political power (Plog 1983, Upham 1982), and those who think pueblo society was more or less egalitarian and based on complicated ritual interaction and leadership based in religious authority (Reid 1989b: 87, Adams 1991). In the latter view, access to religious knowledge and authority might be inherited, but there is no social stratification, and no differential access to the means of production. This paper attempts to show that visual arts deserve more attention in attacking this problem, and that a cross-cultural comparative approach is useful.

Three cases are discussed in which prehistoric population aggregation in non-state agricultural societies was accompanied by an increase in the amount and kind of labor invested in artistic activities. The examples are taken from Europe, Anatolia, and the proto-historic Southwest. It is proposed that intensification of artistic activities in these cases is closely related to the problem of organizing large communities in the absence of social stratification. Visual arts in such communities mark different social groups that are cross-cutting rather than hierarchically ranked. The larger significance of this proposition is that changes in patterns of stylistic and ritual activity over time reflect changing configurations of social, economic, and political power. It has been argued that different configurations of these kinds of power lead to different evolutionary trajectories than have been traditionally proposed (Runciman 1982, Yoffee 1985 and this volume).

Interaction and information in the "New" (Old) Archaeology

Before the "New Archaeology," decorated ceramics and projectile point forms were most often studied as chronological markers and as traits of "culture areas." In the 1960s and 1970s, the "New Archaeology" tried to reconstruct social relationships within and between communities by studying degrees of similarity and difference in artifact form and decoration (see for example, Longacre 1970, Hill 1970). This approach was later referred to as "interaction theory" (Graves 1981; Kintigh 1985; S. Plog 1983; see also S. Plog 1976, 1978, 1980). Such studies treated style as a passive reflection of social relationships.

The question of the *functions* of style was taken up after a 1977 article by Martin Wobst. This approach, called "information theory,"[3] notes that shapes, colors and decoration of material culture items are often actively used to "signal" information about social identities, such as ethnicity. Wobst suggested that visual signalling of social identities facilitated interaction between social groups, reduced stress, and increased efficiency in social encounters. This is a functional approach, but it addresses the function of visual symbols. This approach posits that objects are encoded with information by their makers, and decoded by viewers who know the meanings of the visual signs. In an extension of Wobst's argument, Wiessner (1983, 1984, 1985) argues that all aspects of style have important social effects at any level of consciousness. Art not explicitly aimed at outsiders often functions to provide a "familiar backdrop" for social action, even at the domestic level, thus reducing stress, and enhancing individual adaptation to the social environment (Wiessner 1985).

Ethnoarchaeological studies looking at material culture variation and social boundaries of various kinds and scales (Graves 1981; Hodder 1977, 1978, 1979, 1982; Wiessner 1983, 1984) conclude that different kinds of relationships are signalled by different kinds of objects. Prehistorians have difficulty working with these conclusions because there is no way to observe people using artifacts, nor to ask about the meanings artifacts may have to individuals. Warren DeBoer notes, "At present, archaeologists lack a well-developed theory which specifies the kinds of material remains that are likely to carry different kinds of social information" (DeBoer and Moore 1982: 153).

In practice, those using information theory in style studies are primarily concerned with methods of measuring diversity in design systems, not in studying relationships among the many channels and contexts of visual communication, or the kinds of messages that are sent (see, for examples and discussion, Brunson 1985; Conkey 1978, 1987; Hegmon 1986, 1988; Kintigh 1985; S. Plog 1980, 1983; Pollock 1983). In short, information theory has not been as productive in discerning prehistoric social groups as its early proponents had hoped.

The post-processual critique

Post-processualist archaeology has stimulated an interest in prehistoric symbolic systems, the most obvious manifestation of which is visual art. Hodder, for example, points out that systems of symbolic communication are important in forming and maintaining social, economic, and political systems, and that this is true even in non-state societies. One post-processual axiom is that all material culture items, even garbage, are "meaningfully constituted" by individuals using symbols to "negotiate identity" with different kinds of interest groups, such as ethnic, class, and gender (Hodder 1986, 1987).

Hodder's three kinds of meaning (Hodder 1987: 1) provide a useful framework from which to begin looking at artifacts and decoration as evidence for symbolic communication. Hodder's first kind of meaning is "how the object is used and how it conveys information," which I gloss as "functional" or "pragmatic" meaning. The second kind is "structural meaning," the object's place in a code for communication; and the third is the "historical content of the changing ideas and associations of the object," which I gloss as "symbolic meaning."

But the archaeological record is defined by Hodder, and by Shanks and Tilley (1987a, 1987b), as a "polysemous text" in which symbolic meanings can be "read." *Only* through the study of symbolic systems can archaeologists learn anything of interest. Hodder maintains that the archaeologist must approach all questions about the past by understanding the third kind of meaning, which he sees as the most important. The archaeologist's ability to understand anything about material culture is seen to depend on understanding symbolic

meanings, which have their origins in particular historical processes of assigning conventional meanings to material signs. It is not surprising that most examples given by Hodder, and by Shanks and Tilley, are drawn from modern material culture studies and ethnographic sources.

Hodder is not very concerned with his first two kinds of meaning – functional or pragmatic meaning: what it is people do with material objects as signs; and structural meaning: the sets of oppositions and associations among things and meanings. Hodder's insistence on accessing all levels of meaning, but especially the symbolic, makes his symbolic/contextual approach difficult, if not impossible, to use in prehistoric archaeology. In reference to methods for stylistic analysis of artifacts, he writes, "everything depends on everything else, and the definition of attributes depends on the definition of context which depends on the definition of attributes!" (1986: 141, exclamation original).

Toward "practical" study of prehistoric art

It is here asserted that the *roles* and *functions* of symbolic communication can be of greater interest than the study of symbols for symbols' sake. These can be discussed without, on the one hand, reducing all aspects of symbolic activity to adaptational values, or on the other extreme, insisting that all specific, iconological meanings of art must be known.

Post-processualists note that objects can be invested with meaning for the purpose of negotiating social relationships. This is an improvement over the information-theorists' "signalling" because "negotiation" includes the fact that objects can "act back" on the process of creating and interpreting other symbolically-invested objects. It also recognizes that individuals have more than one kind of social identity, that some of these identities change, and that individuals compete and otherwise interact in a variety of contexts. The degree to which objects are invested with symbolic meanings, and the kinds of symbolic meanings attributed to objects, should proceed from the cultural contexts in which objects are made, used, and discarded. Furthermore, not all meanings are accessible, nor intrinsically interesting, to all prehistoric archaeologists.

We need comparative studies to show what people do with visual symbolic systems in societies with different kinds of socio-political and economic systems. Functions will depend to a large degree on the kind and scale of organization in a society. For example, the possible role of visual messages in boundary maintenance among hunter–gatherers has been discussed (Wiessner 1983, 1984; Soffer 1985: 444–52). Likewise, symbols of political legitimation, including relationships between present rulers and the gods or ancestors, and other aspects of ideology are shown to account for much "artistic" activity in ancient states (Chang 1983, Schele and Miller 1986, Winter 1987).

Another approach to understanding the roles of visual symbolic communication is to trace stylistic behavior through time. The degree and kind of investment by societies in their visual arts changes. Changes cannot be passed off as mere "fashion" which itself is a phenomenon to be explained. Rather, investment of labor and materials in decoration of artifacts is connected in important ways to economy, social organization, and ideology.

In short, investment in visual communication systems can be seen to change over time, and to differ among societies. A search for patterns in stylistic behavior and use of the comparative method to understand such patterns in economic, social and ideological contexts (rather than their total symbolic contexts) is a potentially fascinating process. If certain objects can be shown to play roles as a sort of social tool, that is only one aspect of their context in a larger and vastly complicated system of human activity, cognition, and signification. Function is one kind of meaning that objects have, and it happens to be a kind that is most often interesting and accessible to archaeologists.

Art and population aggregation: case study

The specific questions posed here are: when are changes in social and political organization reflected in "artistic activity"? What conditions of life in such societies lead to periods of increased investment in visual "symboling"? Increased investment in visual arts activities, such as decoration of ceramics, room walls, and textiles, need not be a sign of increased leisure time nor of the emergence of luxury goods controlled by a class of managerial elites, as has often been assumed. Rather, in some kinds of societies, it may signal increased competition and social stress due to changing organizational scale.

The three cases of what might be called "artistic intensification" outlined here are the 6th and 5th millennia in the Hungarian Plain, the 7th–6th millennium site of Çatal Hüyük in Anatolia, and the Pueblo IV period in the American Southwest.[4] The three cases have a few key features in common. First, all sites were populated by agriculturalists who seemed to have joined together following residence in smaller sites. These aggregate sites are much larger than any previous sites in each region, so co-resident populations are of a larger scale than existed previously. In all three cases we have an increase in long-distance trade, including so-called "luxury," "exotic," and "ritual" items, increase in the decoration of domestic architecture (such as murals), increase in decoration on household items, and by inference from various sorts of evidence, an increase in ritual activity.

In no case do we have good evidence for social stratification, significant differences in wealth, for minority control of surplus production, or for control of means to exercise force. There is, however, some evidence for part-time craft specialization, differential access to trade goods, and leadership roles based in religious authority.

Art, ritual, and regional trade in the Hungarian Plain

Sherratt (1982) discusses the 6th and 5th millennia BC developmental sequence in the Hungarian Plain in the Carpathian Basin. In the earliest of three periods (the Körös culture, 6000–5000 BC), settlement is dispersed and population density is low relative to the productive environment of the basin. Therefore, little competition for resources or territory is expected. There are no local stylistic groupings visible in ceramics, which are for the most part undecorated.

In the middle period (the Tisza, 5000 to about 4600 BC), population seems not to grow, but aggregates: there are fewer sites but they are larger and are occupied for longer periods than were early-period sites. Many ceramics are elaborately decorated, "often imitating textile patterns," and are widely traded. Regional styles are distinct and elaborate. Figurines and effigy vessels are numerous, and "household fittings" are also decorated. Many kinds of imported materials are found, and in larger quantities than in the early period. Sherratt speculates that aggregation could have been a response to defense needs, for which there is some evidence, but possibly reflects an enlargement of resident co-operative units for the purpose of breeding cattle as a trade item.[5]

In the late period (the Tiszapolgar, ca. 4600–3500 BC), settlement reverts to a dispersed pattern, pottery is again plain and shows no regional stylistic differentiation, and figurines are no longer produced. To explain this apparent development and loss of "progressive" features such as artistic activity and the formation of large communities, Sherratt points to the regional setting of the phenomenon to be understood. In the middle period, many items came to the population centers in the plain from sites in the edges of the basin. Pottery was traded in both directions. Sherratt proposes that cattle were traded out of the centers by groups who had developed some degree of specialization in breeding and taming cattle as a trade item. Groups who did not have domestic cattle began to trade and incorporate cattle into their own economies. At this time, different regions tried to make their local products, including pottery, very distinctive in order to break into the expanding regional exchange system. There also appears to have been more local craft specialization in this period than in the early and late periods. Decoration of pottery at this time probably reflects labor invested to make the product more desirable and attractive to the consumer, and investment in local style to identify and advertize the maker.

The abundance of figurines and effigy vessels in middle-period household contexts may reflect increased ritual activity, albeit not centralized activity, as there seem to be no specialized ritual locales such as temples. Ritual is an effective means of regulating relations within social groups (Rappaport 1971a). For example, ritual provides a structured set of roles and rules for interaction, an appropriate forum for the negotiation of identities, as a post-processualist might say. Note that in this period settlements were larger, each person had a wider circle of contacts, and social life was more complicated. Relations among communities can be regulated by alliance and trade as well as by ritual. Stylistic expression of identity in this period might be related to economic and political activities as well as to ritual.

By the late period, Sherratt proposes, groups on the periphery were no longer dependent on the center for cattle, and as their wealth increased, they did not participate in active competition with other groups in the trade network. There was not necessarily social devolution, but ritual and stylistic behavior seems to have decreased just when investment in it no longer advanced anybody's interests. Dispersal into smaller settlements could be due to decreased economic stability or other factors, but probably would have had the effect of increasing internal community stability, again lessening the need for ritual mediation.

Art, ritual, and social stress in the Konya Plain

Sherratt proposes that a situation analogous to that in the 5th millennium Carpathian Basin may have pertained at Çatal Hüyük in Anatolia's Konya Plain (1982: 14). Here as well we see evidence for a "precocious" flowering of artistic and ritual activity in a site that is unusually large for its time. It is not likely that all 15 hectares were occupied simultaneously, but excavation of about 2 hectares revealed 12 building levels of contiguous rectangular structures. Levels 6–8, at least, appear to represent a densely inhabited village (Figure 7.1). This large community, occupied from about 6500 BC to 5700 BC,[6] had an economic focus on cattle, and was engaged in extensive regional trade (Mellaart 1962–1967; Angel 1971; Bartel 1972; Cohen 1970; Perkins 1969; Todd 1976).

The excavator of Çatal Hüyük, James Mellaart, felt that the elaborate wall paintings, sculpture, and textiles, and many exotic goods such as obsidian, stones, and pigments, reflected an elite quarter of a fully urban site. Rooms with elaborate decoration were designated "shrines" by Mellaart (Figure 7.2), even though most of these rooms have

domestic features such as hearths, storage features, and sleeping platforms, just like the adjoining rooms, labelled "houses." Mellaart proposed that priests inhabited the houses adjoining the shrines, and that plebeian masses must have lived in some unexcavated neighborhood outside of his "priestly" district. In spite of the excavator's views, the site's inhabitants are unlikely to have had the high degrees of social and economic differentiation implied by the terms "city" and "urban." Site size and occupation density seem to be the primary features cited by Mellaart for such a designation.

But more important, Mellaart seems to have envisioned a system in which everything went along so smoothly that once "necessities" were taken care of, plenty of time and energy were left for matters aesthetic and metaphysical. This romanticized view of antiquity has much to do with creating an idealized past to contrast with our secular, impersonal, industrialized present, and little to do with archaeological facts. For example, Çatal Hüyük paleo-pathology reveals that inhabitants were in remarkably poor physical condition (Angel 1971; Todd 1976: 74). If these diseased and malnourished individuals were elite, how must the lower classes have lived, much less worked to support their betters?

Another interpretation of life at Çatal Hüyük is constructed by Johnson, drawing on Rappaport (1971a: 11, 1971b: 33–7). He cites Çatal Hüyük as a possible example of a large-scale yet non-stratified society in which ritual ameliorates stresses of relatively unstructured social interaction. In contrast to Mellaart, Johnson supposes that an increase in ritual activity in some kinds of societies may indicate a "system in trouble" (Johnson 1982: 406), a system that has outgrown its egalitarian principles of organization. In a later paper, Johnson illustrates a model of two alternative ways of organizing aggregate populations, one egalitarian and one stratified, in a discussion of the Puebloan Southwest (Johnson 1989: 378).

Art, ritual, and instability on the Colorado Plateau

On the Colorado Plateau and in the mountains of the Mogollon Rim region, major demographic shifts in about AD 1300 are accompanied by radical changes in architecture, community layout, and decorative styles. Pueblo IV period sites (AD 1300–1629), in contrast to earlier ones, produce high densities of ceramics, high proportions of decorated over utility wares, high proportions of non-local ceramics, and a proliferation of wares, types, and untypable combinations of decorative features (Reid 1989a; Smith 1962, 1971; Upham 1982). Rock art and textiles also change at about AD 1300 (Schaafsma 1980; Schaafsma and

Schaafsma 1974; Kent 1983a, 1983b). Although all three of these media incorporate at least a few characteristics of art styles thought to have their origins in Northern Mexico, the evidence does not support Mesoamerican colonization, political takeover, nor even direct trade (Carlson 1982: 215). The southern stylistic influence may have been a matter of borrowing some visual forms that were perhaps only vaguely associated with bigger and better, or simply more intriguing, people to the south. Stripped-down images of Tlaloc and Quetzalcoatl probably took on meanings more relevant to their new local, Puebloan, contexts than to their stately origins. Such images include the masked figures known as katsinas. Katsina-like depictions appear on pottery, and in murals and rock art, and represent a new ceremonial complex developing in the 1300s and 1400s. Historically, the katsina religion acts as an overarching Puebloan ideology and promotes community integration (Adams 1991, Ferg 1982, Hays 1989).

In addition to "foreign" stylistic influence, the Pueblo IV period sees a change in the amount and kind of labor invested in craft items: mural painting becomes much more elaborate than ever before (at least by 1400, but not necessarily earlier [Smith 1952]) (Figure 7.3). Elaborate polychrome ceramics become much more common (beginning around 1300) and most may be produced by craft specialists (Carlson 1982). Labor invested in polychrome pots such as Four Mile and Sikyatki Polychromes is greater and evidently more skilled than was characteristic of earlier ceramics (Feinman *et al.* 1981). But unless it can be shown that such specialization was full-time, or that specialists were controlled by a political or economic elite, there is no evidence that stepped-up craft production indicated evolution toward

Fig. 7.1 Plan of Level VI.B of Çatal Hüyük. Not shown is the double-wall construction of all the walls, suggesting that rooms were added singly, and construction was not planned out in advance. (From Mellaart 1967: 9.)

a vertical hierarchy. Recall Sherratt's explanation for elaborate Hungarian ceramics – products had to be distinctive for their makers to break into an expanding regional trade network. They would also have to be well made to survive transport. Their makers did not go on to form urban craft barrios, but reverted to undecorated wares after the regional system broke down or changed its form. Ceramic distributional evidence indicates that Pueblo IV pottery also was most widely traded between regions during this period. For example, the most widely traded ceramic ware of any time in the Southwest is Jeddito Yellow Ware, a fine, coal-fired ware made on and around the Hopi Mesas from AD 1300 to the Spanish entrada. Examples have been found as far away as California and Kansas (Schaefer 1969; Adams, Stark, and Dosh n.d.).

There is also an evident increase in the amount of obsidian traded and the distance it traveled. Mesoamerican copper bells appear occasionally in Pueblo IV sites. Numerous macaw burials have been recovered in Pueblo IV sites, including Grasshopper and Homol'ovi III (Olsen and Olsen 1974; Adams 1989). These birds were native to Mesoamerica, not the Southwest, and were probably obtained by Puebloans for their colorful feathers. Macaws are depicted on ceramics in Northern Arizona as early as AD 1250, and in the Mimbres region of Southwestern New Mexico in the 1100s, but their depiction truly proliferates after AD 1300. Elaborate polychrome effigy vessels of macaws were produced at Hopi and Homol'ovi in the late 1300s (Martin and Willis 1940). There are also innovations in textile techniques (Kent 1983a, 1983b), and an increase in cotton production in areas most favorable for its cultivation, such as Homol'ovi (Adams 1989).

Although there is much evidence for trade and perhaps ritual interaction among communities, there is little evidence that larger Pueblo sites controlled activities at smaller ones, or that there were functionally distinct neighborhoods, craft barrios, or other indications for economic specialization above the level of, for example, the part-time household specialist in pottery or stone-tool manufacture.[7]

In sum, material culture innovations, an increase in the intensity and geographical scale of trade, and an increase in the amount of labor invested in producing and otherwise obtaining decorated and ritual-related items accompanies Pueblo IV population aggregation. At this time, and continuing into the ethnographic present, virtually all Pueblo settlements were aggregated communities. These sites are larger than any earlier Anasazi sites, and are clustered in a few regions. Other areas are completely abandoned. Discussion of the Pueblo IV aggregation can benefit from greater application of the comparative method not only with the historic pueblos, but with archaeological cases outside the usual Southwesternist experience, especially the European Neolithic.

Johnson examines Pueblo organization according to several characteristics of Puebloan archaeological assemblages. For example, Pueblo burials and architecture do not reflect concentration of wealth in the hands of an elite class. Johnson also notes "modularity" in architecture (1989: 378, 380), and the nature of settlement size classes (1989: 380). There are settlement size hierarchies, but size is always a multiple of a basic unit. The evidence suggests that large sites simply had more organizational units of the same type of units found in other Anasazi sites. An Anasazi architectural unit consists of contiguous habitation and storage

Fig. 7.2 "Shrine" room of Çatal Hüyük. Level VI.B, room 8, north and east walls. (From Mellaart 1967, Fig. 35.)

Fig. 7.3 Kiva mural from Pottery Mound in New Mexico. (Hibben 1975, Fig. 38.)

rooms, and a *kiva*, or semi-subterranean ritual structure.[8] In other words, the process of population aggregation seems to have been more like adding dominoes to a pile than it was like constructing a Lego house of functionally different pieces such as bricks, window frames, and roof tiles. Pueblo sites of all periods are for the most part characterized by a repetition of numerous similar units and lack of large central ritual or storage structures. Exceptions, such as Pueblo IV period plazas and Pueblo II and III period "Great Kivas," which are larger than kivas associated with roomblocks, are common but do not represent significant labor investment of the scale seen in, for example, Mississippian temple mounds, Mesopotamian temple structures, or Mesoamerican temples and pyramids. Structures such as Great Kivas may easily represent formal gathering places for the entire community or for visitors from surrounding communities. They were probably supplanted by open plazas when villages grew, as they did in the 1300s (Figure 7.4).

Johnson cites the agricultural marginality of the Southwest as the reason significant economic surplus could not have been accumulated by would-be elite individuals or

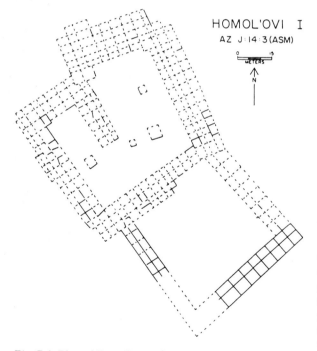

HOMOL'OVI I

AZ J:14:3(ASM)

0 _____ 15

METERS

↑
N

Fig. 7.4 Plan of Homol'ovi I, a 14th century pueblo on the Little Colorado River. The four detached rooms in the northwest plaza are kivas, subterranean ceremonial chambers. (From Adams 1991.)

social groups (1989: 372). It is not just poor yields, but the unpredictability of yields due to rainfall fluctuation, and the nature of arroyo cutting and filling cycles that change the potential of individual fields from year to year. Storable food surpluses are a key prerequisite to the accumulation of economic and political power in the hands of an emergent elite. In addition, potential mobility of individuals and kin groups to other communities or even to other ways of life would have prevented any emergent Pueblo elite from controlling labor to any significant degree.

Social prestige and influence, in contrast, could be accrued through gaining control over ritual knowledge. When communities aggregated, ritual and art could be elaborated in order to enhance communication among members of disparate backgrounds. Leaders achieved and maintained order on the basis of social and ritual power alone, in the absence of an ability to wield economic and political power.

Summary

In summary, all three cases represent the earliest large, aggregated communities of sedentary agriculturalists in their respective regions. All storage structures are associated with domestic structures, so there is no evidence for pooling resources, communal stockpiling, or payment of tribute to a central authority. All evidence for ritual consists of artifacts and "cult fittings" found in multiple structures scattered throughout the community or in houses. There is no evidence for centralized religious practice or authority, as in communities with temples. Graves are also associated with houses or roomblocks, rarely with formal cemeteries. And although some graves have more offerings than others, these offerings consist primarily of tool kits and pottery, in amounts that any individual might conceivably have owned. Offerings of ornaments and ritual items are likewise found in modest amounts. Even the richest puebloan burial appears poor in comparison to elite burials of Mississippian Cahokia in Illinois, or Bronze Age Europe.

In making these comparisons, it is not necessary to discuss the cause of aggregation in any of the cases described. Causes might be of the sort traditionally cited – environmental change (the traditional explanation for Pueblo IV aggregation is the effects of the Great Drought), population pressure, defense – or something a little more imaginative, such as the process of plant or animal domestication coupled with changes in the organization of production, and demands of expanding markets or trade networks (Sherratt's explanation of Tisza culture and Çatal Hüyük aggregation). One could even suggest that aggregation might occur because new religious ideas appeared, appealed, and religion itself became a growing concern with social and economic implications. This is a plausible explanation for the Pueblo IV case, although it would be difficult to demonstrate archaeologically. The cases discussed here pose relationships between some kinds of material evidence, and some *effects* of population aggregation, whatever the cause, on people.

Johnson (1982) argues that aggregation can have three kinds of effects: development of vertical hierarchies, fissioning back into smaller groups, or development of horizontal hierarchies. He draws on studies of the capacity of the human brain for information processing. The results have come to be known as "scalar stress theory."

Aggregation and "scalar stress theory"

Johnson argues that when egalitarian populations aggregate into larger communities, some form of hierarchy must result. According to "scalar stress theory" (Johnson 1982, 1989), increasing group size and the scale of decision-making units causes stress for all individuals involved. A "vertical" hierarchy can develop, that is one group, such as a senior lineage, can consolidate power to allocate land resources, marriage partners, and leadership roles. If no such structure develops, then a likely result is factionalism and competing interest groups. Interest groups might variously be based on ethnic, kin group, economic, gender, or age differences. The group may then fission into smaller communities within which consensus can be reached. Alternatively, if no *vertical* hierarchy appears, the group may instead develop organizational principles that *sequentially* increase the size of basal social units so that decisions can be made by consensus first among many small groups, such as nuclear families, then among a set of fewer, but larger groups, such as extended families, groups of related families, or task-groups, then perhaps clans, moieties, and so on. An example of an increase in basal units would be the threefold increase in household size proposed by Sherratt for the Körös–Tisza transition. Such an increase may represent a change from nuclear to extended family households. Sodalities and age-grade organizations are examples of social groups that cross-cut kin-based social units, and that can be involved in making some kinds of decisions. They too help keep organizational problems within groups of limited size. Johnson calls these organizational networks "sequential" or "horizontal" hierarchies. Decisions in a sequential hierarchy are made consensually by many different sub-groups or their representatives. They are different from "simultaneous" or "vertical" hierarchies in which decisions are made by a small number of elites.

Ritual is very important in organizing a sequential hierarchy. Johnson writes,

Participation in ceremony that prescribes patterns of behavior and interaction may reduce required integrative decision-making, and ceremony may provide a social context for organizations that have non-ceremonial integrative functions (Johnson 1982: 405);

and,

Ritual which may not be evident at smaller organizational sizes becomes increasingly important at larger sizes . . . kivas or ceremonial rooms represent a level of sequential hierarchy above the household in which such matters as interhousehold cooperation and dispute resolution were consensually resolved in a sanctified context (Johnson 1989: 380).

Visual arts may be important in sequential hierarchies for several reasons. First, decoration may be important in signalling and negotiating identity with gender roles, age grades, access to trade partners or other special economic statuses, and membership in sodalities. Second, visual arts may also figure strongly in trade systems which were characterized by competition for goods and for alliance. Finally, ritual activities themselves usually demand "special" objects and costumes. Use of exotic materials and a high investment of labor, time, and skill in making and decorating objects are some of the ways to make objects "special."

Following predictions of scalar stress theory, which is, like information theory, functionalist at heart, it is possible that artistic activities were important in many ways during aggregation, and in efforts to maintain an aggregated state. If populations dispersed again, there may have been less incentive for individuals to invest in decoration and other artistic and ritual activities because there was less need to negotiate one's position in the community. Alternatively, a relatively stable managerial elite may emerge, lessening the need for ritual and symbolic mediation and negotiation of social relationships, or even actively repressing it. For example, in the Hungarian case, burial evidence seems to show the emergence of ranking in the small, dispersed communities of the late period. Development of a principle of ranking could have led to the emergence of vertical hierarchies in any subsequent aggregation.

Conclusions

Art and ritual play different roles in different kinds of societies. Material evidence for these activities is important in challenging traditional models of social evolution and in building new models to outline different evolutionary trajectories. In the 1960s, archaeologists borrowed an outdated model of social evolution (see Yoffee, this volume). The model classified societies according to complexity, i.e. number of institutions making up a social system. In fact, there are many societies (such as the Pueblos of the American Southwest) which cannot be placed in any of these categories. Furthermore, use of this model perpetuates the pernicious notion that there are "primitive" and "advanced" societies.

Not all societies experience increasing differentiation of institutions and vertically hierarchical arrangements of authority (complexity) as they increase in settlement size and in organizational scale (the size of the socially and economically integrated population). Some develop instead very *complicated* networks of religious authority and associations (such as pueblos). There are probably many other evolutionary trajectories, and many important axes of comparison besides scale and complexity (see Yoffee, this volume). Clearly, diversity in human organization is greater than the categories allowed by the traditional classification (bands, tribes, chiefdoms, and states). But comparison of organizational forms across time and space is still rewarding.

What conditions bring about the development of sequential as opposed to simultaneous hierarchies? Is it previously existing "core principles," ideas about authority, inheritance, and so on, that are specific to different historical traditions, as Hallpike (1986) suggests? Or are environmental and economic factors more important, such as trade and availability of resources that can be exploited to produce a storable surplus, as Johnson (1989), Runciman (1982), Sherratt (1982), and Yoffee (1985) seem to suggest?

To address this sort of problem, archaeologists must insist on thorough and meticulous examinations of the archaeological record, and on communication among researchers who, although their material may be separated by oceans and millennia, find themselves beset by similar problems and united by common interests.

Notes

1 Processual archaeology, according to a possibly unbiased Classical archaeologist, is an approach favoring "holistic, systematic frameworks of theory that address themselves to long-run process rather than the activities of individuals or the individual event" (Cartledge 1982: 1011). Post-processual archaeology favors non-generalizing, some would say particularistic, approaches to prehistory and the role of prehistory in present-day political and ideological concerns. In this paper, Hodder 1986, and Shanks and Tilley (1987a and 1987b) are taken as major representatives of the post-processual "program" (see Introduction to this volume).

2 Conkey (1987: 413) forbids use of the term "art" to refer to prehistoric "visual and material imagery." "Art" *is* a value-laden term, but it is a very much shorter one than "visual and material imagery," and may be used to imply "evidence for visual symbolic communication." In the case study presented below, "art" refers specifically to figurines, murals, and decoration of utilitarian objects, such as pots and textiles.

3 The primary pursuit of ecologists using "information theory" appears to be to measure various kinds of diversity, but mainly genetic diversity, in ecological systems (cf. Margalef 1968: 2–5). Archaeologists use the term in at least two ways. Those authors cited in the text appear to have some affinity with the use of the term by ecologists. They primarily try to measure diversity of social information as it is "encoded" in stylistic features of material culture items. The term "information" is also used by Wright (1977: 395), who discusses the flow and control of information about resources, labor, and so on among institutions in states.

4 These examples were chosen because Andrew Sherratt compares his Hungarian Plain sequence with Çatal Hüyük in an article about trade (Sherratt 1982), and Gregory Johnson compares Çatal Hüyük with the American Southwest in two articles about aggregation and organization (Johnson 1982, 1989). I focus here on the Pueblo IV period in Arizona and western New Mexico, AD 1300 to about 1500, also known as the Western Pueblo culture and as the Protohistoric Pueblo period, but Johnson most often refers to Chaco Canyon, a somewhat earlier case of population aggregation in western New Mexico.

5 The plain was evidently a natural habitat for cattle, unlike the surrounding region, and cattle are thought to have been undergoing domestication at roughly this time and place. The fact that cattle are not conventionally classed with trade items is largely a function of our habitual classification and subsequent dismissal of them as food, therefore a subsistence item.

6 Whether or not Mellaart's dates for this occupation are a few centuries too early is not relevant to this discussion, but the reader should be aware that there is doubt about the absolute dating of Çatal Hüyük.

7 Evidence cited by Upham (1982) to support the hypothesis that an elite class at large sites controlled the populations of small sites in the Anderson Mesa and Homol'ovi areas was based on three faulty interpretations of the evidence. First, many of his small sites were not contemporaneous with the later occupations of his large sites. Second, many of his smaller sites probably represent seasonally occupied field-house clusters

(Homol'ovi Research Program, Arizona State Museum, ms. in preparation). Third, ceramic distribution studies were interpreted as showing differential access to "luxury" wares, but most probably are the result of time differences between assemblages. The assertion that the different wares used in the study were contemporaneous was based on a small test excavation in deposits later shown by Downum (1986) to contain mixed fill from several time periods.

8 Lekson (1988) notes that although there is much controversy among Southwesternists about what is a kiva and when and how pithouses "evolved" into kivas, all agree that kivas in the Pueblo IV period are deserving of the name. Their ritual function has been inferred mainly by direct historic analogy with modern Pueblo kivas, where ritual activities and many male craft activities, such as weaving, take place. Features such as benches, hearths, ventilators, storage for ritual paraphernalia, loom fixtures, and symbolic features such as the *sipapu* (symbolic entrance to the underworld) and southern platform (historically, this area represents secular space, and is where women sit) are held in common (see Smith 1972).

References

Adams, E. Charles 1989 Homol'ovi III: A Pueblo Hamlet in the Middle Little Colorado River Valley. *Kiva* 54: 217–30.
   1991 *The Origin and Development of the Katsina Cult.* Tucson: University of Arizona Press.
Adams, E. Charles, Miriam Stark, and Deborah Dosh n.d. Ceramic Distribution and Ceramic Exchange: The Distribution of Jeddito Yellow Ware and the Implications for Social Complexity. ms. on file, AZ State Museum.
Angel, Lawrence 1971 Early Neolithic Skeletons from Çatal Hüyük: Demography and Pathology. *Anatolian Studies* 14: 121–3.
Bartel, Bart 1972 The Characteristics of the Çatal Hüyük Supracommunity. *American Journal of Archaeology* 76: 204–5.
Brunson, Judy L. 1985 Corrugated Ceramics as Indicators of Interaction Spheres. In *Decoding Prehistoric Ceramics*, edited by B. A. Nelson, pp. 102–27. Carbondale: Southern Illinois University Press.
Carlson, Roy L. 1982 The Polychrome Complexes. In *Southwestern Ceramics: A Comparative Review*, edited by A. H. Schroeder, *The Arizona Archaeologist* 15: 201–34.

Cartledge, Paul 1982 A New Classical Archaeology? *Times Literary Supplement* Sept. 12, p. 1011.
Chang, K. C. 1983 *Art, Myth, and Ritual: The Path to Political Authority in Ancient China.* Cambridge, Mass.: Harvard University Press.
Cohen, Harold R. 1970 The Palaeoecology of South Central Anatolia at the End of the Pleistocene and the Beginning of the Holocene. *Anatolian Studies* 20: 119–38.
Conkey, Margaret W. 1978 Style and Information in Cultural Evolution: Toward a Predictive Model for the Paleolithic. In *Social Archaeology: Beyond Subsistence and Dating*, edited by C. L. Redman, M. J. Berman, E. V. Curtin, *et al.*, pp. 61–85. New York: Academic Press.
   1987 New Approaches in the Search for Meaning: A Review of Research in "Paleolithic Art." *Journal of Field Archaeology* 14: 413–30.
DeBoer, Warren and James Moore 1982 The Measurement and Meaning of Stylistic Diversity. *Nawpa Pacha* 20: 147–62.
Downum, Christian E. 1986 Potsherds, Provenience, and Ports of Trade: A Review of the Evidence from Chavez Pass. Paper presented at the Fourth Mogollon Conference, Tucson.
Feinman, Gary, Steadman Upham, and Kent Lightfoot 1981 The Production Step Measure: An Original Index of Labor Input in Ceramic Manufacture. *American Antiquity* 46: 871–84.
Ferg, Alan 1982 14th Century Kachina Depictions on Ceramics. In *Collected Papers in Honor of John W. Runyon, Papers of the Archaeological Society of New Mexico* 7, edited by G. X. Fitzgerald, pp. 13–29. Albuquerque.
Graves, Michael 1981 Ethnoarchaeology of Kalinga Ceramic Design. Unpublished Ph.D. dissertation, University of Arizona, Tucson, Arizona.
Hallpike, C. R. 1986 *The Principles of Social Evolution.* Oxford: Clarendon.
Hays, Kelley A. 1989 Katsina Depictions on Homol'ovi Ceramics: Toward a Fourteenth Century Pueblo Iconography. *Kiva* 54: 297–311.
Hegmon, Michelle 1986 Information Exchange and Integration on Black Mesa, Arizona, A.D. 931–1150. In *Spatial Organization and Exchange: Archaeological Survey on Northern Black Mesa*, edited by S. Plog, pp. 187–223. Carbondale: Southern Illinois University Press.
   1988 Ceramics and Style in Early Integrative Architecture of the North American Southwest. Paper presented at the 53rd annual meeting of the Society for American Archaeology, Phoenix, Arizona.

Hibben, Frank 1975 *Kiva Art of the Anasazi at Pottery Mound*. Las Vegas: KC Publications.

Hill, James N. 1970 Broken K Pueblo. *University of Arizona Anthropological Papers* 18. Tucson: University of Arizona Press.

Hodder, Ian 1977 The Distribution of Material Culture in the Baringo District, Western Kenya. *Man* 12: 239–69.

1978 Social Organization and Human Interaction: The Development of Some Tentative Hypotheses in Terms of Material Culture. In *The Spatial Organization of Culture*, edited by I. Hodder, pp. 199–269. Pittsburgh: University of Pittsburgh Press.

1979 Economic and Social Stress and Material Culture Patterning. *American Antiquity* 44: 446–54.

1982 *Symbols in Action: Ethnoarchaeological Studies of Material Culture*. Cambridge: Cambridge University Press.

1986 *Reading the Past*. Cambridge: Cambridge University Press.

1987 The Contextual Analysis of Symbolic Meanings. In *The Archaeology of Contextual Meanings*, edited by I. Hodder, pp. 1–10. Cambridge: Cambridge University Press.

Johnson, Gregory 1982 Organizational Structure and Scalar Stress. In *Theory and Explanation in Archaeology: The Southampton Conference*, edited by C. Renfrew, M. Rowlands, and B. Segraves, pp. 389–421. New York: Academic Press.

1989 Dynamics of Southwestern Prehistory: Far Outside – Looking In. In *Dynamics of Southwestern Prehistory*, edited by L. Cordell and G. Gumerman, pp. 371–89. Washington D.C.: Smithsonian Press.

Kent, Kate Peck 1983a *Prehistoric Textiles of the Southwest*. Santa Fe: School of American Research.

1983b Temporal Shifts in the Structure of Traditional Southwestern Textile Design. In *Structure and Cognition in Art*, edited by D. K. Washburn, pp. 113–37. Cambridge: Cambridge University Press.

Kintigh, Keith 1985 Social Structure, the Structure of Style, and Stylistic Patterns in Cibola Prehistory. In *Decoding Prehistoric Ceramics*, edited by B. A. Nelson, pp. 362–85. Carbondale: Southern Illinois Press.

Lekson, Stephen 1988 The Idea of the Kiva in Anasazi Archaeology. *Kiva* 53: 213–34.

Longacre, William A. 1970 Archaeology as Anthropology: A Case Study. *Anthropology Papers of the University of Arizona* 17. Tucson: University of Arizona Press.

Margalef, Ramón 1968 *Perspectives in Ecological Theory*. Chicago: University of Chicago Press.

Martin, Paul and Elizabeth S. Willis 1940 Anasazi Painted Pottery in the Field Museum of Natural History. *Anthropology Memoirs of the Field Museum of Natural History* Vol. 5. Chicago: Field Museum Press.

Mellaart, James 1958 Excavations at Hacilar: 1st Preliminary Report. *Anatolian Studies* 8.

1960 Excavations at Hacilar: 3rd Preliminary Report. *Anatolian Studies* 10: 83–104.

1961 Excavations at Hacilar: 4th Preliminary Report. *Anatolian Studies* 11: 39–76.

1962 Excavations at Çatal Hüyük, 1961, 1st Preliminary Report. *Anatolian Studies* 12: 41–65.

1963a Excavations at Çatal Hüyük, 1952, 2nd Preliminary Report. *Anatolian Studies* 13: 43–104.

1963b Deities and Shrines of Neolithic Anatolia: Excavations at Çatal Hüyük, 1962. *Archaeology* 16: 29–38.

1964a Excavations at Çatal Hüyük, 1963, 3rd Preliminary Report. *Anatolian Studies* 14: 39–119.

1964b A Neolithic City in Turkey. *Scientific American* 210: 94–104.

1965 Çatal Hüyük West. *Anatolian Studies* 15: 135–56.

1967 *Çatal Hüyük: A Neolithic Town in Anatolia*. London: Thames and Hudson.

Mithen, Steven 1989 Evolutionary Theory and Post-Processual Archaeology. *Antiquity* 63: 483–94.

Olsen, Stanley J. and John W. Olsen 1974 The Macaws of Grasshopper Ruin. *The Kiva* 40: 67–70.

Perkins, Dexter 1969 Fauna of Çatal Hüyük: Evidence for Early Cattle Domestication in Anatolia. *Science* 164: 177–9.

Plog, Fred 1983 Political and Economic Alliances on the Colorado Plateaus, AD 400–1450. *Advances in World Archaeology* 2: 289–330. New York: Academic Press.

Plog, Stephen 1976 Measurement of Prehistoric Interaction Between Communities. In *The Early Mesoamerican Village*, edited by K. V. Flannery, pp. 255–72. New York: Academic Press.

1978 Social Interaction and Stylistic Similarity: A Re-analysis. In *Advances in Archaeological Method and Theory* 1, edited by M. B. Schiffer, pp. 143–82. New York: Academic Press.

1980 *Stylistic Variation in Prehistoric Ceramics: Design Analysis in the American Southwest*. Cambridge: Cambridge University Press.

1983 Analysis of Style in Artifacts. *Annual Review of Anthropology* 12: 125–42.

Pollock, Susan 1983 Style and Information: An Analysis of Susiana Ceramics. *Journal of Anthropological Archaeology* 2: 354–90.

Rappaport, Roy 1971a Ritual, Sanctity and Cybernetics. *American Anthropologist* 73: 59–76.

1971b The Sacred in Human Evolution. *Annual Review of Ecology and Systematics* 2: 23–44.

Reid, J. Jefferson 1985 Measuring Social Complexity in the American Southwest. In *Status, Structure, and Stratification: Current Archaeological Preconstructions*, edited by M. Thompson, M. Garcia, and F. Kense, pp. 167–73. Calgary: The University of Calgary Archaeological Association.

1989a Pueblo Pots and Potters. ms. University of Arizona.

1989b A Grasshopper Perspective on the Mogollon of the Arizona Mountains. In *Dynamics of Southwestern Prehistory*, edited by L. Cordell and G. Gumerman. Washington D.C.: Smithsonian Press.

Runciman, W. 1982 Origins of States: the case of Archaic Greece. *Comparative Studies in Society and History* 24: 351–77.

Sahlins, Marshall and Elman Service, eds. 1960 *Evolution and Culture*. Ann Arbor: University of Michigan Press.

Schaafsma, Polly 1980 *Indian Rock Art of the Southwest*. Santa Fe: School of American Research.

Schaafsma, Polly and Curtis Schaafsma 1974 Evidence for the Origins of the Pueblo Kachina Cult as Suggested by Rock Art. *American Antiquity* 39: 535–45.

Schaefer, Paul D. 1969 Prehistoric Trade in the Southwest and the Distribution of Pueblo IV Hopi Jeddito Black-on-Yellow. *Kroeber Anthropological Society Papers* 41: 54–77.

Schele, Linda and Mary Ellen Miller 1986 *Blood of Kings: Dynasty and Ritual in Maya Art*. Fort Worth: Kimball Art Museum.

Schiffer, Michael B. and James Skibo 1987 Theory and Experiment in the Study of Technological Change. *Current Anthropology* 28: 595–622.

Shanks, Michael and Christopher Tilley 1987a *Re-Constructing Archaeology: Theory and Practice*. Cambridge: Cambridge University Press.

1987b *Social Theory and Archaeology*. Albuquerque: University of New Mexico Press.

Sherratt, Andrew 1982 Mobile Resources: Settlement and Exchange in Early Agricultural Europe. In *Ranking, Resource and Exchange: Aspects of the Archaeology of Early European Society*, edited by C. Renfrew and A. Sherratt, pp. 13–26. Cambridge: Cambridge University Press.

Smith, Watson 1952 Kiva Mural Decorations at Awatovi and Kawaika-a. *Papers of the Peabody Museum* 37. Cambridge: Harvard University Press.

1962 Schools, Pots and Potters. *American Anthropologist* 64: 1165–78.

1971 Painted Ceramics of the Western Mound at Awatovi. *Papers of the Peabody Museum of Archaeology and Ethnology* 39. Cambridge: Harvard University Press.

1972 Prehistoric Kivas of Antelope Mesa, Northeastern Arizona. *Papers of the Peabody Museum of Archaeology and Ethnology* 39 (1). Cambridge: Harvard University Press.

Soffer, Olga 1985 *The Upper Paleolithic of the Central Russian Plain*. New York: Academic Press.

Todd, Ian 1976 *Çatal Hüyük in Perspective*. Menlo Park: Cummings.

Upham, Steadman 1982 *Polities and Power: An Economic and Political History of the Western Pueblo*. New York: Academic Press.

Upham, Steadman, Kent G. Lightfoot, and Gary M. Feinman 1981 Explaining Socially Determined Ceramic Distributions in the Prehistoric Plateau Southwest. *American Antiquity* 46: 822–33.

Whittlesey, Stephanie 1978 Status and Death at Grasshopper Pueblo: Experiments Toward an Archaeological Theory of Correlates. Ph.D. dissertation, University of Arizona.

1982 Uses and Abuses of Mogollon Mortuary Data. Paper presented at the Second Mogollon Conference, Las Cruces.

Wiessner, Polly 1983 Style and Social Information in Kalahari San Projectile Points. *American Antiquity* 48: 253–76.

1984 Reconsidering the Behavioral Basis for Style: A Case Study Among the Kalahari San. *Journal of Anthropological Archaeology* 3: 109–234.

1985 Style of Isochrestic Variation? A Reply to Sackett. *American Antiquity* 50: 160–6.

Winter, Irene 1987 Legitimation of Authority through Image and Legend: Seals Belonging to Officials in the Administrative Bureaucracy of the Ur III State. In *The Organization of Power: Aspects of Bureaucracy in the Ancient Near East*, edited by M. Gibson and R. D. Biggs, pp. 69-106. *Studies in Ancient Oriental Civilization* 46. Chicago: The Oriental Institute.

Wobst, H. Martin 1977 Stylistic Behavior and Information Exchange. In *For the Director: Research Essays in Honor of James Bennett Griffin*, edited by C. E. Cleland, pp. 317–34. *University of Michigan, Museum of Anthropology, Anthropological Papers* 61. Ann Arbor.

Wright, Henry T. 1977 Recent Research on the Origin of the State. *Annual Review of Anthropology* 6: 379–97.

Yoffee, Norman 1985 Perspective on Trends Toward Social Complexity in Prehistoric Australia and Papua New Guinea. *Archaeology of Oceania* 20: 41–9.

8

Re-fitting the "cracked and broken façade": the case for empiricism in post-processual ethnoarchaeology

MIRIAM T. STARK

A well-established dialogue concerning "post-processualism" reflects a current lack of consensus in archaeological theory. Post-processualists advocate a particularistic, hermeneutic approach to archaeological inquiry and thereby challenge the "explicitly scientific" approach of what has now become known as processual archaeology.[1] This debate has produced a substantial corpus of literature, only some of which will be considered here.[2] Ethnographic data form the foundation for many archaeological interpretations, and have been used in both processual and post-processual frameworks. Moreover, ethnoarchaeology represents a research strategy of increasing importance in supplying both processual and post-processual archaeologists with ideas for interpretation. Accordingly, this analysis broaches the post-processual discussion by focusing on strengths and limitations of ethnoarchaeological research.

In the post-processual spirit of polemic strategies (Shanks and Tilley 1989: 8), this paper challenges the premise that "varieties of empiricism do not form an appropriate medium for a materialist practice" (*ibid.* 1989: 44). Embodied in Hodder's (1986: 79) claim that empirical science is a "cracked and broken façade" (and resounded elsewhere, e.g., Shanks and Tilley 1989: 3), the paper focuses on the domain of current ethnoarchaeological research and argues that archaeologists and ethnoarchaeologists are compelled by the nature of their data to maintain methodological rigor in research.

This paper considers symbolic analyses of material culture that are conducted within traditional (i.e., non-industrialized) societies as post-processual ethnoarchaeological research.[3] Empiricism is neither wrong nor disabling (*contra* Hodder 1989: 345), and ethnoarchaeological data collection must meet basic standards of methodological rigor

and recognize potential interpretive biases, regardless of differing research questions or theoretical frameworks. Issues of validity, reliability, and accuracy are as critical in the construction of ethnoarchaeological data as they are in the construction of ethnographic data (e.g., Bernard *et al.* 1986).

The paper first provides a general introduction to types of ethnographic data that archaeologists use in interpretation. Next, it examines differences in the goals and assumptions of post-processual and processual ethnoarchaeological studies, and evaluates selected symbolic studies in terms of methods and presentation to identify current weaknesses in the post-processual approach. The paper concludes by examining the potential and limitations inherent in the ethnoarchaeological method and the use of empirical ethnoarchaeological data in the course of archaeological inquiry.

Ethnographic data and archaeological interpretation

The use of ethnographic data has a long history in archaeological interpretation. Ethnographic data are used in many ways to establish material correlates of human behavior and to investigate broad relationships with material culture through time. The ethnographic record supplies archaeologists with evidence for continuity between prehistoric and historic cultural traditions in given regions and provides comparative checks on archaeological findings. Ethnographic data also provide cautionary tales from case studies to warn archaeologists away from simplistic interpretations of material assemblages.

The archaeologist can generalize from ethnographic data to reconstruct biophysical conditions that humans manipulated and to which they directly or indirectly responded to produce the archaeological record. With the assistance of bridging arguments based on ethnographic information, archaeologists can also apply precise and well-confirmed generalizations to infer human behavior from archaeological evidence (Trigger 1978: 9). At the broadest (and least powerful) level of analogy, entire systems can be compared and contrasted, using ethnographic and archaeological cases.

The limitations of ethnographic data for directly explaining archaeological phenomena have been repeatedly emphasized elsewhere and will not be reiterated here (but see Gould and Watson 1982 for one such discussion). Excepting the use of a "direct historic approach" (Steward 1942; Strong 1936) in regions demonstrating long-term cultural continuity, many archaeologists emphasize the heuristic value of such data in shaping archaeological questions, in modelling particular archaeological assemblages based on ethnographically-derived information, and in developing broad models of behavior to be tested against archaeological data. Although ethnographic data are still used to derive direct material correlates for prehistoric human behavior in a traditional manner, there is reason to believe that no direct analogs exist among modern societies for prehistoric examples (Kelly and Todd 1988; Schrire 1984). Recent discussions of ethnographic analogy (Gould and Watson 1982; Wylie 1985) underscore the importance of evaluating the questions that archaeologists ask of the prehistoric record as well as the questions that archaeologist-observers ask of the ethnographic record (Wobst 1978).

Ethnoarchaeology as a source of data

The ethnoarchaeological method provides a superior form of ethnographic data for archaeological interpretation because of its greater range of germane topics than those available in traditional ethnographic research. This paper follows Longacre's (1981: 49–50) definition of ethnoarchaeology as the testing of models relating variability of human behavior to material traces among extant groups, where the investigator can simultaneously control for both human behavior and material culture variability.

Ethnoarchaeological studies provide researchers with the means of formulating and testing archaeologically-oriented or -derived methods, hypotheses, models, and theories (Kent 1987: 37). Additionally, ethnoarchaeological research can aid in justifying specific archaeological interpretations (Binford 1987b: 449). The most general goal of ethnoarchaeological research is to provide an ethnographic foundation on which to develop inferences and to base interpretations (Hodder 1982a: 28). One aspect of that goal is the identification of processes of human behavior and their material correlates that help to explain patterns observable in the archaeological record (Gould 1978: 4). Ethnoarchaeology may also explore holistic systems of behavior involved in the production and use of material culture. An increasingly powerful use of ethnoarchaeology is in the realm of generalization. As increasing numbers of ethnoarchaeological studies are published on societies throughout the world, generalizations can be developed on the basis of comparative studies to explore particular culture processes and research themes.

Ethnoarchaeology is not a theory, but rather a research strategy for answering archaeological questions in living societies. While the resultant data can be used in a variety of theoretical frameworks, ethnoarchaeology does not have *explanation* as a goal. Ethnoarchaeological research rather aids in the development of hypotheses regarding the archaeological record, and in the refinement of a particular focus on relevant research topics. Some practitioners believe that ethnoarchaeological data can detail the conditions that underlie specific situations and relationships between humans and material culture (cf. Binford 1987a: 507). No direct relationships, however, can generally be assumed between ethnoarchaeological and archaeological contexts. Yellen's observation that "all archaeological interpretation requires a leap of faith" (1977b: 272) underscores the limitations of ethnoarchaeology in explaining prehistoric behavior.

Ethnoarchaeologists share assumptions that in large part cross-cut different theoretical frameworks. First, ethnoarchaeological research is firmly rooted in an empirical tradition that seeks to build a "theory of material culture" (Trigger 1978: 8). Emerging during a period that Dunnell has characterized as a "methodological revolution" in the 1930s, empirical testing was established as "the criterion by which the correctness of conclusions was to be gauged" (Dunnell 1986: 30). One aspect of the empirical tradition in archaeology is the assumption that humans interact with their material world in observable relationships. These relationships can be studied in ongoing systems to aid in the interpretation of prehistoric human behavior (Kramer 1979: 1).

Secondly, ethnoarchaeologists assume that these interrelationships can be described through empirical research, and can be characterized by a series of loosely-defined generalizations that are described alternately as "low-level theories" (Trigger 1989a: 20) or as "low-level principles" and "experimental laws" (Schiffer 1988: 464). Identifying these patterns entails an understanding that idiosyncrasies in and deviations from the patterns are as important as the similarities (Binford 1987b: 507; Gould 1980: xi–xii). Carefully collected ethnoarchaeological research investigates and accounts for particular cultural and social contexts in which the material culture system is embedded in order to understand the totality of the material culture systems under study.

These loosely-defined generalizations are then linked to the archaeological record through the use of "middle-level" (Trigger 1989a: 21), "middle-range" (cf. Raab and Goodyear 1984) theories that can be tested using archaeological data. The range of systematic relationships from which generalizations are derived is broad, subsuming material correlates of human behavior and formation processes of the archaeological record (Schiffer 1987), principles by which humans construct their worlds (Hodder 1985: 2), and overarching principles of social action based on structuralist premises (Shanks and Tilley 1987). That generalizations are inevitable in the course of archaeological interpretation is clear. What differs in separate interpretive frameworks is the subject of generalization and analysis.

Third, ethnoarchaeologists assume that certain material conditions are instrumental in shaping cultural behavior, insofar as they believe that similarities in material conditions encourage broadly similar cultural expressions. Ethno-archaeological data from comparable situations can thereby be compared and contrasted in both generalizing and particularizing studies of human behavior. In collecting comparative data, ethnoarchaeologists pursue one objective of archaeology: to achieve a "systematic interconnection of facts within the field of archaeological data, and of archaeo-logical data to all other data" (Spaulding 1953b: 589). This form of the comparative method may utilize ethnographic information in the form of "raw data" regarding specific human–object relationships, or in the form of analytical frameworks that are employed to organize the "raw data" into interpretive schemes (cf. McNett 1979). Exactly *how* ethnoarchaeological data may be incorporated into archaeo-logical interpretation is not the subject of this analysis. Alternative discussions of key issues in evaluating and using ethnoarchaeological data (Kramer 1979; Schiffer 1981; Simms 1992) provide a useful starting point on this subject.

Ethnoarchaeology and the post-processual critique

Post-processual studies challenge the processual assumption that the "scientific" (*sensu* Watson *et al.* 1984) paradigm can explain human behavior. Processualist research is criticized for an obsession with "scientific" methods of confirmation and explanation that are narrowly explanatory and thereby unsatisfactory. The "skeptical empiricist, soft functionalist" assumption of processual studies – that culture consists of predictable patterns – dehumanizes participants in prehistoric societies (Shanks and Tilley 1987). Prehistoric individuals are buffeted by the winds of environmental–ecological fate, lacking power to change their respective destinies.

Post-processualists contend that the empirical tradition of processual studies minimizes human intentionality in prehistoric and contemporary societies. Shanks and Tilley have considered the generalizing approach a "disabling orientation" that presents a determinist view of human behavior (1989: 6). So-called "contextual" interpretations are also exemplified in Hodder's (1982a) studies of East African material culture, where social and historical contexts are explored in great detail, and the interpretations offered are based on context-specific factors.

Despite the post-processual insistence on the establish-ment of organizing principles that guide human behavior through space and time, a "contextual" archaeology (and ethnoarchaeology) seemingly holds no place for cross-cultural comparison. Although the generalizing, empirical processual tradition seems a foreign country to post-processualist archaeological interpretation, this search for universal principles is not (cf. Leach 1977; articles in Hodder 1982b). The structuralist foundations of the post-processualist framework identify "internally related sets of structural principles" (Tilley 1982). These principles are expressed in a series of binary oppositions that are reflected in material culture, and may exhibit distinct configurations from one society to another (Hodder 1982a).

Post-processual ethnoarchaeological research shares certain goals with processual studies in the same area. The first is to embed theory into particular ethnoarchaeological data sets by emphasizing both inductive and deductive methods of analysis (Hodder 1987b). The second goal is to salvage relevant information from non-industrial societies whose material culture traditions are rapidly disappearing with the spread of western values and objects. The third objective is to present ethnographic analogs that relate material patterning to adaptive and cultural contexts (Hodder 1982a: 40).

Post-processual studies of material culture in contem-porary societies lie in the realm of ideas and ideology, and their ethnoarchaeological studies share assumptions regarding the relationship between material objects and human interactions. First, since prehistoric artifacts are not simply "things in themselves" but rather are assumed to be representations of ideas (Leach 1977: 167), these post-processual studies attempt to discern non-functional meanings of objects from ethnoarchaeological contexts.

For example, pottery can be actively used in "power strategies" to negotiate gender-based imbalances in Africa (Braithwaite 1982; Welbourn 1984). Similar approaches are used in viewing ceramic decoration as a power strategy among the Endo and Azande in Africa. Relations between ideology and its representations are expressed through use-contexts of pottery: the uses of different kinds of pottery (e.g., decorated vs. undecorated, Braithwaite 1982) or its uses in different social contexts (beer-drinking vs. food-grinding [Welbourn 1984]) are explained through patterns of gender-based inequality. Ceramic ethnoarchaeological research, then, explicates how material culture symbolizes, ritualizes, and reflects important social relations in African societies.

Symbolic studies also seek to identify in ethnographic contexts generative principles and generalizations that can later be tested against archaeological data. These principles help archaeologists to explain the relations between material culture and ideology, to elucidate discursive and non-discursive dimensions of symbolization, and to outline how material culture is structured within – and yet structures – daily practice (Hodder 1982b: 14). Post-processual ethno-archaeological research establishes methods of how to "read" cultures as "texts" (Hodder 1987b: 445). Finally, proper ethnoarchaeological research should be "long-term, participatory and from the inside" (Hodder 1987c: 444).

Pottery can also be used to "frame" social interaction and to dictate appropriate behavior. Miller's study outlines the roles that pottery plays in social strategies in his ethno-archaeological study of the central Indian community of Dangwara. Artifacts provide "enormously rich evidence for social relations" (Miller 1985: 198) and reflect the hetero-geneity of the caste society under study. A "semiotic code" of Dangwara pottery is described, using binary oppositions, in Miller's presentation of a model representing the inter-action between social strategy and artifactual variability and change (1985: 4).

Ethnoarchaeological research by post-processualists shares the same assumptions as does the archaeological research presented by Hodder (1986), Miller and Tilley (1984), and Shanks and Tilley (1987). The post-processualist conception of material culture, for example, assumes that individual artifacts are laden with symbolic meaning and are well ordered in larger cultural systems of artifacts and behavior. Both prehistoric and contemporary material objects as symbols are "irreducibly polysemous with an indeterminate range of meanings" (Shanks and Tilley 1987: 115). Material conditions of existence result from – rather than help shape – practices produced by cultural dispositions and cultural understandings (Hodder 1985: 4) in both archaeological and ethnoarchaeological circumstances. Interpretation is particularistic, richly descriptive (Collingwood 1946: 245), and committed to "long-term" cultural historical reconstructions (Hodder 1987b), rather than to the comparison of cultures with one another.

The post-processual framework holds that proper explanation requires highly inductive "thick description" (Geertz 1973), and is evaluated on the basis of richness, contextualization, internal coherence, and correspondence to a particular data set. Post-processualists also assume that all archaeologists are inescapably biased by contemporary culture concerns and categories. Any comparative enterprise we attempt, therefore, will only tell us about the prevailing ideology in our own culture, rather than providing insights about prehistoric human behavior. Events and observations that processual archaeologists call "facts" (Binford 1988: 392) are culture-bound, and "data" retrieved during research are inextricably tied to a specific theoretical framework. Research by Welbourn, Braithwaite, and Miller (previously mentioned) is used to exemplify current problems in post-processual ethnoarchaeological research.[4]

One fundamental problem is shared by processual and post-processual ethnoarchaeological research: the lack of explicit methodological frameworks. The credibility of archaeological conclusions rests on the techniques by which they were derived (cf. Dunnell 1986: 40). Little explication of field methods is provided, including the duration of field investigation, data collection techniques, interview format, and observational approach.

A few specific comments here on Miller's (1985) study exemplify this lack of methodological rigor. Miller explains that his fieldwork covered "most of the yearly cycle, apart from the monsoon and the preceding high summer, when activities such as potting are comparatively restricted" (1985: 17), but both the duration and seasonality of his two field seasons are unclear. A careful inspection of his data base (including household censuses, recorded vessel categories, photographs and paintings of vessels, actual vessels, and 7,000 measurements from other vessels) yields confusing information regarding the types and origins of vessels used in his symbolic analysis. No explanations are given regarding the appropriateness of the group under study for exploring particular research questions. Despite the insistence that "methodological rigor" (Hodder 1985: 13) constitutes a concern of post-processual archaeology, information essential to evaluating the research properly is omitted.

The failure to make research methodologies explicit in post-processual research leads to a lack of ethnographic accountability, as accepted standards of data collection, analysis and reporting of methods are ignored. Evaluating ethnoarchaeological studies by their own criteria – that post-processual research among traditional societies be "long-term, participatory and inside" (Hodder 1987c: 444) is impossible, since the "long-term" aspect of the studies is never addressed. It is also not clear from the research to what extent the ethnoarchaeologists "participated" in the culture.

A second problem, specific to symbolic ethnoarchaeo-logical research, focuses on articulating the differences between observers' interpretations and what has been called the "native's point of view" (Geertz 1973). Ethnoarchaeo-logical and ethnographic observers alike must grapple with the problem of the influence of the outside ethnographic observer, whose own social status and role affect the allowable degree of integration into different domains of a given society. Field research stressing observational, quantifiable data may be less hindered by this problem than are symbolic analyses, which rely on "inside" information from informants. Particular cultural values may also inhibit access to "non-discursive", material culture-based realms and to knowledge of the symbolic world. Ethnoarchae-ologists are thus inescapably confronted with a fragmentary cultural context from which to draw symbolic inferences, regardless of the duration of the ethnoarchaeological study.

The researcher is generally dependent upon members

of the culture to assist in bridging the linguistic boundary. Previous research has suggested that likely informants (i.e., individuals who are most attracted to and by ethnographers) differ significantly from those in the society's general population. The most likely informants, in fact, are socially peripheral or economic elites, both types being essentially marginal individuals (Honigmann and Honigmann 1955: 285). Elites are often the most articulate and powerful members of a group under study, while being frequent cultural mediators. These individuals perpetuate the culture economically, politically, and ideologically, through restricted access to traditional and ritual knowledge and to formal avenues of education. The ethnoarchaeologist who relies on informants or assistants relies on twice-mediated interpretations, intentionally or unintentionally manipulated to mask existing power relations in the society. Just as the individual cannot be screened out of archaeological analysis (Shanks and Tilley 1987: 210), neither can the individual be screened out of ethnoarchaeological analysis.

The greatest limitation to these studies hinges on Hodder's criterion of an "inside" approach, referred to elsewhere in the annals of anthropology as the "emic" perspective (cf. Pelto 1970). On the one hand, post-processual studies illuminate cognitive aspects of society, in part resulting from informant-supplied motivations (Hodder 1985: 2), and these cognitive aspects have been largely overlooked in processual studies. On the other hand, post-processualist analysis assumes that material culture-based communication goes unrecognized by a culture's participants, so that individuals are denied an interpretive voice.

A few examples from symbolic ethnoarchaeological studies elucidate this problem. Welbourn's study, for instance, notes that "if it is suggested to [the Endo] that such pots might resemble people, they laugh and deny it" (1984: 20). In addition, Braithwaite (1982) decides that the Azande are ignorant of symbolic meanings in their pottery decoration since "those aspects of women's power and influence are implicit . . . in the area of the undiscussed" (1982: 85). Finally, northern Cameroon informants confronted with interpretations of pots as human bodies found these parallels merely coincidental (David *et al.* 1988: 372). Yet the authors concluded that "natives' acceptance or rejection of rationales for their symbolic behavior constitutes neither proof nor disproof" (*op. cit.* 366) of the analysis. Perceptions that ceramic producers, consumers, traders, and disposers have of those material objects under study are dismissed, a criticism already lodged elsewhere (Plog and Richman 1983; Wandiba 1988). Following Joyce's (1988: 382) query, if those individuals using material culture do not find an interpretation compelling, how should we interpret this reaction? Moreover, how are we to reconcile the need for a politicized archaeology with a disavowal of indigenous interpretations?

There is an inescapable difficulty in the symbolic-structuralist quest to discover the unobservable. And when the unobservable is concurrently the uncognized or contested, one wonders how to evaluate conflicting interpretations should they be put forth by the informants themselves. It is precisely this difficulty that weakens the conclusions of the symbolic ethnoarchaeological studies. On the one hand, the post-processualist agenda states that "archaeology, as cultural practice, is always a politics, a morality" (Shanks and Tilley 1987: 212), and demands that we develop a "critical appreciation of different pasts" (Shanks and Tilley 1989: 10). On the other hand, an appreciation of the natives' present is dismissed in post-processual ethnoarchaeological research, a conflict of interests that calls into question the coherence between epistemology and research in post-processual studies.

The paradox – that individuals manipulate objects in their material world whose meanings they do not recognize or understand – is not simply a disjunction between what people say and do (Hodder 1986). If all observation is subjective, and "there is no original meaning to be recovered as the meaning depends on the structured and positioned social situation of the individual" (Shanks and Tilley 1987: 117), one must conclude that the symbolic system of meaning in an ongoing cultural system can never be under-stood.

In situations where questions cannot be answered on empirical grounds, competing explanations naturally abound, and this is especially true in symbolic ethno-archaeological studies. Of vital importance to such studies is the assumption that material culture is a "communicative medium of considerable importance . . . and as a symbolic medium for orientating people in their natural and social environments" (Shanks and Tilley 1987: 96). By unques-tioningly accepting this premise, post-processualists neatly sidestep a rigorous evaluation of their own analyses, which "processual" assumptions nonetheless receive in post-processual hands.

A final problem lies in translating symbolic analyses of material culture relationships into the archaeological record. The post-processual ethnoarchaeological studies lack effective linkages between ethnographic analyses and the expectations that can be derived for the archaeological record. Little attention is given to archaeological correlates for these power relations and strategies, so that the contribution for archaeological studies is limited. In fact, some critiques have observed that the "contextual" (*sensu* Hodder 1987a) approach works most effectively in non-archaeological (i.e., ethnoarchaeological, ethnohistorical, or historical) contexts (Earle and Preucel 1987: 506; Megaw and Megaw 1988: 393).

A related difficulty in the post-processual studies involves determining whether symbolically-laden artifacts are also utilitarian and in perishable in prehistoric societies, and this linkage remains undemonstrated. Meanings vary across different realms of social life, and meanings are manipulated differently, through different media with different motives, by different participants in a given culture. Finally, meanings that are ultimately of interest to archaeologists may bear little relationship to those meanings of importance to individuals within a culture. Translating symbolic analyses from contemporary to prehistoric contexts is fraught with difficulty, and it is not clear how one can successfully operationalize such variables associated with meaning and the negotiations of power relations into the archaeological record.

Although material culture items undoubtedly participate in the negotiation of social strategies, it is unclear whether symbolically laden material culture items in contemporary traditional societies share prehistoric analogs. Miller and Tilley (1984: 4) note that studies of prehistoric and contemporary societies may be directly equated with one another. Here the question of analogy enters: is it possible to assume that the axes of power relations observable in contemporary societies were operative in the distant past? Recently, Trigger has noted that most of the more successful symbolic studies lie in the field of historical archaeology, concluding that "the culturally specific (emic) meaning of artefacts that cannot be embraced by the direct historical approach may for ever lie beyond the realm of scientific study" (1989b: 31).

Summary and discussion

> Obviously there can be no complete objectivity here. To think that it can be achieved is to fool one's self, and to attempt to achieve it is to destroy a greater truth (de Laguna 1957: 181).

Objectivity and subjectivity revisited

The post-processualist manifesto (Shanks and Tilley 1987) dismisses the need to develop generalizations (based on "rabid empiricism," *ibid.*, 1987: 12) and advocates a relativist approach to archaeological interpretation. In response to the radical relativism espoused by post-processualists, a sentiment is growing among archaeologists that not *anything* does go in archaeology (Wylie, this volume). Within cultural anthropology there are now also those who insist that – relativist claims to the contrary – some things do not go and are simply wrong (Keesing 1989).

A radical relativist anthropological perspective, as has been discussed widely in the literature, holds great potential for political misuses regarding human rights in the past and the present. Even in relativist frameworks in archaeology and cultural anthropology, moral values must have their place (Renteln 1988).

The kind of hyper-empiricism that the post-processualists attack is not actually practiced by most archaeologists. Kristiansen (1988) observes that most archaeologists stand on some middle ground that includes "Marxists and non-Marxists, positivists and non-positivists (whatever their breed)" (*ibid.*: 474). It would appear instead that post-processualists themselves practice another extreme of empiricism (Salamone 1979: 50), one in which a type of rationalism assumes that realities lie behind observable phenomena (cf. Shanks and Tilley 1989: 3). Trigger (1989a) points out that some things *are* knowable in archaeology, and archaeological research has produced concrete information about past societies that has withstood the force of competing interpretive paradigms. The past constitutes something more than a "project in the present" (Shanks and Tilley 1987: 211), and archaeologists have the privilege and responsibility to continue to extract knowledge from the archaeological record.

The subjectivist stance of post-processual proponents concludes that data are by no means neutral and archaeological questions are theory-bound. Even given these premises, however, subjectivity "does not grant a license for poor sampling or subjective impressions" in symbolic research (Hassan 1989: 257), including ethnoarchaeological studies. Interpretive ethnographers, actually, have recently argued the same point. Scheff (1986) contends that it is possible to make the Geertzian "thick description" more verifiable and directly falsifiable through providing texts and documentation to readers.

In rejecting empirical evidence and refusing to suggest standard criteria for evaluating research, such studies inhibit access to ideas and frameworks so important to the post-processual enterprise. In part, this problem may stem from the motive of "liberating the oppressed" that takes precedence over a politically neutral search for "factual" evidence (Washburn 1987: 545). Ironically, the failure of such ethnoarchaeological studies to make explicit potential research biases renders the studies subject to the same harsh criticisms lobbed at processual research by Shanks and Tilley (1987) and others.

Is there a recoverable past?

Archaeological interpretation is neither entirely subjective, nor is it determined simply by some sort of polling of archaeologists (Spaulding 1953b: 590; Thompson 1956).

Methods of evaluation exist for ethnoarchaeological interpretations, and post-processual studies are no less subject to requirements of careful scholarship and a close attention to careful and systematic data retrieval than are other forms of theory-guided archaeological research.

Shanks and Tilley (1989) contend that facts are not neutral, but instead "speak to their culturally conditioned audiences in determinate ways" (1989: 3). Our recognition that all "facts" are theory-laden does not, however, necessitate an abandonment of empirical research. Moreover, the post-processual opposition between "objectivity" and "subjectivity" may be a false dichotomy. O'Meara (1989: 366), in fact, argues for parallels between the scientific method and the hermeneutic circle in anthropological research.

Methodological weaknesses currently pose problems for symbolic studies of material culture, and it is in the symbolic realm that much post-processual ethnoarchaeological research has been done. This paper does not dismiss the importance of investigating the relationship between material and non-material aspects of human behavior. Nor does it deny that ethnoarchaeological and archaeological studies may eventually identify this part of culture. Some of the most useful ethnoarchaeological studies to date have focused on methodological issues that could legitimately be subsumed under the rubric of "middle-range research" (Binford 1983).[5] The uniformitarian assumption that underlies these studies provokes no small amount of disdain from the post-processualist camp. Ethnoarchaeological research is also underway, however, that addresses relationships between material culture and the social and ideological domains using a rigorous approach. Some recent examples include studies that focus on material culture vis-à-vis social practice (Larick 1991) or on the effect of social factors in patterns of consumption (e.g., Hayden and Cannon 1984; Larick 1991; Longacre and Stark 1992). Other research emphasizes the articulation of social relations and spatial organization with respect to agricultural production (Stone 1992), commodity distributions (Kramer and Douglas 1992), and site structure (Binford 1991).

In fact, the paper contends that archaeological knowledge cannot develop without intuitively conceived ideas. Useful hypotheses must transcend existing empirical data (Gjessing 1975: 324). What is at stake, however, is the means by which all archaeologists collect their data and present their research, and the set of criteria that may be used for evaluating such research.

Standardizing ethnoarchaeological research strategies

It was previously noted that some of the problems with post-processual ethnoarchaeological research afflict the entire field of ethnoarchaeological research, most especially in the lack of well-defined research and field methods (cf. Schiffer 1978). Consequently, the conclusions derived from such field research are subject to substantial criticism. How might ethnoarchaeological research be improved in general? While acknowledging that theoretical frameworks operate at all levels of observation and measurement, Bernard *et al.* (1986) provide concrete suggestions to improve and standardize the "construction" of primary data in anthropological research. In addressing forms of informant-derived and observational data, the authors conclude:

> Each of us has the responsibility to make sure that data are collected in such a way as to document fully the influence of the particular situation on the results of the research and in such a way that others can use them (1986: 383).

Properly done, the ethnoarchaeological field research strategy involves a dialectic between techniques of field-based data collection, and generalization and evaluation leading to modifications in research design over an extensive time period. But this dialectic should not preclude the necessity for careful research designs, containing explicit ideas or hypotheses to be examined, and the procedures by which they will be tested. Biases – or categories of bias – can thereby be systematically isolated and controlled.

Ethnoarchaeological research requires types of analytical and field expertise at different stages of interpretation that are not common in standard archaeological research. At the most basic level, field techniques – both observational and informant-centered – demand an immediate cultural sensitivity not required of many archaeologists in the course of traditional fieldwork. On a more abstract level, consideration of the ethnographically-observed dialectic between ideology and practice, as expressed through the uses of material objects, requires both the knowledge of the ethnographic context and an understanding of symbolic-structuralist theory that most archaeologists currently lack.

Hodder (1986: 104) claims that this current failing necessitates an "asymmetric dependence of archaeology on anthropology" to be remedied only as ethnographers gain an interest in material culture studies. Ethnoarchaeologists can and must develop the basic field and analytical methods necessary for addressing the range of questions related to assumptions about how materials operate in cultural systems (Hayden and Cannon 1984: 210). Care must be taken in the selection of informants, recognizing, as do ethnographers (Freeman *et al.* 1987), that some informants are better than others. Field assistants should be employed from the local population and selected from a variety of kin or corporate groups to lessen resentment and envy toward those employed. Multi-member research is a traditional part of archaeological fieldwork, and team ethnoarchaeological projects by nature lead to increased reliability and a higher level of confidence in the research.

In conclusion, ethnoarchaeology provides the only means for us to look at the "totality of the relevant environment . . . that is necessary for discerning the object's meaning" (Hodder 1986: 6). In addition, ethnoarchaeological research provides archaeologists with the opportunity to explore the relationships between human behavior and material cultural patterning within an ongoing system. An underlying theme in the paper's construction is that reconciliation at the methodological level is needed between processual and post-processual ethnoarchaeologies, so that ethnographically-derived data can be used by archaeologists asking theoretically different questions.

Archaeologists from a number of cross-cutting theoretical orientations have recently called for the development of a theory of material culture. Rather than the wholesale importation of models from other fields or from within anthropology, it is necessary to produce an archaeologically-specific theory, appropriately suited to archaeological phenomena. At the primary and middle-range domains of archaeological interpretation, this may involve the aggregation of hierarchies of principles about aspects of human behavior and the creation of the archaeological record (Schiffer 1988), or the relationships between humans and material culture in ongoing cultural systems (Raab and Goodyear 1984). A material culture theory must recognize that material objects constitute symbols in a complex communicative system. What remains underdeveloped, however, is an adequate archaeological framework for addressing questions of meaning.

Ethnoarchaeology, rather than being a theory, is a research strategy for answering archaeological questions in living societies, providing descriptions rather than explanations of human behavior. What ethnoarchaeology can offer to a theory of material culture is a most useful tool for collecting ethnographic data to be used in archaeological interpretation. Cultural anthropologists have long appreciated the necessity for both cross-cultural regularities and context-specific cultural particularities (Basso 1971: 997). Both of these goals can be realized through ethnoarchaeological research, and ethnoarchaeological data can be used in the formulation of archaeological research problems.

To understand the extent to which the interpretive framework determines the nature of the data collected, a critical assessment of our methodologies is needed. This is only made possible through the explicit presentation of methodological issues in published materials. Long-term ethnoarchaeological field research offers at least two advantages over short-term projects: the development of rapport with the participants in the culture under study, and the ongoing evaluation of interpretations that are subject to in-field revision with the help of informants. Long-term field research allows the ethnoarchaeologist to contextualize the data, strengthening the accuracy of the observations collected by documenting the wider range of variability in behavioral and social realms over time.

The recent call for a re-examination of archaeological theory has brought competing approaches to archaeological interpretation into direct conflict. Many processualists and post-processualists insist that there are few points of convergence between the approaches and dismiss attempts to find common ground. Yet archaeological research has demonstrated that generalizations about human behavior and cultural processes *and* analyses of idiosyncratic (and hence, unpredictable) influences represent indissolubly linked processes, both of which must be studied in the course of archaeological interpretation (Trigger 1989a: 374–5). Rowlands and Gledhill (1977: 144) recognize the struggle that archaeologists must continually wage both against unsubstantiated historical imagination and against an elevation of factual presentation into dogma.

The focus of this paper has been on processual and post-processual conceptions of the ethnoarchaeological approach. More attention must be paid to the ways in which archaeologists collect, classify and interpret ethnographically-derived data in their analysis of archaeological problems to enhance the analytical sophistication and versatility of the use of such data in archaeological interpretation. Just as archaeologists must decide what questions are appropriate to ask of the available ethnographic data (i.e., relevant, and amenable to study), so ethnoarchaeologists must decide how to address these questions most systematically and usefully in the context of an ongoing material culture system. This paper asserts that archaeological interpretation moves forward only with the recognition of a multiplicity of interpretive voices, all reliance upon a broad base of systematically collected ethnographic and archaeological information. Ethnoarchaeological studies provide a valuable source of information and a potential point of convergence for post-processual and processual archaeological interpretation.

Acknowledgments

This paper was originally presented at a graduate seminar in the University of Arizona's Department of Anthropology, and seminar members provided helpful comments on the paper, as did Norman Yoffee and Michael Schiffer. I am indebted to the Department of Anthropology Writers' Group at the University of Arizona for valuable comments, suggestions, and stimulating discussion regarding the paper in its various incarnations.

Notes

1 This analysis subsumes a large group of archaeological studies under the "post-processual" banner, following Hodder's (1985) article of that title. The author acknowledges that the use of the category "post-processualist" artificially unites several competing theoretical stances whose theoretical premises differ markedly from one another, and whose advocates disagree vigorously with one another (cf. Hodder 1989). For the purposes of this analysis, however, the important unifying elements in post-processual studies are: (1) the rejection of an empiricist approach to research; (2) a resulting emphasis on non-observable aspects of society; and (3) the assumption that material culture has a "recursive" role in human societies.

2 The following publications have been included within this critique: Binford 1987a, 1987b, 1988; Earle and Preucel 1987; Hodder 1985, 1986, 1989; Kristiansen 1988; Megaw and Megaw 1988; Plog and Richman 1983; Shanks and Tilley 1989; Trigger 1989a, 1989b; Washburn 1987.

3 This analysis thereby excludes various studies of modern material culture by post-processualists (e.g., Shanks and Tilley 1987).

4 Because previous critiques have addressed aspects of extensive ethnoarchaeological research by Hodder (1982a, 1986, 1987c), this analysis excludes Hodder's research. The studies that were selected for this appraisal – namely, Braithwaite 1982; David *et al.* 1988; Miller 1985; Welbourn 1984 – were chosen in order to evaluate a cross-section of ceramic ethnoarchaeological research conducted within symbolic frameworks. The term "post-processual" is applied to these works because the nature of the research questions addressed conforms to Hodder's (1985) definition of "post-processual" archaeology.

5 Ethnoarchaeological research on methodological issues feeds directly into archaeological studies on issues such as site formation (e.g., Chang 1988, O'Connell 1987; Siegel and Roe 1986), artifact use-life (e.g., Nelson 1991), and refuse disposal (e.g., Hayden and Cannon 1983; Sutro 1991). Within ceramic ethnoarchaeology, research on aspects of ceramic manufacture (e.g., D. Arnold 1985; P. Arnold 1991; Stark 1985) has been particularly useful for archaeologists interested in identifying ceramic production and source areas.

References

Arnold, D. 1985 *Ceramic Theory and Cultural Process.* Cambridge: Cambridge University Press.

Arnold, P. J. 1991 *Domestic Ceramic Production and Spatial Organization: A Mexican Case Study in Ethnoarchaeology.* Cambridge: Cambridge University Press.

Basso, K. 1971 Anthropological Strategy. *Science* 171: 996–7.

Bernard, H. R., P. J. Pelto, O. Werner, J. Boster, A. K. Romney, A. Johnson, C. Johnson, and A. Kasakoff 1986 The Construction of Primary Data in Cultural Anthropology. *Current Anthropology* 27: 382–96.

Binford, L. 1983 *Working at Archaeology.* New York: Academic Press.

1987a Data, Relativism and Archaeological Science. *Man* 22: 391–404.

1987b Researching Ambiguity: Frames of Reference and Site Structure. In *Method and Theory for Activity Area Research*, edited by S. Kent, pp. 449–512. New York: Columbia University Press.

1988 Correspondence: Archaeology and Theory. *Man* 23: 374–6.

1991 When the Going Gets Tough, the Tough Get Going: Nunamiut Local Groups, Camping Patterns and Economic Organisation. In *Ethnoarchaeological Approaches to Mobile Campsites: Hunter–Gatherer and Pastoralist Case Studies*, edited by C. S. Gamble and W. A. Boismier, pp. 25–138. Ethnoarchaeological Series 1. Ann Arbor: International Monographs in Prehistory.

Braithwaite, M. 1982 Decoration as Ritual Symbol: A Theoretical Proposal and Ethnographic Study in Southern Sudan. In *Symbolic and Structural Archaeology*, edited by I. Hodder, pp. 80–8. Cambridge: Cambridge University Press.

Chang, C. 1988 Nauyalik Fish Camp: An Ethnoarchaeological Study in Activity Area Formation. *American Antiquity* 53: 145–57.

Collingwood, R. 1946 *The Idea of History.* Oxford: Oxford University Press.

David, N., J. Sterner, and K. Gavua 1988 Why Pots are Decorated. *Current Anthropology* 29: 365–89.

de Laguna, F. 1957 Some Problems of Objectivity in Ethnology. *Man* 228: 179–82.

Dunnell, R. 1986 Five Decades of American Archaeology. In *American Archaeology, Past and Future*, edited by E. Meltzer, D. Fowler, and J. Sabloff, pp. 23–48. Washington: Smithsonian Institution Press.

Earle, T. and R. Preucel 1987 Processual Archaeology and the Radical Critique. *Current Anthropology* 28: 501–38.

Freeman, L., A. K. Romney, and S. C. Freeman 1987 Cognitive Structure and Informant Accuracy. *American Anthropologist* 89: 310–25.

Geertz, C. 1973 *The Interpretation of Cultures*. New York: Basic Books, Inc.

Gjessing, G. 1975 Socio-archaeology. *Current Anthropology* 16: 323–41.

Gould, R. 1978 From Tasmania to Tucson: New Directions in Ethnoarchaeology. In *Explorations in Ethnoarchaeology*, edited by R. Gould, pp. 1–10. Albuquerque: University of New Mexico Press.

  1980 *Living Archaeology*. Cambridge: Cambridge University Press.

  1985 The Empiricist Strikes Back: Reply to Binford. *American Antiquity* 50: 638–44.

Gould, R. and M. Schiffer 1981 *Modern Material Culture: The Archaeology of Us*. New York: Academic Press.

Gould, R. and P. Watson 1982 A Dialogue on the Meaning and Use of Analogy in Ethnoarchaeological Reasoning. *Journal of Anthropological Archaeology* 4: 355–81.

Hassan, Fekri 1989 Review of Archaeology of Contextual Meanings. *American Anthropologist* 91: 255–6.

Hayden, B. and A. Cannon 1983 Where the Garbage Goes: Refuse Disposal in the Maya Highlands. *Journal of Anthropological Archaeology* 2: 117–63.

  1984 *The Structure of Material Systems: Ethnoarchaeology in the Maya Highlands*. SAA Papers No. 3. Washington, D.C.: Society for American Archaeology.

Hodder, I. 1982a *Symbols in Action*. Cambridge: Cambridge University Press.

  1982b (ed.) *Symbolic and Structural Archaeology*. Cambridge: Cambridge University Press.

  1985 Post-processual archaeology. *Advances in Archaeological Method and Theory*, Vol. VIII, edited by M. B. Schiffer, pp. 1–26. New York: Academic Press.

  1986 *Reading the Past*. London: B. T. Batsworth Ltd.

  1987a (ed.) *The Archaeology of Contextual Meanings*. Cambridge: Cambridge University Press.

  1987b The Contextual Analysis of Symbolic Meanings. In *The Archaeology of Contextual Meanings*, edited by I. Hodder, pp. 1–10. Cambridge: Cambridge University Press.

  1987c The Meaning of Discard: Ash and Domestic Space in Baringo. In *Method and Theory for Activity Area Analysis*, edited by S. Kent, pp. 424–48. New York: Columbia University Press.

  1989 Review of What is Archaeology? An Essay on the Nature of Archaeological Research, by Paul Courbin. *Journal of Field Archaeology* 16: 345–8.

Honigmann, J. and I. Honigmann 1955 Sampling Reliability in Ethnological Field Work. *Southwestern Journal of Anthropology* 11: 282–7.

Joyce, R. 1988 Comments on N. David *et al.* "Why Pots are Decorated." *Current Anthropology* 29: 383–4.

Keesing, R. 1989 Exotic Readings of Cultural Texts. *Current Anthropology* 20: 459–80.

Kelly, R. L. and L. C. Todd 1988 Coming into the Country: Early Paleoindian Hunting and Mobility. *American Antiquity* 53: 231–44.

Kent, S. 1987 Understanding the Use of Space: An Ethnoarchaeological Approach. In *Method and Theory for Activity Area Research*, edited by S. Kent, pp. 1–62. New York: Columbia University Press.

Kramer, C. 1979 Introduction. In *Ethnoarchaeology: Implications from Ethnography for Archaeology*, edited by Carol Kramer, pp. 1–20. New York: Columbia University Press.

Kramer, C. and J. E. Douglas 1992 Ceramics, Caste and Kin: Spatial Relations in Rajasthan, India. *Journal of Anthropological Archaeology* 11: 187–201.

Kristiansen, K. 1988 The Black and the Red: Shanks and Tilley's Programme for a Radical Archaeology. *Antiquity* 62: 473–82.

Larick, R. 1991 Warriors and Blacksmiths: Mediating Ethnicity in East African Spears. *Journal of Anthropological Archaeology* 10: 299–331.

Leach, E. 1977 A View from the Bridge. In *Archaeology and Anthropology*, edited by M. Spriggs, pp. 161–76. Oxford: BAR Supplementary Series 19.

Longacre, W. 1981 Kalinga Pottery: An Ethnoarchaeological Study. In *Pattern of the Past: Studies in Honour of David Clarke*, edited by I. Hodder, G. Isaac, and N. Hammond, pp. 49–66. Cambridge: Cambridge University Press.

Longacre, W. A. and M. T. Stark 1992 Ceramics, Kinship and Space: A Kalinga Example. *Journal of Anthropological Archaeology* 11: 125–36.

McNett, C. 1979 The Cross-cultural Method in Archaeology. In *Advances in Archaeological Method and Theory*, Vol. II, edited by M. B. Schiffer, pp. 39–76. New York: Academic Press.

Megaw, J. V. S. and M. R. Megaw 1988 Review of Archaeology of Contextual Meanings and Archaeology as Long-Term History, edited by I. Hodder. *Antiquity* 235: 392–4.

Miller, D. 1985 *Artefacts as Categories*. Cambridge: Cambridge University Press.

Miller, D. and C. Tilley 1984 Prehistory: An Introduction. In *Ideology, Power and Prehistory*, edited by D. Miller and C. Tilley, pp. 1–15. Cambridge: Cambridge University Press.

Nelson, B. A. 1991 Ceramic Frequency and Use-life: A Highland Mayan Case in Cross-cultural Perspective. In *Ceramic Ethnoarchaeology*, edited by W. A. Longacre, pp. 162–204. Tucson: University of Arizona Press.

O'Connell, J. F. 1987 Alyawara Site Structure and its Archaeological Implications. *American Antiquity* 52: 74–108.

O'Meara, J. T. 1989 Anthropology as Empirical Science. *American Anthropologist* 91: 354–69.

Pelto, N. 1970 *Anthropological Research: the Structure of Inquiry*. New York: Harper and Row Press.

Plog, S. and K. Richman 1983 Review of *Symbols in Action: Ethnoarchaeological Studies of Material Culture* by Ian Hodder. *American Anthropologist* 85: 718–20.

Raab, L. and A. Goodyear 1984 A Review of Middle-range Theory in Archaeology. *American Antiquity* 49: 255–68.

Renteln, A. D. 1988 Relativism and the Search for Human Rights. *American Anthropologist* 90: 56–72.

Rowlands, N. and J. Gledhill 1977 The Relations between Archaeology and Anthropology. In *Archaeology and Anthropology*, edited by M. Spriggs, pp. 143–60. Oxford: BAR Supplemental Series 19.

Salamone, F. 1979 Epistemological Implications of Fieldwork and their Consequences. *American Anthropologist* 51: 46–60.

Scheff, T. 1986 Toward Resolving the Controversy over "Thick Description." *Current Anthropology* 27: 408–10.

Schiffer, M. 1978 Methodological Issues in Ethnoarchaeology. In *Explorations in Ethnoarchaeology*, edited by R. Gould, pp. 229–47. Albuquerque: University of New Mexico Press.

1981 Some Issues in the Philosophy of Archaeology. *American Antiquity* 46: 899–908.

1987 *Formation Processes of the Archaeological Record*. Albuquerque: University of New Mexico Press.

1988 The Structure of Archaeological Theory. *American Antiquity* 53: 461–85.

Schrire, C. 1984 Wild Surmises on Savage Thoughts. In *Past and Present in Hunter–Gatherer Studies*, edited by C. Schrire, pp. 1-26. New York: Academic Press.

Shanks, M. and C. Tilley 1987 *Social Theory and Archaeology*. Oxford: Polity Press.

1989 Archaeology into the 1990s. *Norwegian Archaeological Review* 22: 1–14.

Siegel, P. E. and P. G. Roe 1986 Shipibo Archaeo-ethnography: Site Formation Processes and Archaeological Interpretation. *World Archaeology* 18: 96–115.

Simms, S. R. 1992 Ethnoarchaeology: Obnoxious Spectator, Trivial Pursuit, or the Keys to a Time Machine? In *Quandaries and Quests: Visions of Archaeology's Future*, edited by L. Wandsnider, pp. 186–98. Occasional Paper No. 20. Carbondale, Illinois: Center for Archaeological Investigations, Southern Illinois University.

Spaulding, A. 1953a Statistical Techniques for the Discovery of Artifact Types. *American Antiquity* 18: 305–14.

1953b A Review of Ford's "Measurements of Some Prehistoric Design Developments in the Southeastern States." *American Anthropologist* 55: 588–91.

Stark, B. 1985 Archaeological Identification of Pottery Production Locations: Ethnoarchaeological and Archaeological Data in Mesoamerica. In *Decoding Prehistoric Ceramics*, edited by B. Nelson, pp. 158–94. Carbondale: Southern Illinois University Press.

Steward, J. 1942 The Direct Historical Approach to Archaeology. *American Antiquity* 7: 337–43.

Stone, G. D. 1992 Social Distance, Spatial Relations, and Agricultural Production among the Kofyar of Namu District, Plateau State, Nigeria. *Journal of Anthropological Archaeology* 11: 152–72.

Strong, W. 1936 Anthropological Theory and Archaeological Fact. In *Essays in Anthropology in Honor of Alfred Louis Kroeber*, edited by R. Lowie, pp. 359–70. Berkeley: University of California.

Sutro, L. D. 1991 Where the River Comes: Refuse Disposal in Diaz Ordaz, Oaxaca. In *The Ethnoarchaeology of Refuse Disposal*, edited by E. Staski and L. D. Sutro, pp. 13–22. Anthropological Research Papers No. 42. Tempe: Arizona State University.

Thompson, R. 1956 The Subjective Element in Archaeological Inference. *Southwestern Journal of Anthropology* 12: 327–32.

Tilley, C. 1982 Social Formation, Social Structures and Social Change. In *Symbolic and Structural Archaeology*, ed. by I. Hodder, pp. 26–38. Cambridge: Cambridge University Press.

Trigger, B. 1978 *Essays in Archaeological Interpretation*. Edinburgh: Edinburgh University Press.

1989a *A History of Archaeological Thought*. Cambridge: Cambridge University Press.

1989b Comments on Archaeology into the 1990s. *Norwegian Archaeological Review* 22: 28–31.

Wandiba, S. 1988 On why Pots are Decorated the Way They Are. *Current Anthropology* 29: 740–1.

Washburn, W. 1987 A Critical View of Critical Archaeology. *Current Anthropology* 28: 544–5.

Watson, P., S. LeBlanc, and C. Redman 1984 *Archaeological Explanation: The Scientific Method in Archaeology*. New York: Columbia University Press.

Welbourn, A. 1984 Endo Ceramics and Power Strategies. In *Ideology, Power and Prehistory*, edited by D. Miller and C. Tilley, pp. 17–24. Cambridge: Cambridge University Press.

Wobst, H. M. 1978 The Archaeo-ethnography of Hunter–gatherers or the Tyranny of the Ethnographic Record in Archaeology. *American Antiquity* 43: 303–9.

Wylie, A. 1982 An Analogy by Any Other Name is Just as Analogical: A Commentary on the Gould–Watson Dialogue. *Journal of Anthropological Archaeology* 1: 382–401.

1985 The Reaction against Analogy. *Advances in Archaeological Method and Theory* 8: 63–112. New York: Academic Press.

Yellen, J. 1977a *Archaeological Approaches to the Present*. New York: Academic Press.

1977b Cultural Patterning in Faunal Remains: Evidence from the !Kung Bushmen. In *Experimental Archaeology*, edited by D. Ingersoll, J. Yellen, and W. MacDonald, pp. 271–331. New York: Columbia University Press.

9

Communication and the importance of disciplinary communities: who owns the past?

TIM MURRAY

Since the 1960s archaeology has become more disputatious than at any other time in its history. Practitioners openly debate conceptual and epistemological issues which lie at the core of the discipline. Archaeology exhibits such internal dissension that we are entitled to ask whether there are any disciplinary cultural norms left, whether there are any bedrock goals and understandings that can survive such disputation, and whether these norms of disciplinary behavior are necessary for there to be a productive future for the discipline. By extension, if what has served in the past as a basis for discourse is outmoded, can we replace it with a new account of disciplinary approach and purpose which facilitates communication and recognizes the diversity of the community of producers and consumers of archaeological knowledge?

Ironically, the prime cause of dissension, a positivist move to establish firmly that archaeology could be both scientific and relevant to the analysis of human affairs, was seen by its proponents as having the clear potential to *reduce* dispute by providing a generally agreed-upon basis for archaeological logic, archaeological epistemology, and archaeological ontology. Instead of this, our contemporary experience is of debates where archaeological logic is contextual, where archaeological epistemology veers wildly between varieties of positivism and relativism, and where archaeological ontology is a quicksand of mutually exclusive "common-sense" propositions about human behavior and the nature and significance of the archaeological record (see for example Patrik 1985; Sabloff *et al.* 1987). Overarching these debates is a more general question: is archaeology no more than methodologically distinct from other disciplines involved in the analysis of human affairs? If this is the case,

does the discipline really need a distinctively archaeological logic, epistemology, or ontology?

Archaeologists have been forcefully made aware of an increasing diversity of approach and purpose which may be directly sourced to the wide variety of interests held by practitioners, and to significant variations in the social and cultural conditions of practice. It is worth noting that this wide range of interests probably always existed among practitioners and the public audience of archaeology, but that the presence of such divergence was masked by a general adherence to positivist epistemologies, where (to follow the rhetoric) objectivity was both the guarantor of, and guaranteed by, the process of doing science.

Significantly, we now have increasing evidence, drawn from newer histories of archaeology (Murray 1987, 1989a; Trigger 1989), that, notwithstanding the positivist rhetoric of nineteenth-century archaeology, practitioners made judgements based primarily on the cognitive plausibility of rival knowledge claims. In other words, archaeologists consistently violated their own explicit epistemological and methodological principles, doing so without penalty because they were delivering culturally meaningful science to their colleagues and to the general public. It is worth noting that there are no good grounds to reject a claim that much the same situation obtains among all the varieties of contemporary archaeology. Furthermore, while the number of interest groups has multiplied and the determination of cognitive plausibility has become somewhat more complicated, the traditional disjunction between rhetoric and practical performance remains a powerful force in contemporary archaeology. In this sense, critical self-reflection is generally applied only to those programs we disagree with (Binford 1987; Shanks and Tilley 1987, 1990)!

With the collapse of positivism in archaeology, and the growth of a more widespread understanding of the theory-ladenness of observation and the nature of science as a social and cultural product, practitioners have begun to find most of the core concepts and categories of archaeology to be deeply problematic. Furthermore, much of its disciplinary agenda seems to be an artifact of nineteenth-century preoccupations with ethnicity and succession, and the bulk of its concepts and categories seem to be retained mainly because of institutional inertia and an absence of alternatives, rather than because of any real utility.

The same sense of problem clearly applies to a more general concern about the social and political consequences of archaeological knowledge claims. Some practitioners are, for example, clearly troubled by a posited link between positivism, functionalism/systems thinking, and conservative ideologies underwriting neocolonialism, the creation of national mythologies, and attacks on liberty (see, for example, Hodder 1984; Shanks and Tilley 1987, 1990: 5). While archaeologists have long understood that archaeo-logical knowledge can have significant cultural and political ramifications (see, for example, J. Allen 1987; Childe 1933; Silberman 1982), these new attitudes express a more encompassing disquiet, a feeling that archaeology will remain a catspaw as long as its practitioners fail to under-stand the fact that doing archaeology is a political act (see especially Shanks and Tilley 1990).

Other practitioners reject what they see as a clear link between science and a constraint on the exploration of new meanings (hence new bases of relevance) for archaeological data. In this account, challenging new ideas and approaches, being archaeologically underdeveloped, are difficult to nurture when their empirical content is either low or questionable, and their appeal rests firmly on cognitive plausibility. To go further, challenges to the existing fabric of archaeology generally come from the politically less powerful (nonetheless, successful challengers generally survive to assume positions of power). Consequently we are presented with a devastating scenario: no political power, conviction seemingly based more on ideology than archae-ology, underdeveloped theoretical apparatuses with few unambiguous empirical consequences. Given this kind of outcome, is it any wonder that some practitioners reject those disciplinary structures which seem (to them) to exclude the development of an archaeology that is relevant to their contemporary needs?

These objections raise related divergences stemming from the fact that archaeology is also a social institution, it socializes practitioners, it enculturates them (see Murray 1987: Chapter 1). Tensions based on conflicts between disciplinary traditions and contemporary concerns (see, for example, Conkey and Spector 1984; Ehrenburg 1989), age and gender differences, differential access to publication venues, grant moneys, and employment opportunities, and a wide variety of political and cultural agendas, all constantly throw up new interests and combinations of interests among practitioners and their audience. Reaction to this state of affairs is also varied. In some quarters it is felt that these sectional interests may have supplanted a belief in "objective" archaeology – that the achievement of contem-porary political goals has become more important than a credible expansion of our understanding of human behavior, leading to a reduction in the reliability of archaeologists' knowledge claims (e.g., J. Allen 1987; Binford 1987). In other assessments, the very fact that practitioners see no necessary break between doing archaeology and living in society is a cause for celebration rather than alarm, a guarantee that the discipline continues to be relevant and will

therefore survive into the next generation (albeit in an altered state).

Added to this is an increasing divergence of interest and approach among our *non-professional* audience. This divergence spans the gamut of views about the reliability of archaeological knowledge claims, the elitism of knowledge commodified by practitioners and controlled for the advancement of archaeologists, the "objectivity" of archaeologists, and the ease (or difficulty) with which archaeological statements can be incorporated into personal world views (Chippindale 1986).

The significance and power of cultural resources management (CRM) archaeology has also multiplied points of divergence within the discipline (e.g. Lipe 1984). While archaeologists may cherish a growing pluralism in approach and purpose, or perhaps simply recognize that the old order has been shaken and that we may well be living through a chaotic period before the new order emerges, the managers of cultural resources understand that divergence can have negative outcomes. Decisions made by managers, based on significance assessments and balancing other land-use options, obviously affect the physical parameters of the archaeological record they bequeath to our successors. Furthermore, in most instances those decisions can lead to litigation. Consequently management decisions have to be defensible, explicable, and empirically justifiable.

Again, while it may be possible that older approaches have no greater credibility than newer ones, the fact remains that this environment tends to give an advantage to conven-tional approaches to archaeology, simply because they do not challenge traditional and popular understandings of the nature and significance of the archaeological record. This greater (frequently undeserved) credibility may act to structure the archaeological record available to future generations in such a way as to constrain further the poten-tial for different accounts of the past to be proposed, and for different disciplinary approaches to be developed. Notwith-standing this concern, managers also have a more pressing worry: how to find a way of convincing other interest groups that divergences within archaeology do not indicate a conflict between *equally improbable* accounts which provide no justification for claims of significance.

Finally, there are distinct regional traditions within archaeology (Trigger and Glover 1981; Trigger 1989). The genesis of such traditions is still not clearly understood, but they are probably the product of a complex interplay between sociopolitical contexts and the nature of the archaeological record in different parts of the world. These different kinds of disciplinary contexts have also tended to inspire their own subdisciplinary standards and preoccu-pations. It is, for example, very difficult to convince an archaeologist who is confronted with a record of 32,000 years of human action in 80 cm of deposit that he or she should pursue an analysis of paleoideology. By the same token the excavators of the ruins of 19th century factory housing would reject the explanatory repertoire of lower paleolithic archaeology as being wholly reductionist and dehumanized. Can we then properly speak of archaeology being more than a congeries of data collection and reduction methodologies, given that its theoretical instruments and its underlying principles have to deal with widely differing analytical contexts spanning several millions of years? Furthermore, given all this divergence, is it realistic to speak of a community of archaeologists, or are we really observing shifting patterns of relationship between many communities which either happen to number archaeologists among their members or have an interest in the data and issues habitually discussed by archaeologists?

The advent of a world prehistory (a direct consequence of radiometric dating) has, when linked to the ever-broadening world-wide cultural and political milieu in which it is practiced, also placed great pressure on the previous consensus about goals and approaches which derived from European and North American records and preoccupations. By the same token it also sets limits to the power of critiques of traditional archaeology. For example, notwithstanding the appeal of the scenario painted by Shanks and Tilley of an unholy alliance between positivism, universalism, and Thatcherism, the fact remains that in other parts of the world traditional archaeology (and its radical critiques) operate in dramatically different cultural and political contexts (Gathercole and Lowenthal 1989; Layton, ed. 1989a, 1989b). The danger here is to continue the tradition of colonial science and have the specificities of these local contexts excised in favor of the view from the first world. In this sense there is some opposition to the notion that *Antiquity*, *American Antiquity*, *Academic Press*, or *Cambridge University Press* "owns" the past.

In this paper I want briefly to explore some of the implications of this increasing diversity of approach and viewpoint among the producers and consumers of archaeological knowledge for the construction and constitution of archaeological theory. While we might be able to enumerate some of the more prominent sources of divergence, it is a more complex matter to identify and address their consequences. I have chosen to concentrate on one small aspect of the loss of disciplinary innocence, or as Wildersen (1984) might put it, the attainment of disciplinary maturity – claims for ownership of the past made by post-colonial peoples. Naturally, the question of who owns the past can be asked of anyone, archaeologist or aboriginal person. Clearly aboriginal peoples are not the only ones who feel that their

voice is not being heard, and I will return to a broader construal of ownership and interest in the closing sections of this paper.

I will argue that all claims about ownership of the past direct our attention to two pressing questions in theoretical archaeology. First, whether a relativist account of archaeological epistemology can be sustained, and second, whether contemporary archaeology, notwithstanding the presence of divergence, can communicate with itself and with the rest of the world in a way which will enhance the potential for the discipline to make a significant contribution to human self-perception. The resolution of both questions is clearly beyond the scope of this paper, but I will seek to use debates about ownership of pasts and presents (and their means of production) to further an understanding of the consequences of diversity within disciplinary communities.

Some general issues

It is a commonplace that "Who owns the past" is a difficult problem, made worse by the fact that it is a rarely-mastered trick to defend the archaeologist's right to investigate the past without running the risk of being accused of positivistic or neocolonialist leanings. The major problem here is that there are other histories, other ways of knowing about the past, other senses in which past and present link together in a kind of seamless web, but that these alternatives to archaeology are generally the domain of the disenfranchised or less-powerful. Thus to assert the rights of archaeology and its practitioners is taken to imply a denial of other rights and interests. Added to this is the implication that archaeology is colonial science and, as such, its practice enhances the domination of colonial culture, because that which *produces* the past and *controls* its dissemination, *owns* the past.

I reject this implication, although it would be pointless to deny that archaeologists have been insensitive to and perhaps simply disinterested in alternative histories. Practitioners have been reminded by governments, by their colleagues, and by minority groupings that their discipline (or at least their discipline with its current set of preoccupations) is not the only route to an understanding of the past, and that practitioners should understand that alternative pasts (i.e. those produced by indigenes, minority groups, women, the disenfranchised) are valuable and meaningful and should be respected as such.

Indeed, we have seen above that there is no monolithic archaeological past – rather a myriad of pasts produced by archaeologists of various persuasions and by the public. Such alternative pasts (archaeological ones included) become the touchstones of community identity; in other words they are both the products and the producers of community identity. It is also important to remember that pasts are always debatable, and that these debates are not abstracted from everyday life – they are an essential part of it.

By the same token some commentators, perhaps overcome by a desire to make amends for past insensitivities, have produced accounts which subtly privilege these alternative pasts by rehearsing the links between our discipline and imperialism, racism, and the silencing/ suppression of minorities on the grounds of gender, political persuasion, class, or race (see, for example, Layton 1989). Such accounts have tended to emphasize conflicts between archaeology and these alternative pasts which have centered around struggles to "own" or control the physical resources from which such pasts are held to be produced. Post-colonial peoples typically identify a control over the physical remains of pasts with a control over the production of interpretation *about* those pasts (H. Allen 1988; Layton 1989; Mulvaney 1986, 1989).

These are serious matters raising issues of censorship, objectivity, and sensibility which have appeared in other arenas, such as general anthropology, in the post-colonial period (Berreman 1974; Palmer 1987; Sutton 1986; Valentine 1975). While it may be a nonsense to speak of owning the past, given that the past does not exist in ownable form, the fact remains that the right or ability to produce and disseminate accounts of the past can be constrained by law, custom, the existence of socially sanctioned competitors, and by financial resources. Although it would be wrong to claim that a denial of access to physical resources would silence unpopular interpretations, it would most definitely privilege those interpretations which could engage more directly with physical data. By the same token, poorly resourced alternative pasts are difficult to produce, let alone disseminate.

There is no need to multiply examples of how pasts have served national ends and suited cultural preoccupations (McBryde 1985a; Fowler 1987; Gathercole and Lowenthal 1989; Groube 1985; Murray 1989a, 1989b; Trigger 1980, 1984). *What is more important is to understand how post-colonial peoples have construed ownership, why a control over interpretation is so important to them, and to investigate strategies for reconciling potential hostility between archaeologists and those peoples.* The remainder of this paper will be directed towards a discussion of those issues.

It is time that we defined the issues which have and continue to cause conflict between the science of archaeology and the Aboriginal people. To date, the issues have been confused; archaeologists feel unfairly criticised and feel hurt because they say they are doing their best to develop an understanding of our culture, and we are angry because we are treated to token moves to obtain our approval and consent to what you are doing.

The issue is control. You seek to say that as scientists you have a right to obtain and study information of our culture. You seek to say that because you are Australians you have a right to study and explore our heritage because it is a heritage to be shared by all Australians, white and black. From our point of view we say that you have come as invaders, you have tried to destroy our culture, you have built your fortunes on the land and bodies of our people and now, having said sorry, want a share in picking out the bones of what you regard as a dead past. We say that it is our past, our culture and heritage, and forms part of our present life. As such it is ours to control and it is ours to share on our terms. That is the Central Issue in this debate. (Langford 1983: 2)

R. F. Langford's powerful statement outlining what she considers to be the rights of Australian Aboriginal people to own their heritage has been echoed in the councils of indigenous peoples all over the world (see, for example, Condori, 1989; Richardson 1989; Hammil and Cruz 1989). It is a clear and unequivocal statement of a perspective which emphasizes the right of indigenous peoples to retain (regain?) control of their identities, by controlling the products (both past and present) of those identities. There is also a straightforward explanation for this desire to control – it is the product of long periods of cultural and political oppression, denigration, and exclusion, continuing with recent experience of a more subtle colonialism, where aspects of indigenous identities are being defined and articulated by dominant colonial cultures. Aboriginal ownership (or control) of the physical remains of the past has also been seen as a way for Aboriginal people to learn management and administrative skills, to gain an "insider's view" of bureaucracies, and to gain employment and financial returns from the management of heritage.

In essence claims of ownership reflect a widespread rejection of a relationship with colonial culture which controls both the pasts and the presents of indigenous peoples and replaces them with a spurious nationalism or multiculturalism. In Australia this rhetoric is exemplified in statements by European Australians that Aboriginal people are Australians first, and Aboriginal people second, or that in a multicultural Australia, Aboriginal identity is equivalent to ethnic identity. These statements include the kind of catchall rhetoric which argues anti-racism and internationalism by stating that the objects or contexts of concern are not the heritage of a particular group but a common human heritage (see, for example, Mulvaney 1986, 1989). Aboriginal people have not been the only ones to note that these kinds of assertions are generally made by those in power or by those of the dominant cultural group who want something the less powerful are keeping from them by ethical arguments of a different kind (H. Allen 1988; Bowdler 1988; Langford 1983).

But the matter is more complex than this. Anthropologists and archaeologists act as representatives of the dominant culture in two ways. First, they are, in the main, part of that culture and therefore pursue archaeological and anthropological puzzles and problems generated by tradition and experience (the nineteenth-century emphasis on racial and cultural typology and socio-cultural evolution is an example). Second, practitioners act as validators of what is worth knowing and indeed knowable about indigenous pasts and presents because they are widely believed (by other members of the dominant culture) to produce objective, reliable, scientific knowledge about those pasts and presents. Indeed, very often archaeology and anthropology provide the instruments with which indigenous peoples are *understood* by other members of society (sometimes even by Aboriginal peoples themselves).

Consequently, indigenous peoples living in countries like Australia, Canada, the United States of America, and New Zealand frequently control neither their pasts, their presents, nor indeed the language of communication about themselves. Attempts made to establish new ways of communicating about collective experiences frequently fall foul of European rules of spelling, terminology, or categorization. For example, the very concepts powering much of the conflict between archaeology, anthropology, and indigenous peoples – identity, continuity, and survival – are seen by the non-indigenous community as being inherently problematic. One could lose count of the debates between the "professionals" about the meaningfulness/lessness of concepts like ethnicity (Keefe 1988 and references; Palmer 1987). Yet those concepts are absolutely central to the indigenous position.

Identity is a complex (and endlessly debatable) concept and indigenous peoples have stressed survival and continuity as two of its most crucial elements. It is worth remembering that this is no abstract difference of opinion about identity and arguments for its justification. Claims for control over land and resources are involved, as are perhaps more deeply rooted emic issues. Can one ever justify to outsiders what is simply "natural" to insiders? On the other hand is it proper to speak of a continuous Aboriginal culture in Australia since the first occupation of Sahul some 50,000 years ago?

Australian archaeologists are perplexed by such notions, especially when all the available evidence indicates great change in Aboriginal culture over the history of human occupation of the continent. What do these changes mean if not some notion of cultural discontinuity, replacement, change of essence or extinction? Aboriginal people see it differently. All evidence of change and variation is evidence that Aboriginal societies have histories, and there can be no inheritors of these cultural traditions other than contemporary Aboriginal people – even if many of them no longer lead traditional lives.

Consequently an assertion of Aboriginality, and a desire to control the very production of identity so that Aboriginal people can recreate themselves, lie at the heart of claims for ownership of the past. Notwithstanding the fact that many archaeologists and anthropologists have sincerely worked for Aboriginal advancement and have become locked in conflict with their colleagues over issues of objectivity (Mulvaney 1986; Palmer 1987), archaeology has traditionally sought other goals and followed other concerns. But it is also true to say that archaeology and anthropology have provided a means by which non-Aboriginal people have begun to learn about Aboriginal society (Barlow 1985). This knowledge has done much to overcome the ignorance and disinterest which has obtained until recent years. Although there is a great deal of contested ground, surely some accommodation is possible?

An Australian perspective on ownership and control

> Aboriginal antiquities, now that they are useful to European society, are now taking on an importance that is far greater than any accorded to Aboriginal society while it existed in viable form. Has Aboriginal life dignity now that most Aborigines have left it? (H. Allen 1988: 86)

There is no single Australian perspective on the core issues of this paper, but it seems to me that a discussion of issues using some Australian examples should at the least reduce the impact of sermonizing about the commodification of the past and of there being an inevitable conflict between archaeologists and indigenous peoples about *whose* past and *what* past. Consultation with Aboriginal people is a legislative reality in all states if Australia (Ward 1985) and Aboriginal people are keen to develop their own accounts of Aboriginality (Atkinson *et al.* 1985; Keefe 1988; Palmer 1987).

While there have been major conflicts between archaeologists and aboriginal people, particularly over the excavation and reburial of skeletal materials (J. Allen 1983, 1987; Ewing 1990; Lewin 1984; Pardoe 1985; Webb 1987), consultation and legislative recognition of Aboriginal interest has tended to reduce the potential for hostility. Furthermore, notwithstanding the fact that the politics of heritage are fluid, there have been some shining examples of the recognition of mutual interest and regard in this heartland of stones-and-bones positivist archaeology.

Perhaps the most important of these have been the establishment of management data for the Kakadu world heritage area (H. Allen 1978; Jones 1985; Neijie 1984; Sullivan 1984); Pardoe's consultation with Aboriginal communities of the Murray–Darling Basin explaining the context of research on skeletal remains (Pardoe 1985); and the links forged between Tasmanian Aboriginal people and the archaeologists in their joint efforts to save the archaeological resources of southwest Tasmania (J. Allen 1983, 1987; McQueen 1983). These have been high-profile campaigns which express the significance of change in the fundamental context of Australian archaeology and anthropology, covering areas as diverse as consultation procedures (Davidson *et al.* 1983; Lewis and Rose 1985; Palmer 1987; Sullivan 1984; von Sturmer 1981), the design of data recording forms (Ward 1986), through to the promotion of research specifically requested by Aboriginal people (Egloff 1981; Ucko 1983).

All Australian governments have enacted legislation which seeks to conserve cultural aspects of the natural estate through close consultation with Aboriginal people and other interested parties, but Aboriginal *ownership* of Aboriginal culture and heritage is recognized in only one State of Australia. The core provisions of the Aboriginal and Torres Strait Islander Heritage Protection Amendment Act 1987 reveal a number of significant tensions which relate to the point about the overarching importance of the political context of land rights and heritage.

> WHEREAS it is expedient to make provision for the preservation of the Aboriginal cultural heritage of Victoria:
>
> AND WHEREAS the Government of Victoria acknowledges:
>
> (a) the occupation of Victoria by the Aboriginal people before the arrival of Europeans;
>
> (b) the importance to the Aboriginal people and to the wider community of the Aboriginal culture and heritage;
>
> (c) that the Aboriginal people of Victoria are the rightful owners of their heritage and should be given responsibility for its future control and management;
>
> (d) the need to make provision for the preservation of objects and places of religious, historical or cultural significance to the Aboriginal people;

> (e) the need to accord appropriate status to Aboriginal elders and communities in their role of protecting the continuity of the culture and heritage of the Aboriginal people:
>
> AND WHEREAS the Government of Victoria has requested the Parliament of the Commonwealth to enact an Act in terms of this Act:
>
> AND WHEREAS the Commonwealth does not acknowledge the matters acknowledged by the Government of Victoria, but has agreed to the enactment of such an Act (pp. 1–2).

The first tension has to do with the fact that this Act could not be passed through the Victorian state parliament, due to the opposition of conservative parliamentarians in the Upper House. While voting essentially conformed to party lines, conservative opposition largely centered around objections to affirmative action and the need to protect the interests of the farming lobby. In this sense the notion of Aboriginal ownership of *sites* (as parcels of land) could be used as a *de facto* recognition of land rights.

The second tension has to do with the different constraints (Aboriginal and European) of the concept of heritage. Debate here centers around issues of continuity and identity. Is Aboriginal heritage part of a living tradition, or are the bits and pieces of it protected under legislation, the physical remnants of what was once a living society? Furthermore, which source of information about the meanings of such items is the most reliable – the archaeologist's "objectivity," or the Aboriginal person's mythologizing about a past that they have no real memory of (Johnson 1983)?

This is necessarily a fairly crude pastiche of some complicated arguments, but the core of the dispute – a conflict between authorities – is close to the mark. Therefore, while there has been great progress within the practice of Australian archaeology in the areas of consultation and training, deep-seated conflicts of this kind can still produce outcomes which would simply be stupid if they were not so insulting (Mowljarlai and Peck 1987; see also Bowdler 1988). They can also lead to head-on clashes between the parties over the fate of skeletal remains which may well be tens of thousand of years old. Does the continuity of culture also involve the application of contemporary Aboriginal notions of reverence for the dead to these human remains?

> However, in relation to Aboriginal sites, prehistorians are placed in another bind. Even at the risk of a new paternalism, prehistorians are obliged to inform Aboriginal owners about the significance and meaning of much ancestral data. Due to cultural and population changes through time, for example, sites of great archaeological

significance possess no traditional or current community relevance, or their ancient art forms are meaningless (Mulvaney 1979: 213).

Mulvaney's comments clearly emphasize an element of cultural essentialism which is the flip side of arguments about continuity and identity. Again, while it is quite probable that many archaeological sites were unknown to contemporary Aboriginal people prior to their analysis by archaeologists, and equally probable that contemporary Aboriginal people would not necessarily be uniquely qualified in interpreting the meaning of such sites, it is nonetheless equally true that the significance archaeologists might attach to those sites need not necessarily be the same as that established by Aboriginal people.

The same observation applies to skeletal remains where the strength of an Aboriginal interest is more widely recognized and acted upon. There have been cases of repatriation, and there are also extremely strict guide-lines issued by government departments and grant-awarding bodies. Yet should all these legislative and administrative remedies allow contemporary Aboriginal people to rebury the remains of their ancestors – even if they are thousands of years old? It is absolutely characteristic of the complexities of the issue to say that there is no simple yes or no answer, and certainly no way of maintaining a thoroughly consistent position.

On the one hand if we accept that contemporary Aboriginal people are the inheritors of a living culture some 50,000 years old, then we cannot deny them the right to protect the remains of their ancestors. On the other hand, the argument for cultural continuity is largely one of assertion, and if taken seriously could entail the enforced reburial of all skeletal material from the Australopithecines onwards simply because a group of individuals felt that their cultural prohibitions against the disturbance of mortal remains were being flouted. The second position is obviously an extreme one, but it does make the point that if cultures, though continuous, are dynamic, then current cultural preoccupations may mean permanent loss to the descendants of this generation of Aboriginal people – the very first who have had to confront such issues.

Although this view entails a recognition of European notions of change, history, and succession, future Aboriginal culture may well be the product of such a cultural accommodation. The point is that we cannot predict the future course of any culture, but to argue that it should remain as today would surely seal its fate. That is why the compromise position – reinterment in a keeping place under the control of Aboriginal people – can be (and has been) developed. Such compromise positions can arise and be implemented only when the disputing parties effectively recognize that other interests are also legitimate, and where the parties are prepared to communicate.

Aboriginal communities have taken the challenge of defending their interest in their heritage seriously enough for this issue to be a major focus of Aboriginal politics. In Australia the link between heritage and identity has been fostered in an environment where self-determination has been very difficult to achieve. As Palmer (1987: 87–8) points out, Aboriginal people have never become economically or politically independent from European society. As such there have always been practical limitations to the extent of self-determination, notwithstanding the rhetoric of Aboriginal and white politicians. This struggle for control and for self-definition has spawned the emphasis on ownership of the past, because it has been felt that a control over the physical aspects of pasts confers a control over what can be said or written about those pasts. At least here, it is argued, Aboriginal people can defend themselves and gain status as having worthwhile knowledge and expertise.

But there is a high price to pay for such control, or indeed ownership, and this refers to the responsibilities of power. Leaving aside the matter of skeletal remains, any attempts at censorship of unpopular people or opinions, or the extension of claims of control or ownership to claims that only Aboriginal people should write Aboriginal history or archaeology, might give the illusion of power and value, but they have the more devastating effect of closing off communication and losing Aboriginal people a moral ascendancy in Australian society. It is, of course, bitterly ironic that Aboriginal people have themselves been the victims of similar abuses of power.

> Along with the Aboriginal historians I accept that Aboriginal people "are the guardians and custodians of our history and culture, and it is our responsibility to pass onto future generations our set of truths." If, however, those guardians and custodians also act as gaolers, while claiming infallibility in interpreting their source materials, based upon race, totalitarianism is just down the road (Mulvaney 1986: 56).

This is all well and good, but the requirement for access and understanding clearly has to cut both ways. At present Aboriginal people are beginning to gain a greater insight into the nature and purpose of archaeology, mainly because consultation is occurring. Furthermore, many Aboriginal people regularly gain employment working as informants, consultants, and field crew for archaeological research projects. Aboriginal people are also studying archaeology at the tertiary level and managing cultural resources. So communication is occurring, views are being more clearly expressed, and the intentions of both groups are somewhat better understood. Whether this can be considered to be a dialogue is another matter. European archaeologists perceive that Aboriginal people do not read the past as they do, but few archaeologists engage those divergent perceptions in a way which might feed back into their own interpretations. It is also difficult for practitioners to accept that Aboriginal people might seek to construct their own (different) stories for sites excavated and analysed by archaeologists, and that these stories might show scant regard for the knowledge claimed by practitioners.

Consequently some elements of dispute remain, as they are likely to do when the past is contested ground, and when there is so much at stake for Aboriginal people. The maintenance and extension of dialogue between the parties is one crucial pathway towards resolving outstanding matters. Another, related, pathway stems from an understanding of *how* divergent perceptions are generated. In this sense it is simply not enough to say that we are all socially constructed. What we need to do is to understand how, and what effect, particular modern social constructions have on the production of knowledge about the past. While it may be true that conflicts over interpretation will probably be inevitable, at least we should understand the bases of such conflicts and recognize the legitimacy of rights and interests other than our own. An effective dialogue of this kind may well allow us an alternative to a created "Australianness" based on a subsumption of an Aboriginal past into a spurious national past, and thus perform a valuable service to our fellow citizens, both European and Aboriginal.

Some aspects of relativism and disciplinary communities

We have seen that one of the central issues raised by the question: Who owns the past? is that of the place of relativism within the philosophy of archaeology. One of the core features of what has been described as (self-) critical archaeology, post-modernist/post-processual archaeology, or even post-positivist philosophy of science, is an active engagement with relativism (Shanks and Tilley 1987; Hollis and Lukes 1982; Bhaskar 1989; Feyerabend 1987). The heightened interest in relativism is not a sign of disciplinary paralysis. Rather it is a demonstration of maturity and vigor as philosophers and archaeologists work through the implications of Wittgenstein's observations on language and forms of life, the perception that there are minds and cultures other than our own, and the fact that archaeologists and philosophers as practitioners seek to recreate their disciplines in ways which are more personally meaningful. Thus the proliferation of interests and the contemporary focus on relativism are both cause and product of one another.

The real problem seems to lie in claims that relativism entails that judgements must be arbitrary and that there exist no viable means of deciding between alternative views. Practitioners are presented with the specter of an archaeology where there exists no rational basis for judgement about the merits of knowledge claims, and no strong foundation for management of the archaeological record so that it might continue to provide a focus for debate between practitioners, and between practitioners and other groups who have an interest in the archaeological past. In this account, the discipline is at the mercy of political forces, forces which may use censorship (or political and economic domination) to produce pasts which ultimately serve only as the bases of mythologies rather than as frameworks wherein we might expand our understanding of humanity by challenging those taken-for-granteds which structure our experience (see Murray 1987).

Notwithstanding the fact that the history of archaeology exhibits many examples of manipulation and mythologizing, which were the products of positivism rather than relativism, the prospect of censorship, domination, or arbitrary judgement should give no one, archaeologist or indigenous person, any comfort. What seems to be at stake here is the absence of any overarching "objective" calculus of rules and procedures which would ensure that we would all agree about what meaningful and valuable accounts of the past would look like. Indeed, one of the lessons we can draw from the current debates between archaeologists and post-colonial peoples is that concepts and categories such as past, present, and future (along with time) are not cross-culturally valid. Agreement is thus an unlikely prospect while mutual understanding is still rare and difficult to achieve.

Of course all groups that have an interest in the past have bases for judgement about the virtues of accounts produced either by their own members or by others. Judgement may result from the application of a wide range of tests: conformity to cultural, ideological, or religious tenets; political utility; ease of exposition to lay publics; empirical fruitfulness; refutability; confirmability; cognitive plausibility; elegance, synoptic power. There are many others. Naturally all interested parties do not agree about which of these tests is the most convincing, or the most powerful. By the same token, few would be foolhardy enough to argue that their chosen test is entirely problem-free and necessarily privileged under all conditions (Murray 1990).

There is no need to argue that a relativist epistemology is the natural or appropriate theory of archaeological knowledge, and that all archaeological judgements need to be arbitrary or be ordained by ideological prejudice. Obviously practitioners and the general public need to understand how these judgements operate, and they need to understand some of the implications of whatever knowledge claims might arise from them. To go further, judgements that are broadly based, i.e. those that might include a number of tests, probably carry increased conviction mainly because it is perceived that they have been more at risk.

Most important, however, is an understanding of the context of the knowledge claim itself – not of its justification, but of its discovery. Why we find some arguments convincing and others not usually has more to do with the traditions of archaeological research than with some philosophical calculus of explanation, or the political affiliations of the archaeologist concerned. Why else would archaeologists accept theories which, while they might be valuable in sociology or social anthropology, require really intensive redefinition before they can be sensibly applied to the bulk of archaeological contexts, and why does that development occur so rarely? Why indeed would archaeologists seriously discuss theories which have undimensioned empirical consequences, or are at such a tentative stage of development that viable test implications cannot even be proposed?

The answer lies, of course, within the culture of archaeology, and with the fact that archaeologists still produce culturally meaningful accounts of the past that neither effectively engage the past nor pass methodological muster. The fear of a past which may not be intelligible in the same terms as we understand present experience overcomes most objections to mythologizing and story-telling. Most of what passes for archaeological theory supplies scant basis for judgements over and above those of cultural or disciplinary tradition and cultural prejudice. Clearly we have a great deal to learn from the compromises effected between archaeologists and Aboriginal people.

Two points need emphasis. First, that much of our difficulty lies in accepting the special challenges of relativism – particularly that we must accept the responsibility as a community for making locally-rational judgements about issues which concern us. Here we see the problems which can arise in the absence of timeless philosophical verities, but also the possibilities which arise from negotiated epistemologies. Second, there is a real fondness for philosophical absolutes among the adherents of our current archaeological factions. For example, empiricism is absolutely bad, relativism is absolutely bad, functionalism is absolutely bad, or post-positivism is absolutely good.

This kind of talk is a nonsensical by-product of an overly reverent attitude to philosophy and philosophers. They play a different game than we do. For me an understanding of the history and sociology of archaeology provides the most solid foundation for the judgements we have to make as archaeologists. While I strongly support the legitimacy of a philosophical analysis of archaeology, I give equal support

to the notion that our goals as archaeologists might well require us to give philosophers something new to make rules about. Einstein put the argument clearly:

> No sooner has the epistemologist, who is seeking a clear system, fought his way through such a system, than he is inclined to interpret the thought content of science in the sense of his system, and to reject whatever does not fit into his system. The scientist, however, cannot afford to carry his striving for epistemological systematicity that far . . . ; the external conditions which are set for him by the facts of experience, do not permit him to let himself be too much restricted in the construction of his conceptual world by the adherence to an epistemological system. He therefore must appear to the systematic epistemologist as a type of unscrupulous opportunist (Feyerabend 1987: 189).

Archaeology is an evolving discipline, and the special challenges posed by the fact that there is no unified account of disciplinary approach and purpose, and by the fact that non-archaeologists have rights and interests in the archaeological past, are critical aspects of the context of disciplinary evolution. Significantly, while we might seek guidance on matters of theory and philosophy from a wide range of disciplines, and, through our membership of society, bring a desire to make the past meaningful in terms of our own lives and preoccupations, we should be clear that it is archaeologists, through their practice, who create the philosophy of archaeology. Building a community of archaeologists (whose primary commitment as archaeologists is the expansion of our understanding of humanity via archaeological analysis) from the myriad of communities of practitioners and consumers of archaeology is perhaps the greatest challenge of all.

Concluding remarks

In this paper I have attempted, albeit in a cursory (and polemical) way, to broaden the focus of discussion of a wide range of issues which can be shown to be directly related to core debates between archaeologists and aboriginal peoples about ownership of the past. Clearly the debates are extremely complex and it is probably a first mistake to speak in terms of monolithic interest groupings such as "indigenous peoples believe . . . ," or "Aboriginal people think . . . ," or "feminist archaeologists contend . . . ," or even "followers of critical theory in archaeology all claim . . . ," despite the superficial confidence it gives by convincing us we are dealing with manageable and predictable blocks of interest and interaction. Such amalgams clearly mask significant variation; they also serve as debating points in themselves, and thus deflect us from making much progress by committing us to an endless reinvention of the wheel.

Having said this, I think that it is all too easy to burlesque the proliferation of interest groups as being the result of a footrace among archaeologists, and between archaeologists and indigenes, to claim the moral high ground. Whatever the motives of the producers or consumers of archaeology, the fact remains that no formula account of the nature or purpose of archaeology (even allowing for agreement over whether there should even be a discipline of archaeology) is going to satisfy all parties now, or at any other time.

The history of archaeology is littered with examples of the suppression of disciplinary dissent, the manipulation of argument and principles and, most important, the culturally-sanctioned production of archaeological knowledge which violates the methodological principles of its producers. The broad issues briefly canvassed in this paper are frequently deeply personal and certainly fraught with dangerous inconsistencies even in the most fully self-realized individuals. But does the recognition of wide varieties of opinion and a sense that many of those opinions (no matter how deeply held) may be undisciplined (hence messy), mean that reaching a basis for action and mutual understanding is impossible?

I have argued that this is not the case, indeed, that it cannot be the case if archaeology is to survive. I have maintained that the most effective strategy for dealing with relativism is to foster communication, thereby more clearly establishing the grounds of dispute and forcing under-developed (or simply outmoded) approaches into the open. The same strategy applies to disputes which, while they may be superficially centered on a celebration of the right of interest groups to produce archaeological knowledge which accords with their particular ideological, cultural, or social preoccupations, have much more to do with a defence of positions from the possibility of disturbance by a thorough-going engagement with empirical data.

> I like visitors to come to Ubirr to look at the paintings and learn the stories about the paintings. The outside [or public stories] are good to tell visitors and are very good for children to know. It's good for *balanda* [white people] to learn about the Aboriginal way of life.
>
> Some *balanda* who come to Ubirr don't really understand what they see. They rush through the sites and then back to their buses. They don't stay long enough at the sites. How can they understand? Some ways to make them understand better are:
>
> 1. I would like more signs like the ones already at Ubirr to tell the *balanda* what the painting is and the Aboriginal story about the painting. But I would like

the *Gagadju* and other Aboriginal languages from around here on the signs as well as English. It's important that the right names are used.

> 2. The stories about my country should be made bigger. My family are the last people with the story for these places. I would like a big history book to be written where the stories could all be told. This could be sold to visitors. I think the *balanda* story about the old people [prehistory] could also be told in the book. (Neijie 1984: 41).

Bill Neijie is right, survival depends on being relevant and having a clear understanding of goals and purposes. In this sense a willingness to communicate, to learn, to develop theories and preoccupations to the extent where judgements can be broadly based, and to be critically self-reflective, may yet provide the basis of a versatile and relevant archaeology. I think these are positive options for us. However, they will come to nothing if archaeologists do not engage in critical self-reflection about all areas of their practice, particularly their disciplinary predisposition to borrow without development and to accept the historical position accorded archaeological knowledge on the cognitive map of the human sciences. It is high time that both were changed.

Part and parcel of this self-criticism is an examination of how our discipline behaves as a community. Here I mean both the good and potentially bad aspects of community behavior – codes of practice, language, professional standards, who we include and who we exclude, and the ways in which knowledge is both adjudicated and disseminated. Thus, conflicts between archaeologists and aboriginal people mirror conflicts among archaeologists about matters of identity and judgement. The stage is set for a more detailed sociology of archaeological knowledge and for this exploration to become a crucial element of a developing philosophy of archaeology.

References

Allen, Harry 1978 Training for a Career in Public Archaeology. *Australian Institute of Aboriginal Studies Newsletter* 10: 21–8.

1988 History Matters – A Commentary on Divergent Interpretations of Australian History. *Australian Aboriginal Studies* 1988(2): 79–89.

Allen, Jim 1983 Aborigines and Archaeologists in Tasmania, 1983. *Australian Archaeology* 16: 7-11.

1987 *The Politics of the Past*. Professorial Inaugural Address. La Trobe University, Bundoora, Victoria, Australia.

Atkinson, W., M. Langton, D. Wanganeen, and M. Williams 1985 A Celebration of Resistance to Colonialism. In *Black Australia* 2, edited by M. Mill and A. Barlow, pp. 14–22. Canberra: Australian Institute of Aboriginal Studies.

Australian Parliament 1987 *Aboriginal and Torres Strait Islander Heritage Protection Amendment Act.*

Barlow, A. 1985 Aboriginal Studies in Tertiary Australian Studies. *Australian Aboriginal Studies* 1985(2): 79–81.

Bernstein, R. J. 1983 *Beyond Objectivism and Relativism.* Oxford: Basil Blackwell.

Berreman, G. D. 1974 Bringing it all back home: Malaise in Anthropology. In *Reinventing Anthropology*, edited by D. Hymes, pp. 83–98. New York: Vintage Books.

Bhaskar, R. 1989 *Reclaiming Reality.* London: Verso.

Binford, L. R. 1987 Data, Relativism and Archaeological Science. *Man* 22: 391–404.

Bowdler, S. 1988 Repainting Australian Rock Art. *Antiquity* 62: 517–23.

Childe, V. G. 1933 Races, Peoples and Cultures in Pre-historic Europe. *History* 18: 193–203.

Chippindale, C. 1986 Stoned Henge: Events and Issues at the Summer Solstice, 1985. *World Archaeology* 18: 38–58.

Condori, C. M. 1989 History and Prehistory in Bolivia: What About the Indians? In *Conflict in the Archaeology of Living Traditions*, edited by R. Layton, pp. 46–59. London: Unwin Hyman.

Conkey, M. and J. D. Spector 1984 Archaeology and the Study of Gender. *Advances in Archaeological Method and Theory* 7: 1–38. New York: Academic Press.

Davidson, G., B. Hansford, and M. Moriarity 1983 Listening to Aborigines: Some Communication Requirements for Non-Aboriginal–Aboriginal Contact. *Australian Aboriginal Studies* 1983(1): 48–9.

Egloff, B. 1981 *Wreck Bay: an Aboriginal Fishing Community.* Canberra: Australian Institute of Aboriginal Studies.

Ehrenburg, M. 1989 *Women in Prehistory.* London: British Museum.

Ewing, T. 1990 Emphasis on "Aborigine Rights." *Nature* 344: 697.

Feyerabend, P. K. 1987 *Farewell to Reason.* London: Verso.

Fowler, D. 1987 Uses of the Past : Archaeology in the Service of the State. *American Antiquity* 52: 229–48.

Gathercole, P. and D. Lowenthal (eds.) 1989 *The Politics of the Past.* London: Unwin Hyman.

Groube, L. 1985 The Ownership of Diversity. In *Who Owns the Past?*, edited by I. McBryde, pp. 49–73. Melbourne: Oxford University Press.

Hammil, J. and R. Cruz 1989 Statement of American Indians before the World Archaeological Congress. In *Conflict in the Archaeology of Living Traditions*, edited by R. Layton, pp. 195–200. London: Unwin Hyman.

Hodder, I. 1984 Archaeology in 1984. *Antiquity* 58: 25–32.

Hollis, M. and S. Lukes (eds.) 1982 *Rationality and Relativism.* Oxford: Basil Blackwell.

Johnson, C. 1983 *Doctor Wooreddy's Prescription for Enduring the Ending of the World.* Melbourne: Hyland House.

Jones, R. (ed.) 1985 *Archaeological Research in Kakadu National Park.* Canberra: Australian National Parks and Wildlife Service.

Keefe, K. 1988 Aboriginality: Resistance and Persistence. *Australian Aboriginal Studies* 1988(1): 67–81.

Langford, R. F. 1983 Our Heritage – Your Playground. *Australian Archaeology* 16: 1–16.

Layton, R. L. 1989 Introduction: Conflict in the Archaeology of Living Traditions. In *Conflict in the Archaeology of Living Traditions*, edited by R. Layton, pp. 1-21. London: Unwin Hyman.

Layton, R. L. (ed.) 1989a *Who Needs the Past? Indigenous Values and Archaeology.* London: Unwin Hyman.

  1989b *Conflict in the Archaeology of Living Traditions.* London: Unwin Hyman.

Lewin, R. 1984 Extinction threatens Australian Anthropology. *Science* 225: 393–4.

Lewis, D. and D. B. Rose 1985 Some Ethical Issues in Archaeology: a Methodology for Consultation in Northern Australia. *Australian Aboriginal Studies* 1985(1): 37–44.

Lipe, W. D. 1984 Value and Meaning in Cultural Resources. In *Approaches to the Archaeological Heritage*, edited by H. Cleere, pp. 1–11. Cambridge University Press.

McBryde, I. 1985a Introduction. In *Who Owns the Past?*, edited by I. McBryde, pp. 1–10. Melbourne: Oxford University Press.

McBryde, I. (ed.) 1985 *Who Owns the Past?* Melbourne: Oxford University Press.

McQueen, J. 1983 *The Franklin – Not Just a River.* Ringwood (Vic.): Penguin.

Mowljarlai, D. and C. Peck 1987 Ngarinyin Cultural Continuity: a Project to Teach the Young People the Culture, Including the Re-painting of Wandjina Rock Art Sites. *Australian Aboriginal Studies* 1987(2): 71–8.

Mulvaney, J. 1979 Blood from Stones and Bones. Aboriginal Australians' Australian Prehistory. *Search* 10: 214–18.

  1986 "A Sense of Making History": Australian Aboriginal Studies 1961–1986. *Australian Aboriginal Studies* 1986(2): 48–56.

1989 Aboriginal Australia: Custodianship or Ownership? *Heritage News* 11: 11–12.

Murray, T. 1987 Remembrance of Things Present: Appeals to Authority in the History and Philosophy of Archaeology. Unpublished Ph.D. dissertation, Department of Anthropology, University of Sydney.

1989a The History, Philosophy and Sociology of Archaeology: the Case of the Ancient Monuments Protection Act (1882). In *Critical Traditions in Contemporary Archaeology*, edited by V. Pinsky and A. Wylie, pp. 55–67. Cambridge University Press.

1989b Sociopolitics and Archaeological Research: a Rejoinder to Tangri. *Australian Archaeology* 29: 53–60.

1990 Why Plausibility Matters. *Australian Archaeology* 31: 55–60.

Neijie, Bill 1984 Visitors to Sites: a Traditional Owner's Perspective. In *Visitors to Aboriginal Sites: Access, Control and Management*, edited by H. Sullivan, pp. 41–2. Canberra: Australian National Parks and Wildlife Service.

Palmer, K. 1987 Anthropologists in Aboriginal Australia: the Case for Negotiated Anthropology. *Australian Aboriginal Studies* 1987(1): 86–92.

Pardoe, C. 1985 Cross-cultural Attitudes to Skeletal Research in the Murray–Darling Region. *Australian Aboriginal Studies* 1985(2): 63–78.

Patrik, L. 1985 Is there an Archaeological Record? *Advances in Archaeological Method and Theory* 8: 27–62.

Richardson, L. 1989 The Acquisition, Storage and Handling of Aboriginal Skeletal Remains in Museums: an Indigenous Perspective. In *Conflict in the Archaeology of Living Traditions*, edited by R. Layton, pp. 185–8. London: Unwin Hyman.

Sabloff, J. A., L. R. Binford, and P. A. McAnany 1987 Understanding the Archaeological Record. *Antiquity* 61: 203–9.

Shanks, M. and C. Tilley 1987 *Re-constructing Archaeology*. Cambridge University Press.

1990 Archaeology into the 1990s. *Norwegian Archaeological Review* 22: 1–12.

Silberman, N. A. 1982 *Digging for God and Country*. New York: Knopf.

Sullivan, H. (ed.) 1984 *Visitors to Aboriginal Sites: Access, Control and Management*. Canberra: Australian National Parks and Wildlife Service.

Sutton, P. 1986 Anthropologists and Development in Arnhem Land. *Australian Aboriginal Studies* 1986(1): 34–7.

Trigger, B. G. 1980 Archaeology and the Image of the American Indian. *American Antiquity* 45: 662–76.

1984 Alternative Archaeologies: Nationalist, Colonialist, Imperialist. *Man* 19: 355–70.

1989 *A History of Archaeological Thought*. Cambridge University Press.

Trigger, B. G. and I. Glover (eds.) 1981 Regional Traditions of Archaeological Research, vol. 1. *World Archaeology* 13(2).

Ucko, P. 1983 Australian Academic Archaeology: Aboriginal Transformation of its Aims and Practices. *Australian Archaeology* 16: 11–26.

Valentine, C. A. and B. L. Valentine 1975 Making the Scene, Digging the Action, and Telling it like it is: Anthropologists at Work in the Dark Ghetto. In *City Ways*, edited by J. Friedl and N. J. Christman, pp. 118–29. New York: Crowell.

von Sturmer, J. 1981 Talking with Aborigines. *Australian Institute of Aboriginal Studies Newsletter* 15: 13–30.

Ward, G. 1985 The Federal Aboriginal Heritage Act and Archaeology. *Australian Aboriginal Studies* 1985(2): 47–52.

1986 "Aboriginalization" of Site Recording Forms. *Australian Aboriginal Studies* 1986(1): 65–9.

Webb, W. 1987 Reburying Australian Skeletons. *Antiquity* 61: 292–6.

Wildersen, L. 1984 The Search for an Ethic in Archaeology. In *Ethics and Values in Archaeology*, edited by E. L. Green, pp. 3–13. New York: Free Press.

PART IV

Epilogue

10
The relativity of theory

ANDREW SHERRATT

With prehistory we enter a world of few facts and much guesswork, a world moreover which is ruled by the archaeologists. This is worrying; while field-work has become an exact and exacting craft, archaeological discussion is often as much an indulgence as a discipline; where they might exchange hypotheses archaeologists are apt to demand adherence and to hurl polemics or even charges of corruption.

(McEvedy 1967: 9)[1]

The brilliant compiler of *The Penguin Atlas of Ancient History* quoted above, Colin McEvedy, set himself the task of constructing a set of maps illustrating the development of Europe and the Near and Middle East from prehistoric times. In so doing, he had to make use of the evidence of archaeology, and his continued characterization of the subject is worth pondering.

In prehistory . . . the archaeologist has been on his own; he has not only discovered the unlettered past, he has read it out, for all to hear; he has made pronouncements in a dozen fields, from metallurgy to sociology; he has had flights of fancy and fits of bad temper; he has been generally unlovely.

The great pioneers who led archaeology beyond the frontiers of recorded history invested very considerable personal fortunes in their chosen sites; striding confidently around their estates they would label an unexpected pot as an import and expect obedience. The habit of omnipotence spread to lesser men . . . amazingly it proved possible to give blow by blow accounts of prehistoric battles and, in more tender mood, tell how Woman shaped the First Pot.

Inevitably poetic license bred a puritan reaction within the profession, the puritans gained power and there was a ruthless clean-up. Not only was speculation condemned, but intellectual activity of any sort came to be frowned upon. The new style archaeologist showed signs of distress if he uncovered an object of beauty or value; salvation lay in the meticulous description of humbler finds. Classification was allowable; sub-classification was better; attempts at synthesis or interpretation were met with stony silence.

We have been through several cycles since these words were written; while puritanism is still advocated (Courbin 1988), the debate within archaeology – while often still conducted in terms of polemic rather than exchange – has embraced both optimistic determinism and pessimistic relativism, and extended to shifting patterns of alliance with other subjects and disciplines – geography, anthropology, history, and literary criticism – and different conceptions of the nature of theory and its authority. It is still not clear, however, whose judgements we should obey, or whose theories should control our disciplinary agenda. We are still unsure what form the answer should take, when faced with the question: "What happened in (pre)history?"

Archaeology is now a world-wide operation: and there are more archaeologists working today than in the total sum of all previous generations. For a variety of reasons, human societies of the late second millennium AD have come to devote a larger proportion of their resources to allow these people to practice their skills than ever before – now often aided by the expensive apparatus of the natural sciences. Yet there are new problems and growing pressures which are fundamentally altering the contexts within which they work, often taking the interpretation of archaeological evidence out of the hands of archaeologists, and dividing them into potentially hostile groupings. Should these different communities be allowed to fragment into local patterns of activity, or can we try to answer McEvedy's questions – on a global scale – with confidence and coherence?

The role of archaeology in the production of the past

The various practices of archaeology, and the very existence of an entity with a common name, are embedded in expectations about the nature and uses of the past. Consciousness of the existence of a discoverable past, different from the present but nevertheless open to investigation, has been a feature of the expansion of western societies since the sixteenth century. It arose both from the attempts of European states to establish their own national identities, and from Europeans' encounters with a diversity of other cultures. While these motivations have interacted, they have given rise to identifiably different traditions of archaeological thought and practice, which still animate our pronouncements and polemics.

Activities that can formally be described as archaeological can be identified in many civilizations with a long literary tradition, whether in the investigative tourism of Pausanias or in the more practical form of excavation – as when Edward I of England excavated the supposed tomb of King Arthur in Glastonbury Abbey in 1278 in an attempt to link the prestige of his own royal house to that of a semi-mythical ancestor (MacDougall 1982: 13). The effective genesis of an institutionalized practice of archaeology – and the invention of the word itself – took place, however, in the context of the rising economic and political importance of the nations of northwest Europe and their dominance of Mediterranean trade in the seventeenth century.

Consciousness of the classical world had been part of northwest European education for the previous centuries; but the opportunity to collect physical remains of classical antiquity and so to promote a reputation for refinement and scholarship was now a practical possibility. The initiative was taken first by aristocratic collectors in search of sculpture for country houses, then in the eighteenth century by an increasingly bourgeois range of imitators who found smaller objects such as painted pots ("vases") more appropriate for the furnishing of their more modest establishments. The spread of connoisseurship of classical antiquities was intimately linked with growing industrial production of distinctive items of bourgeois material culture, as exemplified for instance by Josiah Wedgwood and the manufacture of porcelain. The incorporation of earlier artistic traditions in the material production of European societies was paralleled by the intellectual growth of a mythology of continental origins based on descent from an increasingly idealized vision of classical Greece (Bernal 1987). It is significant that the interest in "classical" culture and antiquities (for that is what the term archaeology originally meant)[2] showed a successive devolution from royalty through the aristocracy to the middle classes. This phenomenon is of interest not only because its results are still with us, but also as a model for understanding the cultural role of archaeology in other contexts.

The term archaeology was only secondarily applied to the study of the material culture of non-European civilizations. As with the classical world, European knowledge of other ancient urban cultures came primarily from literary sources and notably from the Bible. Egyptian and Assyrian antiquities were acquired in the eighteenth and nineteenth centuries in the same way as classical ones, though primarily for national museums, from the various provinces of the Ottoman Empire. Their influence on industrial culture, though discernible (the "Empire" style!), was minor by comparison with the classical; and their study was initially largely on a private basis, through collection and decipherment of their inscriptions, and through excavations undertaken by private subscription from a Bible-reading middle class. The centres of scholarship were established primarily in museums, and only secondarily in universities, in departments of oriental studies often (like the non-national museums) endowed by wealthy interested patrons. As with classical studies, "archaeology" was very largely an adjunct to documentary history.

Consciousness of non-urban cultures in the rest of the world was not explicitly linked to an appreciation of their potential age. The term "archaeology" thus had no meaning in this context (cf. Wolf 1982). Contemporary items of material culture were acquired as curiosities, and often associated with the collection of specimens of natural history. Nevertheless the intellectual impact of the encounter with technologically less advanced cultures had a marked effect on philosophical speculations about the early history of mankind, and the formation of evolutionary ideas in the Enlightenment which were to become of major significance in the invention of a global archaeology (Sherratt 1989: 1990).

The transformation which potentially joined these separate enterprises was, paradoxically, itself an ideology of nationalism. The Romantic Movement, whose intellectual expression was rooted in northern Germany in a reaction to the abstract sociological speculation of the .French Enlightenment, stressed the uniqueness and specificity of individual cultures.[3] The territorial definition of an emerging network of nation states gave these scholarly speculations a particular relevance. In its search for the origins of the non-classical peoples of Europe, the Romantic Movement turned attention to the indigenous antiquities of the heathen inhabitants of northern Europe, going beyond the descriptions of classical authors to the collection and classification of their material remains, and the comparative study of their languages. At the same time, it provided a culture-historical model within which to interpret the remains of non-literate peoples throughout the globe, as well as re-writing the early history of the classical world itself as an expression of the inherent qualities of the Indo-European peoples. "Ethnology" thus became joined to "archaeology" as the study of the total culture of particular "peoples." Prehistoric Europe was given a time depth through the successive arrival of new peoples with increasingly sophisticated technologies, and national museums now collected the heritage of the prehistoric inhabitants of their countries; but the same methodology could also be applied in other areas to overcome the limitations of the written record. Archaeology had become the medium through which large and hitherto unclaimed parts of the past could be re-created.

Archaeological activity thus extended its role from art history to the ethnology of early peoples, and by the end of the nineteenth century was accommodated to another genre, that of science. The growth of industrial technology and its scientific base had developed by the mid-century to the point where it could challenge revealed religion with a new conception of earth history and human origins. The growth of geological and biological knowledge opened up a vast niche for archaeology to fill by providing an account of early human history, using the antiquarian descriptions of heathen Europe and accumulated ethnographic information to construct a new Enlightenment model which could now be filled with real material and examples. Like many other contemporary social models, this was typically a series of stages (*Stufentheorie*). A new generation of museums combined prehistoric archaeology and ethnology (often including the indigenous American civilizations) in an evolutionary framework. The new science of prehistoric archaeology came into being as a result, ranging from handaxes and shell-heaps to Celtic hillforts and Indian mounds. Its contribution to wider conceptions of human society, however, was limited: Marx learned little from archaeology, though Engels drew to some extent on evolutionary anthropology.

By 1900, therefore, archaeology had three role-models: art connoisseurship, cultural history, and positivist science. Each existed for a different reason, and produced its own types of literature; though all had a range of techniques and methods in common. Apart from the Palaeolithic, the evolutionary paradigm lost its appeal as the liberal vision of industrial progress faded in the experience of depression and World War I, and varieties of culture-history came to predominate. Archaeology was represented in museums, state or local services for the protection of monuments, and – tenuously – in universities. Outside these institutions, it was represented by amateurs, private collectors, and by intellectuals of independent means. Archaeology was predominantly a European and North American pursuit, with other areas investigated on an expeditionary basis. During the twentieth century, its operations increased in scale, and its corpus of information increased in volume, with major excavations that often gained public attention. Good methods were often pioneered for bad reasons – as with Kossinna's school of settlement archaeology in Germany, closely linked to nationalistic interests. New areas of the world were opened up to archaeological investigation, and syntheses of the culture-history of Europe and the Americas were written from archaeological materials. A coherent account of human existence from the Stone Age to written history was compiled, though little analytical use was made of these results except by Gordon Childe, whose writings stand out from those of contemporary archaeologists by their vision of the wider significance of this material; and it was in Marxism that he found the most satisfactory framework for interpreting his conception of the prehistoric and historic past.

The social context of archaeological activity in the middle years of the twentieth century was profoundly altered by changes in the world economy and political reactions to them. The Great Depression and World War II had a decisive effect on the nature of archaeology in the advanced countries. While some of this was due to technological developments (like aerial photography and other military-related surveying techniques), a more important aspect was the increased centralization and degree of state intervention which resulted, and was continued in the post-war period as the welfare state. This affected both educational and cultural institutions, and the administration of major public projects which were increasingly funded by the state. Management of the environment and cultural remains became part of the process of planned economic development. The practical effect of these processes was to employ more archaeologists, both as practitioners and as teachers or researchers; the intellectual effect was to imbue archaeology with the technological and managerial attitudes which suffused western culture in general, much as geography was transformed over the same time span from the study of specific landscapes and their natural and cultural characteristics into the study of comparative patterns and processes, or architecture abandoned local styles in favor of technological modernism.

An important threshold in the development of archaeology was its expansion in the universities. This allowed archaeologists the opportunity to become familiar with a greater range of archaeological activity in different parts of the world, and also with the kinds of ideas which were prevalent in other subjects which were likewise casting their disciplines in a generalizing and comparative mode. Biology and geography, with a common emphasis on ecological processes, provided a model for the rationale which was now perceived as missing from the particularist emphasis of regional studies and culture history. This was strengthened by the methodological innovations which were common to these disciplines. The growing market for textbooks (especially for Anthro. 101 courses in the USA) provided a vehicle for the dissemination of these views. Within their cellular structure, more specialized archaeologies (often linked to literary studies) survived relatively unchanged in their explanatory frameworks, though slowly transformed in their practical methodologies. Prehistory, which since the

1880s had been primarily a local activity sustained by regional interests, now emerged as a leading sector of archaeological enterprise – in tune with the spirit of the times and capable of absorbing the new technologies within a broadly scientific methodology and attitude to the past. Along with this new positivism came a revival of evolutionism as the narrative form appropriate to writing its major texts. With its claim to have developed a distinctive theoretical basis of global relevance, this model of archaeology established a virtual hegemony throughout the English-speaking world.

Like other attempts to conceptualize the past as a scientific investigation, this attitude did not survive unchanged beyond the social circumstances which had generated it; though the continuing power of cultural materialism in American cultural anthropology should not be underestimated (Demarest 1989: 91–4). The centralized political structures which had emerged alike in Europe, the USA, and the USSR began to be dissolved (slowly in the west, catastrophically in the Russian dominions) in the two decades following the Oil Crisis. Newly independent nations, and ethnic minorities within older ones, challenged this monolithic conception in a variety of ways, at the same time as internal criticisms within the western intellectual community (mainly European rather than American in origin) reasserted a new and often aggressive relativism. Ethnicity assumed a new relevance as large political entities began to fragment. Privatization succeeded nationalization as America, Britain, and Germany reversed the tendency towards state provision of welfare, education, and cultural provision, and entrepreneurial models of popular entertainment – stressing leisure rather than learning – spread from the mass media to transform archaeological sites and museums into tourist-oriented theme parks. A consumer culture, emphasizing choice, began to erode the elitist conception of higher culture established in the eighteenth and nineteenth centuries. Archaeological theorists, responding to the temper of the times, advocated a plurality of pasts.

Archaeology today

Archaeology has grown up as an aspect of industrial capitalism, promoted by the expansion of material production both as a model for contemporary culture and to provide a sense of identity and continuity with previous cultures – often where none actually existed (cf. Hobsbawm and Ranger 1983). It has been the instrument of various nationalities and sectional interest groups, from the aristocracy to the middle classes, and now to mass consumers or social minorities. Although it has been intellectually stimulated by the contact of cultures and attempts to understand their differences in a comparative or historical way, it has rarely been a disinterested investigation of the unknown. At the same time, it has revealed unsuspected facts about the past, whose interpretation may be disputed but whose importance for an understanding of the human condition cannot be doubted. Several largely unsuccessful attempts have been made to accommodate this information to larger intellectual enterprises, either philosophical, sociological, or scientific.

Archaeology exists today on a larger scale than ever before; not necessarily free from the motivations and biases which have provided the opportunities and determinants of its growth, but through its accumulated literature available for scrutiny, criticism, and constructive use. The question then arises: to what use or uses should it be put?

There is a consistent pattern to the long-term growth of information about the past as it has been acquired by western cultures, not unrelated to the economic fortunes of the societies concerned. From the Renaissance through the Enlightenment to Positivism and Neo-evolutionism, it has been approached as a detached, comparative exercise and interpreted as the consistent growth of order and complexity. As a counterpoint, in the intervening periods and to some extent from alternative geographical foci, it has been treated as a search for roots and cultural origins: from the Reformation, through Romanticism to Nationalism and Postmodernist relativism. These intellectual positions have been expressions of the more general contexts in which western societies have had recourse to the past, and have been reflected in institutional and practical forms as well as in explicit conceptualizations of social origins and development. There is no reason to believe that present and future changes affecting archaeology will be different in kind. The settings within which archaeology is and will be practiced are dependent on such larger changes within society as a whole. If we are now entering a period of cultural fragmentation, it is as well to recognize that the maintenance of a broader picture must be actively defended as part of the future agenda; and that only archaeologists can specify what this ought to include.

While archaeology may be portrayed as no more than a reflection of these wider social currents, it can also be seen as oscillating within a possible range of applications of its developing methodology and information. There is no reason why it should not be applied as a tool in the rational and comparative analysis of social and cultural change, systematizing the undoubted regularities that it has revealed. On the other hand, as a record of human societies and the product of individual actions, it will inevitably be viewed from a diversity of perspectives by observers with a similarly diverse range of interests and sensibilities. It could indeed be argued that these two approaches are inherently complementary, in that system-builders need constantly to be confronted by particularity and the alternatives of interpretation (notably issues such as class-based assumptions, ethnocentricity, and gender bias), and relativists need to be reminded of the common constraints under which past societies have been created. There is no necessary conflict between these objectives, and a recognition of this could help to overcome the cyclical social pressures to cast archaeology in one mould or another. The sophistication of local understanding must always be balanced by a consciousness of the relevant framing of the inquiry. In this respect, archaeology is no different from history itself, or anthropology. As the western world loses its monopoly of these practices, and they are redefined in a broader context, the question becomes of primary importance.

History and anthropology face similar choices, having been created in comparable contexts and facing comparable alternative futures. Indeed, it becomes increasingly irrelevant to see the problem in terms of categories which are peculiar to the western experience. Theory (in the sense either of a critical awareness of the nature of practice or of conscious model-building) emerges as a more general opposition to routine work and the unthinking reproduction of existing structures, rather than simply as the creation of modes of thought appropriate to specific disciplines. The major theoretical task which archaeology, history, and anthropology face in common is how to overcome the contradictions which the changing social contexts of their practice have created, in generating artificially contrasting conceptions of the nature of their activity: the production of specific cultural genealogies or accounts of emerging social complexity.

How might archaeology fit into such an enterprise? With hindsight, it is remarkable how marginal archaeology has been to the main episodes of systematic social theory-building. Enlightenment social theories had no archaeological content (taking their categories from the comparison of contemporary cultures), Positivist conceptualizations were based ultimately on a racist (or at least biology-led) model of cultural differences, while Neo-evolutionary models relied on ecological and economic factors to drive their managerial machinery. Marx and Weber wrote their classics of sociological analysis largely on the basis of the conventional ancient history of their times, and there is little point in trying to provide archaeological exemplification for categories constructed from such a partial basis.[4] This problem is endemic to all attempts to accommodate archaeology to such conceptions of social science. From this perspective it is the material nature of archaeological evidence as a record of practice that is its distinguishing

characteristic. Apart from a crude technological determinism, there has been remarkably little integration of material evidence in larger social syntheses, by comparison with the continuous contribution which archaeology has made (albeit in the humble role of illustration) to the culture-historical expression of the search for identity through tracing roots and origins. This failure to make use of archaeological evidence stems from the dichotomy which has been created in western thought between "society" and "culture," and between sociology and history (Trigger 1989a).

Society, and particularly its economic aspects, has been traditionally conceptualized by abstraction: the discourse of the classical social sciences is highly theoretical in a comparative and model-building way, evolving in the direction of increasing quantification. Cultural history is essentially empirical, and its discourse largely descriptive. This complementary and mutually reinforcing specialization has led to a virtual flushing out of cultural specificity from disciplines such as economics, so that while models of production costs and price-related behavior have a high degree of abstract sophistication, the reasons why consumers actually want to acquire the goods concerned are largely ignored. It is not that such motivations are not well understood by those practically involved such as marketing managers (from Josiah Wedgwood onwards): it is that model-building as a conscious process has been conceived in terms of a "scientific" analysis derived from natural phenomena. The problem is not so much in the construction of comparative models, but in a particular conception of comparability. Structuralism, by exploring the internal logic of culture, has created an opportunity for filling in these missing areas – in approaches to the past as well as to the present – and at the same time to avoid both relativism and the relegation of culture to idiosyncratic variation. Through its culture-historical inheritance, archaeology is well placed to provide the diachronic perspective which has been the chief limitation to structuralist analysis. This aspect of the post-processualist analysis has been a lasting contribution. Through its emphasis on particular categories of material culture that are prominently represented in the archaeological record, archaeology is also capable of redressing the deficiencies of accounts of the past based solely on the partialities of documentary description. The emergence of a focus of interest within anthropology on "commodities and the politics of value" points to a convergence of current interests along these lines (e.g. Appadurai 1986). Archaeology, history, and anthropology appear as increasingly arbitrary partitions of the necessary elements of comprehensive understanding.

Far from being an activity of marginal theoretical relevance, therefore, archaeology is arguably central to a future configuration of disciplines capable of transcending the limitations of their cultural origins. The question of what use should be made of archaeological information and disciplinary competence resolves itself into a practical adaptation of existing institutions, and an intellectual accommodation to the potential re-definition of the nature of the inquiry.

The practical setting

If the prospects for archaeology as a crucial component of such a future intellectual consortium are high, the practical constraints remain formidable. The reasons for which the majority of archaeologists are paid to carry out their activities are only distantly related to these goals, and the motivations of their paymasters are rooted in precisely the conceptions which it is now important to overcome. The three models to which archaeology has come to be accommodated, those of art connoisseurship, culture history, and positivist science, remain powerful factors in determining which aspects of archaeological activity receive funds to carry out their work, and are amplified by misunderstandings in the media. They are backed, respectively, by the international market in (often looted) antiquities as art, by what in "developed" nations has become a heritage industry for the culture of consumer contentment but in "developing" nations is still often infused with nationalist and territorial significance, and by the measurable productivity of hard science whose funds are disproportionate to those available to the humanities. There is a danger that archaeology as a whole will come to be dominated by these stereotypes of art, leisure, and science.

Archaeologists engaged in pure research are a small minority of the professional community. Those who wish to gain employment in the subject must look principally to "heritage management" (CRM/rescue excavation) units or to museums and other institutions concerned with monuments and public collections. Those lucky enough to teach must be conscious of the employment opportunities of their students, and cannot afford to be insensitive to the pressures of the outside world, so archaeology is unusually dependent on these constituencies for its continued survival. Since research funds, too, are limited in scope, the same agencies may provide a substantial proportion of the money available for discovery and innovation, or for any sustained program of work. These stereotypes of archaeological activity thus exercise an unusual influence on its practice.

While the model of art connoisseurship might be thought to be merely a passing episode in the history of the subject, its influence is still considerable in the study of the ancient civilizations whose objects are canonized in museums – for instance through the monies disbursed through the Getty Foundation; and this influence has in fact been extended to new spheres of collecting and the commoditization of decontextualized antiquities and ethnographic objects.[5] Dealing in antiquities is now big business, and such an industry is not without its intellectual consequences. The auction houses dealing with antiquities, for instance, sponsor publications by museums which possess quantities of the types of objects which they sell. It seems unlikely that they would subsidize a book suggesting – say – that Greek vases were essentially downmarket substitutes for long-remelted dining sets in precious metal, and controverting the view that they could be studied by the techniques of Renaissance art history by identifying named artists (whose works command a higher price); or that they would sponsor a conference to examine the effects of these prices on the destructive looting of archaeological sites throughout the world. Yet it is perhaps the former which is the more insidious, since it serves to perpetuate a particular view of the ancient world which is compatible with their commercial interests, and is not counteracted by the national interests of the countries concerned.

The culture-historical model of national and ethnic origins, too, is no antiquarian irrelevance. The scholarship of certain countries of the east Mediterranean is still permeated by the motivations which fuelled the interest in archaeology among the emerging European nations of the nineteenth century. The breakup of the Soviet Union has indeed replicated these conditions in a dozen republics now struggling to establish independent identities. Archaeologists are presented with a moral dilemma of either withdrawing from archaeology or of necessarily operating within the restrictions that such a context imposes. At a personal level, there is also a conflict between sympathy for justifiable cultural aspirations to accompany political independence and its responsibilities, and the need to protest at the perversion of scholarship which has featured all too prominently in the European experience of archaeology, and can easily be used to disenfranchise other cultures in polyethnic nation states.[6] State funds are disproportionately available to points of view compatible with political orthodoxy, and the archaeological literature from countries where the past seems immediately relevant to the present is charged with issues where political and archaeological agenda are hopelessly entangled.

The provision of "leisure" facilities in the advanced capitalist countries in the form of public exhibitions and reading material is not immune to such current preoccupations. *Die Hallstatt-Kultur: Frühform europäischer Einheit* (The Hallstatt culture: early form of European unity) was the title of an international exhibition in 1980 based on material from an Iron Age site in Austria. In such a medium it is easier to contribute to the mythology of a Celtic unity prefiguring the emerging federal structure of the European Community than it is to deconstruct a bogus image of the pre-Roman Iron Age in western Europe and replace it with something better. Popular perceptions of prehistory and early history encourage "common-sense" ethnic attributions, packaging archaeological information in terms of pub-lications such as "The Peoples of Europe," in which infor-mation is already categorized in terms of the nationalist ideologies of the nineteenth century. Even when there is no overt message to convey, public archaeology often favours the easy options of ancestry and exoticism as convenient categories for presenting its material, especially when the commercial objectives of mass tourism and entertainment are as prominent as those of academic inquiry.[7]

Science, too (in the sense of the application of natural-scientific techniques to archaeological problems), has tended to subvert the nature of archaeological research by its access to funds and consequent tendency to define the problems for research as those to which archaeological science can be applied. In Britain it has even begun to swallow up funds otherwise available to archaeology itself; and while it is a good servant, it is a poor master. It is especially dangerous when combined with the view that archaeology itself is simply a science, and that possession of a correct method-ology is necessary to make any valid assertion; or that to get a research grant at all, it has to be formatted to suit the NSF. At a time when politicians demand measures of productivity, the mindless solution of trivial problems is a tempting *modus vivendi*.

The cumulative effect of these contexts of archaeological practice is to produce a routine accumulation of information, packaged within often stereotyped conceptions of how this information ought to be used. Much archaeological activity is data-driven, reproducing with increasing technological sophistication the interests of the immediate sponsors of the projects within which it is undertaken. Nor does it often contribute to wider debates in the area of popular education and general culture: even for colleagues in other subjects, archaeology is all too often seen as an unproblematic technique of acquiring information about the past by simply digging it up. There is little consciousness of how the accumulated evidence of archaeology might be mobilized in pursuit of the major questions which might be addressed to this body of observations about the past.

The roots of the problem lie in the contexts within which archaeological theory is produced – in the structure within which archaeology is formulated as a self-conscious practice and a coherent body of knowledge: the universities them-selves. The fragmentation of archaeological practices is reproduced at the core of the institutions within which theoretical coherence ought to be sought. It is here that the problem must be addressed.

Archaeology in academe

The nature of the problem is immediately apparent. "Archae-ology" exists within such a diversity of institutional settings that it is amazing that it should be considered a coherent enterprise at all. It is perhaps symptomatic that a recent volume entitled *Archaeological Thought in America* (Lamberg-Karlovsky 1989), although excellent in its survey for instance of Asian archaeology, managed to omit entirely any consideration of North America, or for that matter of most of Europe. On the other hand, a similar partiality is evident in the content of ambitious titles of edited volumes on (say) "the interpretation of burial practice," which turn out to be re-shufflings of well-known examples from tiny segments of the archaeological record. Here it is Egypt and Mesopotamia which might have provoked new thoughts. It is not that every volume which pretends to be more than a regional survey should be universalist in scope; it is that "archaeology" in practice means a set of isolated discursive communities deployed over a tiny fraction of their potential evidence.

These inefficiencies have been compounded by a belated post-colonial guilt in which any consideration of supra-local problems has been written off as inherently racist and colonialist, thereby ruling out any investigation of "the origins of humans, human societies and civilizations in the past" (Moran and Hides 1990: 212). The inherently parochial tendencies of culture-historical archaeology are here elevated to the status of principle, in a way which is entirely consistent with Post-modernism's continuation of the Romantic conception of the past. The post-processualist prescription – an introverted critique of archaeology as currently carried out, on a local basis – is an inherently conservative acceptance of the structural settings within which archaeology is currently reproduced and theorized, shorn of the element of comparison associated with the Enlightenment tradition represented most recently by (but not limited to) New Archaeology. It largely precludes an effective application of the most valuable insights of post-processualism to do with the role and meaning of material culture and the creation of value, by restricting its study to isolated regional instances; and it debars archaeology from any critical insights into the larger structures which underlie the growth of political hegemony and the emergence of capitalism.

These problems are particularly acute in the area of "protohistory" – an inadequate label surviving from its nineteenth-century evolutionary origins – when complex societies existed side by side with non-literate ones. It makes no sense to canonize the study of contemporary and inter-related societies into disciplines of prehistoric archaeology and ethnology on the one hand, and ancient or modern history with a pendent art-historical archaeology on the other. The material remains themselves are often eloquent of connections, even when the documentary sources remain silent; while ethnography itself is increasingly being revealed as the product of an extended interaction between urban and non-urban cultures (Wolf 1982; Sahlins 1988). But such larger structures are also evident within the pre-historic record. The spatial scale of phenomena such as the Bell-beaker culture or the Lapita complex render inadequate any methodology based solely on "case studies" which privilege local understanding at the expense of wider settings. By continuing this procedure of New Archaeology (where it was supported by a framework of comparative pigeonholing and environmental determinism), and fore-closing research into "grand themes" (Tilley 1990: 143), such a methodology actively impedes an understanding of the larger structures within which local manifestations occur. Archaeology cannot be limited to a particular spatial scale: it must encompass grand extents as well as individual habitations, just as it deals with both long durations and single moments.

If archaeology is to fulfill its potential, it must transcend the limitations of the institutions within which it has been created. At present it is often no more than an aggregation of unreflective specialisms, divided by region and period and the craft skills which they require. Because of the need to differentiate archaeology from subjects which were already represented in universities, and under whose patronage it was originally established, archaeologists have emphasized their institutional independence from history and anthropology; and they have often drawn the disciplinary boundaries of their subject so as to exclude those archaeologists still working within departments of classics or oriental studies. The rapid growth of archaeology since 1960 – fuelled by the practical incentives discussed above – has largely taken place within institutional frameworks established in the earlier years of this century, or even in the previous one; and in order to acquire funds and space it has been necessary to differentiate archaeology from potential competitors. In consequence archaeology has grown up in such a way as to accommodate itself to the existence of established subjects by avoiding their territories. This disciplinary competition has been responsible for many of its intellectual characteristics: in order to promote solidarity and legitimate their practical everyday existence, archaeologists have sought to create a body of "archaeological theory" that is peculiar to their discipline as institutionally defined.[8] Since this strategy of departmental growth typically proceeds by collecting new specialisms, theoretical archaeology was often treated as an additional specialism, like Roman archaeology or Southwestern archaeology. Nor surprisingly, "archaeological theory" has been characterized by a constant importation of bodies of ideas from what are seen as other subjects, and typically by a theater of aggressive paradigm display as each was introduced as a new pattern for archaeology to follow.

Considered in perspective, however, archaeology is not an independent domain of autonomous knowledge. In each period and area of its application, it is fundamentally dependent on membership of another community, whether biological anthropology, social anthropology, or the various text-dependent disciplines necessary to reconstruct the history of complex societies. Conversely, each of these other subject areas is itself deficient without archaeological input; and, moreover, input from an archaeology which is itself not just a period specialism, but open to ideas from the whole range of its application. As a discipline with its own specific types of evidence, archaeology generates its own concepts which are not necessarily congruent with those of any other discipline. These need to be systematized and articulated across a range of contexts. A healthy archaeology requires a diversity of types of subject-matter, both to heighten the contrasts and to maintain links with relevant debates in neighboring subject areas. From this point of view, archaeology needs to be configured as a set of open networks, rather than compartmentalized as a series of specialist studies; or, in a different metaphor, to exist in a balanced community within an ecology of disciplines.

Archaeological agenda therefore need to be specified within problem domains rather than just disciplinary fields. This requires a more sustained attention to what historians and anthropologists are actually saying than just a quick summary and dismissal of their work as the potential answer to archaeology's current preoccupations (Lewthwaite 1986; 1988). Each "school" of thought in related subjects has its own context in relation to its raw material and past or current debates; each needs to be situated in an intellectual matrix before an intelligent dialogue can begin (Knapp 1992). Only then can areas of complementarity and advantage be defined. Since each discipline is rooted in mastery of a particular type of evidence, none is necessarily subservient to the other: each has conceptualized its problems in relation to its own material; and the end-product of dialogue is ours as much as theirs.

This can be illustrated by an example from precisely that area of the Old World where "archaeologie" had its origins. On the basis of (inevitably partial) documentary sources, and a sociology derived from Max Weber, ancient historians dealing with the Graeco-Roman world have erected a model of the ancient economy (Finley 1985). This has provided a framework within which classical archaeologists have interpreted their results (e.g. Snodgrass 1987). At the same time, archaeological observations have served to undermine it (compare, for instance, Hopkins' *Introduction* to Garnsey *et al.* [1983] with the following papers by Garlan, Tchernia, Pucci, and Carandini). The end product should be a re-writing of Weber, not disillusionment with the documentary record and a cessation of negotiations, nor an unconscious continuation of archaeological research within a now inadequate Weberian paradigm (Sherratt and Sherratt 1991).

This, after all, is what universities are supposed to be for, and what distinguishes them from vocational training establishments. Archaeologists can educate and learn from their colleagues as much as clone their own competences and partial understandings. A historian or anthropologist sensitized to the importance of material culture or the perspective of deep time is as much a gain to archaeology as the production of a new pottery or flint specialist: we may succeed as viruses even if we fail as bacteria.

The relativity of theory

Theory is, of course, immanent in all that we do; but it can be consciously or unconsciously related to practice. "Practical men who believe themselves to be quite exempt from any intellectual influences are, as Lord Keynes pointed out, usually the slaves of some defunct theorist" (Clarke 1973: 18). Problems arise when the two are out of step; or when bodies of theory, while related to types of practice, are unrelated to each other. This is the question of the relativity of theory.

Individual areas of archaeological, anthropological, and historical theory have achieved considerable sophistication; while they were not initially self-evident, they are now sufficiently well understood to be treated merely as matters of methodology or *Quellenkritik*. For archaeology, this would include many of the areas recognised by Clarke as priorities in 1973: pre- and post-depositional processes, sampling and retrieval, analytical procedures. The problems currently under discussion lie rather in the realm of interpretation, which relates bodies of theory to each other and determines what further observations should be collected, and how they should be described.

A first step in understanding our own interpretative narratives should be to situate them in their historical contexts: it is not surprising that the history of archaeology should be enjoying a current burst of activity (e.g. Trigger

1989b). This must expose the degree to which currently used concepts were created in the specific conditions during which archaeology emerged in the preceding centuries – concepts which are now engrained in popular perception as much as in the everyday practice of archaeology (cf. Kuper 1988). This includes not only convenient ethnic labels, but concepts such as autonomy, migration, and diffusion which (albeit under different names) continue to underlie attitudes to interpretation – if only by avoidance and guilt by association.[9] Such criticism extends to comparative categories like foragers and farmers (and the supposed revolutionary transition between them), which are little more than reifications of Enlightenment anthropology projected into the past (Sherratt 1980: 404). Comparable criticisms apply to the crucial transitions of Marxist historiography (Frank 1991), which now appear as local episodes, canonized as the precursors of the coming revolution of socialism. These discussions have often been initiated outside archaeology, and it is important that they should be incorporated into our own debates so that inappropriate concepts are not unconsciously recycled. This level of theorization extends beyond the boundaries of disciplines, and contributes to common conceptions.

Within individual disciplines, it is important not to be trapped by metaphors. If the past can be read, it can also be interrogated. There is no need to model archaeological procedures on those of historians, mostly working in richly documented periods, who believe the past speaks for itself and that these speeches have only to be integrated in plots (e.g. Paul Veyne *Comment on écrit l'histoire: essai d'épistémologie* 1971: see Ricoeur 1980: 34). Archaeology's raw materials, too, write their own plots, in the way in which the evidence offers itself already structured in buildings and tomb-groups, and it is important to understand their messages; there is an urgent need to confront the structures identified by earlier pre- and proto-historians, in uniformitarian notions such as "cultures," and to relate them to the processes of communication taking place at different times in the past. But archaeologists are not restricted to simply re-telling their histories in the context of present concerns; they can be analysed and confronted with unconscious records of quite a different character, such as environmental information, and compared with quite unrelated episodes from other times and periods. This is a more active intervention in the interpretative process than that implied in the notion of reading a text.

On the other hand there can be no naive recourse to the equally metaphorical concept of "laws." When seventeenth-century scientists wrote of the "laws of nature," they were imagining a universe created by a divine legislator, whose laws resembled those passed by the King in Parliament. It is an irony of intellectual history that the scientists' success in understanding the regularities of the natural world has periodically led social scientists to seek laws of human behavior more fundamental than those which human societies themselves have consciously created. There are no such universals. This means that observations of present human behavior cannot be transferred to the past by reference to any postulated system of "laws."[10] The relevance of one observation to another has to be established via a network of local understandings. This is why connections within archaeology, and across its entire time range, are so vital.

Archaeology has two unique resources: its access to the microstructures of daily life, the pattern of "small things forgotten" (Deetz 1977), and its ability to survey the grand sweep – 10,000 times the length of Braudel's *longue durée*. The question "what happened in (pre)history" can be answered both at the small scale of the *petites histoires* of objects and occupation levels, and at the level of the *grand récit* of larger themes. Archaeology's objective should be to link these two domains, neglecting neither the one nor the other, in a way that goes beyond both "history" and "evolution," genealogy and *Stufentheorie*; resisting the imposition of inappropriate models from outside its own field but participating in the construction of an understanding that reaches beyond its disciplinary boundaries.

At a time when politicians and bureaucrats, art collectors, scientists, media folk, and tourist managers are all too ready to write our job descriptions for us, it is as well to set out our *agenda*: things to be done.

Acknowledgements

I am indebted to all the contributors to this volume and to Jim Lewthwaite, Tim Taylor, and Sue Sherratt for helping me to form my perspective, and to Ian Hodder for widening it; to John Baines for his electronic and personal networking; and to Norman Yoffee for his superhuman patience. Finally, I must apologize to Einstein for imitating in the title of this chapter what Marx did in his refutation of Proudhon (*La philosophie de la misère/La misère de la philosophie*), so providing a model which E. P. Thompson adapted further (*The Poverty of Theory*) in circumstances not dissimilar to those of the present essay. However, as will be clear, this chapter is not intended as a refutation of *The Theory of Relativity*.

Notes

1 Reproduced by permission of Penguin Books Ltd.
2 The *Oxford English Dictionary* conveniently charts the usage of this word in the English language: 1607 *archaiology* (Jewish history); 1669 *archeologie* ("or [Greek] antiquity"); 1731 *archaeologick* (antiquarian); 1782 *archaeological* (antiquarian); 1803 *archaeography* (Greek antiquities); 1824 *archaeologist* ("English historical archaeologists"); 1837 *archaeology* ("theoretical geology has a strong resemblance to philosophical archaeology": Whewell); 1849 *archaeologian* (ecclesiastical architecture: Freeman); 1851 *archaeologer* (in *Journal of the Asiatic Society of Bengal*); 1851 *archaeology* ("the closing epoch of geology is that in which archaeology has its beginning": Wilson); *archaeological* ("archaeological inference from the remains of prehistoric tribes": Tylor). These usages reflect the successive influences of ancient (Mediterranean) history, Romantic antiquarianism, Victorian ecclesiology, imperial tourism, and positivist science.

3 It is noteworthy that this tradition was strongly influenced by Protestant Biblical hermeneutics, and that J. G. Herder himself called for "lebendige lesen, Divination in die Seele des Urhebers" (living reading, divination of the soul of the author).

4 It is a fascinating experience to have one's material reinterpreted in terms of a "Germanic Mode of Production" (Thomas 1987: 411). For an alternative reading, see now Sherratt (1991).

5 In November 1988 an Early Cycladic marble head, broken from a third millennium figurine, was sold for $2,000,000 at Sotheby's in New York. Collectors forced out of the market for modern art by rising prices moved their money into archaeological items. An advertisement which appeared in the following month in the magazine of the British *National Art Collections Fund* (a public body) speaks for itself: "On Monday, 29th November at 11.00 am a new art market opens for business, at Bonhams, with a sale of artifacts rarely encountered in our civilised world, let alone just across from Harrods. [!] Tribal art. It's highly compelling, whether for collecting, interior decorating, or for its own sake. It has exceptional interest as products of exotic, human cultures. And it can be visually startling." In the previous year, figures from the (UK) Department of Trade and Industry (reported in the same magazine) revealed that the United Kingdom imported "cultural objects" (their definition) from 103 countries to a value of £974,640,857, and that it exported the same commodity to 102 countries to a value of £1,211,339,338 – some 2% of the country's total export earnings.

6 Such considerations apply with equal force to the archaeology of ethnic minorities within longer established states with native or former slave populations now economically and politically subordinate to dominant

cultures with roots elsewhere. Yet the pressure to support such ethnic minorities can also be hegemonic, if self-appointed spokespeople for recognized "tribal" interests can exert political pressure to appropriate value-laden objects in public institutions for their own purposes. Such cases present more moral dilemmas than the simple commercial appropriation of the art market.

7 How many exhibitions of ethnographic material, especially art objects, raise the question of the genocide of native populations? Do not museums have a responsibility to raise these issues?

8 In the same way, sociologists invented functionalist theory, which claimed to reveal truths about the behavior of individuals of which they were unaware. This was necessary to separate their discourse from the "common-sense" observations of historians and political scientists. Now, secure in departmental chairs, they can proclaim their subjects to be once again "knowledgeable actors."

9 Much of the interest in core–periphery concepts, for instance, has little to do with world-systems theory but rather serves to legitimate an interest in problems of long-distance contacts effectively outlawed under the dominant autonomist paradigm. For a discussion of the relation of ideas of autonomy, diffusion, and migration to nationalist interests in the nineteenth century and earlier, see Sherratt (1990), which argues that they should be seen as reflections of the regional aspirations of early modern Europe, as different parts of the continent struggled to connect their national pre-histories to the prestige associated with the classical world: either in Latin Europe as areas of continuity, in central Europe as its Indo-Germanic originators, or in Atlantic Europe as favored western outposts.

10 At another level, of course, the two metaphors coincide: consider legislator, legible, intellectual – *lex*, *lego*, *intellego*.

References

Appadurai, A. (ed.) 1986 *The Social Life of Things: Commodities in Cultural Perspective*. Cambridge: Cambridge University Press.

Bapty, I. and T. Yates 1990 *Archaeology after Structuralism: Post-structuralism and the Practice of Archaeology*. London: Routledge.

Bernal, M. 1987 *Black Athena: the Afroasiatic Roots of Classical Civilisation*. Vol. I, *The Fabrication of Ancient Greece 1785–1985*. London: Free Association Books.

Clarke, D. L. 1973 Archaeology: the Loss of Innocence. *Antiquity* 47: 6–18.

Courbin, P. 1988 *What is Archaeology?* Chicago: Chicago University Press.

Deetz, J. 1977 *In Small Things Forgotten: the Archaeology of Early American Life*. New York: Anchor Press.

Demarest, A. 1989 Ideology and Evolutionism in American Archaeology: Looking beyond the Economic Base. In Lamberg-Karlovsky (1980), pp. 89–102.

Finley, M. 1985 (2nd edn.) *The Ancient Economy*. London: Hogarth Press.

Frank, A. G. 1991 Transitional Ideological Modes: Feudalism, Capitalism, Socialism. *Critique of Anthropology* 11: 171–88.

Garnsey, P., K. Hopkins, and C. R. Whittaker (eds.) 1983 *Trade in the Ancient Economy*. London: Hogarth Press.

Hobsbawm, E. and T. Ranger (eds.) 1983 *The Invention of Tradition*. Cambridge: Cambridge University Press.

Knapp, A. B. (ed.) 1992 *Archaeology, Annales and Ethnohistory*. Cambridge: Cambridge University Press.

Kuper, A. 1988 *The Invention of Primitive Society: Transformations of an Illusion*. London: Routledge.

Lamberg-Karlovsky, C. C. (ed.) 1989 *Archaeological Thought in America*. Cambridge: Cambridge University Press.

Lewthwaite, J. G. 1986 Archaeologists in Academe: an Institutional Confinement? in *Archaeology at the Interface*, edited by J. L. Bintliff and C. F. Gaffney, (BAR Int. Ser. 300), pp. 52–87. Oxford: British Archaeological Reports.

1988 Living in Interesting Times: Archaeology as Society's Mirror. In *Extracting Meaning from the Past*, edited by J. Bintliff, pp. 86–98. Oxford: Oxbow Books.

MacDougall, H. A. 1982 *Racial Myth in English History*. Montreal: Harvest House.

McEvedy, C. 1967 *The Penguin Atlas of Ancient History*. Harmondsworth: Penguin Books.

Moran, P. and D. S. Hides 1990 Writing, Authority and Determination of a Subject. In I. Bapty and T. Yates (1990), pp. 205–21.

Ricoeur, P. 1980 *The Contribution of French Historiography to the Theory of History* (Zaharoff Lecture 1978–9). Oxford: Clarendon Press.

Sahlins, M. 1988 Cosmologies of Capitalism: the Trans-Pacific Sector of "The World System" (Radcliffe-Brown Lecture in Social Anthropology), *Proceedings of the British Academy* 74: 1–51.

Sherratt, A. G. 1980 Interpretation and Synthesis: a Personal View. In A. G. Sherratt (ed.) *The Cambridge Encyclopedia of Archaeology*, pp. 404–14. Cambridge: Cambridge University Press.

1989 V. Gordon Childe: Archaeology and Intellectual History. *Past and Present* 125: 151–85.

1990 Gordon Childe: Patterns and Paradigms in Prehistory. *Australian Archaeology* 30: 3–13.

1991 Sacred and Profane Substances: the Ritual Use of Narcotics in Later Prehistoric Europe. In *Sacred and Profane: Proceedings of the Oxford Conference on Archaeology, Ritual and Religion*, edited by P. Garwood, D. Jennings, R. Skeates, and J. Toms, pp. 50–64. (Oxford Monographs in Archaeology 32). Oxford: Oxbow Books.

Sherratt, A. G. and Sherratt, E. S. 1991 From Luxuries to Commodities: the Nature of Mediterranean Bronze Age Trading Systems. In *Bronze Age Trade in the Mediterranean*, edited by N. Gale. (Studies in Mediterranean Archaeology, 90), pp. 351–86. Jonsered: Paul Aströms Förlag.

Snodgrass, A. 1987 *An Archaeology of Greece: the Present State and Future Scope of the Discipline*. Berkeley: University of California Press.

Thomas, J. 1987 Relations of Production and Social Change in the Neolithic of North-west Europe. *Man* (NS) 22: 405–30.

Tilley, C. 1990 On Modernity and Archaeological Discourse. In Bapty and Yates (1990), pp. 127–52.

Trigger, B. G. 1989a History and Contemporary American Archaeology: a Critical Analysis. In Lamberg-Karlovsky (1989), pp. 19-34.

1989b *A History of Archaeological Thought*. Cambridge: Cambridge University Press.

Wolf, E. 1982 *Europe and the People Without History*. Berkeley: University of California Press.

11
Archaeology: the loss of nerve

RICHARD BRADLEY

We begin with some notes from a hospital ward:

> At midnight the police found Patient wandering on the Embankment near Waterloo Bridge. They took him to the station thinking he was drunk or drugged. They describe him as Rambling, Confused, and Amenable. Brought him to us at 3 a.m. by ambulance. During admittance Patient attempted several times to lie down on the desk . . . Patient was well-dressed but had not changed his clothes for some time . . . He is an educated man . . . He was talking loudly (Lessing 1971: 9).

Those are the opening words of a novel by Doris Lessing, *Briefing For a Descent into Hell*. It is not a novel that I like, but its theme is curiously apposite to this volume, for the man found wandering beside the Thames has experienced a mental breakdown, and the book follows his case history. Eventually the patient is identified as a Cambridge Professor of Classics. His crisis begins when he meets an archaeologist who has come to doubt whether he can know anything at all about the past: so much so that whenever he tries to lecture he is afflicted by terrible attacks of stammering. His experience has a familiar ring:

> The thought he had had . . . struck at his confidence as an archaeologist – that was how he experienced it. That he had the equivalent of a religious person's "doubts", and it was necessary to dismiss them before going on. The chief thought was that our society was dominated by things, artefacts, possessions, machines, objects, and that we judged previous societies by artefacts – things. There was no way of knowing an ancient society's ideas except through the barrier of our own . . . This experience's effect on him he decided was "unhealthy" and "morbid" (*ibid.*: 164).

Both men, the classicist and the archaeologist, suffer an intellectual crisis and cease to believe that they can talk about the past. What was a pathological condition in a novel twenty years ago can be an article of faith today.

However, my title "Archaeology: the loss of nerve" is not a reference to Doris Lessing's story. It refers to David Clarke's famous paper "Archaeology: the loss of innocence," published in 1973 and in a very different intellectual climate. Clarke was optimistic about the future of the subject. There might be sharp disagreements about the nature of archaeology, but these would tend to evaporate. What has actually happened is that such brisk self-confidence has gone now. Our loss of innocence has turned into a loss of nerve.

How can we diagnose the complaint? When David Clarke was writing, he identified five main areas of archaeological thinking: pre-depositional and depositional theory: post-depositional theory; retrieval theory; analytical theory; and interpretative theory. The first two of these embrace the study of formation processes, and the last extends to the question of explanation. What seems to have happened is that the two extremes have pulled apart, leaving something of a vacuum in between. We can sense a common element in both cases: a frustration with the archaeological record itself, so that at one pole we find increasingly detailed studies of the physical properties of artifacts, and at the other we find that the subject-matter of archaeology is the work of other archaeologists. We are suspended in space somewhere between animal bones and agit-prop.

Both developments spring from a common cause, which is hardly ever admitted: a loss of faith in the raw material of archaeology; and whatever their differences, some of the opinion-makers have undergone a similar metamorphosis. The Law and Order archaeologists of the sixties and early seventies say less and less about the human past, and write with equal passion about the properties of archaeological things. Schiffer has become an expert on traditional technologies; Binford is a faunal analyst, the Mousterian controversy unresolved. For all the fighting talk of Middle Range theory, I feel an uneasy suspicion that this emphasis on the minutely physical is because here at least we are dealing with constants – the thermal properties of pots, the fracture mechanics of flint, the densities of animal bone – and this allows us to pass as scientists for just a little longer. These are regularities some distance away from any human activity; and if this is science, it is a routine science, a science of technicians. We find the same tendency when we talk of "science-based archaeology." In reality what we mean is an archaeology informed by a closer understanding of the properties of particular classes of data. Such scientific methods – of characterization, measurement, or dating – never touch the essential character of the subject: those processes by which we talk about the behavior of human beings in the past. They apply powerful analytical tools to their data, but they serve theories whose heart is altogether elsewhere. The alternative is to discuss the theories but never the data themselves. This is the other path that opinion-makers have followed. Some have maintained a consistent position for a long time – Mark Leone's work is an example – but others have gradually distanced themselves from the archaeological record, as if contact with the dead left them somehow appalled.

As a result, I suggest that archaeological activity is in danger of polarizing, with one faction who hold on to the methods and aspirations of the scientist, and another who are engaged in fervent introspection and regard that aspiration to scientific method as a political position in itself. I have suggested that both groups have reached that position from a common starting point – a disenchantment with the archaeo-logical record – but I do not wish to argue that these positions are disingenuous or even that they are unprofitable. We can learn from both, and, surely, we must do so. My concern is with the effect of this polarization on other archaeologists, and in particular on those who are just coming into the subject.

I submit that this polarization has had two unwelcome effects. The first is a moral earnestness that I find entirely distasteful. Too often the debate is unreal, a rhetorical posturing over reputations rather than ideas. The second is more significant, for now the archaeologists who believe in researching the human past have been forced onto the defensive, and we face a new development that could be the most crippling of all: a critical self-consciousness so acute that it saps individual creativity.

There is too much pressure from both sides. One group urges us to relate any idea about the past to more general principles of human behavior. These should have test implications, which preferably employ measurement and can be examined for statistical significance. Without that we are not scientists, and for them science is a moral quality – witness the animosity with which other positions are discussed. The other group scrutinizes every thought for gender, class, or racial bias, concluding that the main function of studying the past is to criticize the present. Our judgements of such ideas are formed along political lines. Now both are extreme positions, but they are positions that have powerful and persuasive advocates. Caught between them, imagination and talent can be crushed.

We are forgetting about creativity, but without it archaeologists will be left with nothing new to say. Unless we nurture the creative imagination, there is no point in teaching archaeology at any level, and little pleasure in practicing it at all. But we are strangely innocent about the creative process itself. In a television interview in 1962, the sculptor Henry Moore said this:

> Recently there was a book published on my work by a Jungian psychologist; I think the title was *The Archetypal World of Henry Moore*. He sent me a copy, which he asked me to read, but after the first chapter I thought I'd better stop because it explained too much what my motives were and what things were about. I thought it might stop me from ticking over if I went on and knew it all . . . If I was psychoanalysed, I might stop being a sculptor (James ed. 1966: 50).

Note that Moore is not saying that he objects to this analysis or that he disbelieves it; merely that if he were too self-conscious, he might suffer a creative block. I have heard a similar sentiment from a well-known novelist with an interest in archaeology. He was bemused by the range of interpretations that had been placed on his work by critics: interpretations that he had never intended consciously. More worrying was the fact that nearly all of them seemed so plausible when he read them.

I suggest that we are courting the same dangers. Our first thoughts can be twisted out of shape by the attempt to make them explicit before we are ready to do so. We can become so aware of the historical contingencies shaping our very thought-processes that we are frightened of what political vices others may find in them. That is why my novelist was so worried by his interpreters.

I began with a fictional professor. It is no coincidence that I have just mentioned a novelist. Consider how often archae-ology and archaeologists feature in modern literature, in plays, in poems, and in fiction. This is not because all archae-ologists are colorful characters, or because excavations provide exotic settings. Some authors see archaeology itself as a metaphor for human knowledge and experience. The archaeological recovery of the past is compared with the workings of memory and the unconscious mind: with the creative process itself. This is not a new idea. Freud used that very metaphor to describe psychoanalysis (Chippindale 1989: 3), and in 1982 an American writer, Cynthia Ozick, returned the compliment with a story in which a refugee living in New York interprets the character of Freud himself from a photograph of the collection of antiquities that he kept in his Vienna consulting room: paleopsychology indeed! Still more recently, Graham Swift's new novel juxtaposed the psychoanalysis of one character and the professional career of another – a photojournalist turned archaeological air photographer. The book makes an explicit link between the ways in which one of them comes to terms with her past experience and the other brings the prehistoric landscape to light (Swift 1988).

I could discuss further examples, but to do so would distract me from my theme. The reason that such authors have turned so naturally to archaeology as a metaphor may be that it seems so similar to their own experience as creative writers. Rightly or wrongly, they sense an affinity between their creative processes and the ways in which *we* work. We all engage in acts of intuition, in pattern recognition, in linking previously unrelated observations and ideas: the very processes that are fundamental to imaginative thought. Where archaeologists differ from writers – or believe that they do – is that this process is beset by inhibitions, and is very easily disrupted.

I have mentioned the act of imagination from which ideas can grow. Ian Hodder (1986) talks of "reading the past," of archaeology as text, but do we think enough about how we write? I believe it was Albert Camus who said that an author should write the first draft as a poet, relying on instinct and intuition, but the second draft should be written by a school-teacher, carefully, with an eye for construction and logic, and with absolute clarity of expression. As archaeologists we are accustomed to that second stage, for we work within the conventions of our discipline and the expectations of the audience for whom we write. At that stage we bring our assumptions into the open, we link method and theory explicitly, we present our evidence as objectively as we can, and we rely on reasoned argument. My worry is that we may have become so self-aware that we are trapped in a debilitating solipsism. Beset by scientists on one side and Critical Theorists on the other, we shall find nothing to say. Like the fictional archaeologist of Lessing's novel, we shall stammer when we talk about the past.

It is usually said that archaeologists should restrain their imaginations. David Clarke's paper, which I referred to earlier, talks of the dangers of "an irresponsible art form" (1973: 6), although his own imaginative leaps were unsurpassed. In any case, I do not think that this is true. We do have rules, and they are there to be used; otherwise we cannot communicate and we cannot evaluate ideas. But we need to lose our inhibitions if we are to have ideas in the first place, and in the present crisis it would do no harm if we accepted that archaeology is more closely allied to the creative arts than it has seemed respectable to say. Creativity is not incompatible with rules, for rules bring those ideas into the light and facilitate their clear expression. That is true of musical forms from the passacaglia to the fugue, from the note row to the twelve-bar blues; and it is true of poetry, from the iambic pentameter to the haiku. The conventions of archaeological argument could, and should, exert a similar discipline, no matter which epistemology we choose.

It would be easy for a critic to insist that I am advocating a return to subjectivity, that we should simply carry on as before, regardless of any problems of theory. I do not believe that at all. Theory provides the framework in which all our activities are set, and it must always do so. It gives our imagination its muscle, our creative impulses their goal, but there is a growing danger that we shall lose sight of something else that *is* essentially archaeological – the very process of discovery recognized by creative writers; that first-hand contact with past lives from which everything else follows. That may well have brought us into the subject in the first place. It is why archaeology is still so popular and why it has tempted so many people away from more lucrative careers. We are not so remote from those experiences that we can discount their reality altogether.

I began with the story of an archaeologist who had lost his faith, who could not speak in public because he was no longer sure that he had anything to say about the past. I suspect that we are in a different position now. Those who are disenchanted with the prospect of studying the past have seized the initiative, and they are not silent but strident. Those who still adhere to a doctrinaire conception of science can mount a formidable counter-attack. That is as it should be, for the ideas have to be discussed, but the future lies with other people, those who have kept their imaginations alive and still aspire to write human history. They may be processualists or post-processualists; the brand names are entirely unimportant. If Colin Renfrew has reopened the Indo-European problem, it is Ian Hodder who has asked us to consider the cultural meaning of domestication. It is that openness to ideas, and feeling for the archaeological record, that we must develop further. We must never put our creative drive at risk. Otherwise, like that fictional professor, the next generation will find us "rambling and confused." We shall not be "talking loudly" any more.

References

Chippindale, C. 1989 Editorial. *Antiquity* 63: 1–10.

Clarke, D. 1973 Archaeology: The Loss of Innocence. *Antiquity* 47: 6–18.

Hodder, I. 1986 *Reading the Past*. Cambridge: Cambridge University Press.

James, P. (ed.) 1966 *Henry Moore on Sculpture*. London: Macdonald.

Lessing, D. 1971 *Briefing for a Descent into Hell*. London: Cape.

Ozick, C. 1982 *Levitation*. New York: Knopf.

Swift, G. 1988 *Out of this World*. London: Viking.

Index